FOREWORD

Since the day I translated the first poem from my mother tongue to English twelve years ago, I have dreamed of introducing Canadian readers (and English-speaking readers in general) to the riches of Modern Greek poetry through an anthology of selected representative Greek poems from the period of the Heptanesian School, 1750 to today, in my own translations. After many years of intermittent work, including a dozen collections of individual poets in translation and three years of continuous dedication to the anthology, I am finally able to present what I consider my best and most valuable translation work up to now, as well as my most valuable contribution to Canadian literature.

It wasn't without a strong sense of responsibility that I undertook the task of this translation with its multifaceted intricacies and the clarity of presentation required. Indeed, a certain sense of wonder and self-doubt hung over me for a long time before I decided to proceed with this project. In the end, the desire to make and publish the first-ever Canadian translation of such beautiful poetry, totally unknown even to most Anglophones, even poetry lovers, convinced me to embark on the voyage in the hope that the end result would vividly convey a body of graceful, thoughtful, unique literature to enrich and beautify the lives of Canadian readers.

NEO–HELLENE POETS: An Anthology of Modern Greek poetry begins with the middle of the eighteenth century Heptanesean School and ends with a selection of contemporary Greek poetry. The anthology includes work by 60 of the most prominent men and women of Greek letters of the past two hundred years. I've previously translated and presented some of these poets in individual volumes, but this anthology includes not only established and often-translated poets such as Constantine Cavafy, George Seferis, Odysseus Elytis, Yannis Ritsos, Katerina Anghelaki Rooke, Kiki Dimoula, and Tasos Livaditis, but also many poets whose work is quite unknown, including some who have not yet published a collection of their own.

I am grateful to the poets who gave me permission to translate their work and to the literary executors who permitted me to translate poets who are no longer alive. I truly appreciate their timely and generous re-

9

sponse to my requests. Their cooperation enabled me to finalize and release this book on schedule. There were a few other poets whose works I would like to have included in this volume, but the distance and time difference between British Columbia and Greece created difficulties in communicating and, since a dozen poems each from 60 poets was already a substantial body of work to translate, I drew a line at what I had. I am satisfied that the present collection provides as broad-ranging and thorough an overview of Modern Greek poetry as can reasonably be expected from a single volume. In any case, although not planned up front, this edition ended up being the most extensive English translation of modern Greek poetry to date.

In this volume, the reader will encounter the two Greek Nobel Prize winners, George Seferis and Odysseus Elytis, the Star of Lenin Prize winner Yannis Ritsos, the "National Poet" of Greece, Kostis Palamas, and the author of the poem adopted as the national anthem of Greece, Dionisios Solomos. There are poets from the modern renaissance of Greek poetry, from the Greek Romantic movement, from the Greek version of European Surrealism, and many less easily classifiable poets. All are poets whose work has been recognized not only in Greece but also internationally.

I have taken various approaches in these translations. Sometimes the English version is very close to the original, but at other times it deviates substantially in order to make the style or the sense more accessible to the English-speaking reader. When it comes to *accuracy*, I believe these to be my best translations up to now even if, in places, a poem's original form or imagery could not be reproduced exactly. In general, I tried to stay as close to the original as possible even when this meant that some of the beauty or zest of the Greek text was lost in English translation. In a few cases, where a literal translation would have sacrificed too much of the original character of a poem, I tried to find English expressions or idioms that captured the spirit of the Greek text even if they departed somewhat from the *letter*. I'm proud to include some of my own poems as the final section of this anthology. Although I have been a Canadian citizen since 1975, when I write in Greek, I consider myself a Cretan poet.

After the Introduction, I have chosen to present, in an additional section called "In Their Own Words," some statements, including excerpts from interviews, by contemporary poets as an answer to questions such as what is poetry and what is its purpose for each of them. These opinions serve to open the reader to the psyches of the poets and make

NEO — HELLENE POETS

An Anthology of Modern
Greek Poetry: 1750-2018

NEO — HELLENE POETS

An Anthology of Modern
Greek Poetry: 1750-2018

TRANSLATED
BY
MANOLIS ALIGIZAKIS

libros libertad

Ekstasis Editions

Published in 2018 by:
Ekstasis Editions Canada Ltd.   Libros Libertad Publishing Ltd.
Box 8474, Main Postal Outlet   2244 154A Street
Victoria, B.C. V8W 3S1   Surrey, B.C. V4A 5S9

ISBN: 9781926763514

Canada Council   Conseil des Arts   Funded by the   Canadä
for the Arts   du Canada   Government
                                      of Canada

Ekstasis Editions acknowledges financial support for the publication of *Neo-Hellene Poets* from the government of Canada through the Canada Book Fund
and the Canada Council for the Arts, and from the Province of British Colum-
bia through the Book Publishing Tax Credit.

Printed and bound with kdp.amazon.com

Contents

With admiration and solemn reverence I bow before the invincible creativity of the Hellenic Pneuma and I wish it will continue offering its beauty to the world *ad infinitum*

Manolis Aligizakis, Cretan Translator

their voices more tangible and "alive." I chose this approach as a means of communicating the kaleidoscopic vibrancy and complexity of the contemporary Greek poetic scene more vividly than a short review of each poet could have provided.

I hope Canadian readers will embrace this volume with the love, understanding, and appreciation it deserves as an important contribution to Canadian literature and make it part of their libraries. After all, it contains poetry from the place where poetry was first created. Let us not forget the Minoans who wrote poetry four thousand years ago. I'm proud to claim that I come from those roots. This compilation is offered as a chalice to the invincible creativity of the Hellenic pneuma.

Manolis Aligizakis, Cretan
Translator

INTRODUCTION

Compiling a poetry anthology is always a remarkable challenge as well as an exciting undertaking. One of the most crucial points in establishing a chronological cohesion for such a book is what to consider as the starting point of a poetry tradition. This is especially true of Modern Greek poetry, because of the great gap that existed between mainland Greece, which was occupied for centuries by the Turks, and areas such as Crete and the islands of the Ionian Sea, which were mostly under the influence of the Venetians. Various starting points for truly "modern" Greek poetry have been suggested. Some scholars trace the commencement of the modern period to the 16th century Cretan Renaissance and particularly to the works of Vitsentzos Kornaros and George Hortatzis. Others, myself included, prefer to see the Heptanesean School as the most accurate starting point.

The term *Heptanesean School* literally means "The School of the Seven Islands". Sometimes also known as the Ionian School, it refers to the literary production of the Ionian Islands off the western coast of Greece from around the middle of the 18th century to the end of the 19th century. The Ionian Islands, or the Heptanese, were a distinct historic region ruled for centuries by Venice rather than by the Ottomans who governed the rest of Greece. As a result, they developed their own cultural identity and were not incorporated into the Modern Greek state until 1864, some 44 years after Independence from the Ottoman Empire. The Heptanesean School started well before the liberation of Greece from the Turkish occupation and continued for more than half a century after the liberation. In this way, it can be said to have both opened the gates to, and ushered in, the first truly modern poetry of a free Greek people and a free country.

The main figures of the Heptanesean School include poets such as Lorentzos Mavilis, Dionisios Solomos, Nikolaos Mantzaros, Aristotelis Valaoritis, Andreas Kalvos, Andreas Laskaratos, and Nikolaos Polylas, among many others. Of all these, Dionisios Solomos is generally recognized as the greatest figure in Heptanesean literature, and perhaps in Modern Greek literature in general. He is best known for the monumental *Hymn to Freedom*, a 158-stanza anthem inspired by the Greek War of Independence of 1821. The first two stanzas were set to music by Nikolaos Mantzaros and adopted as the Greek national anthem in 1865. Solomos is considered the "national poet" of Greece not only because he wrote the national anthem but also because he contributed crucially to the preservation of the earlier poetic tradition of Crete and the Ionian Islands, known as Pre-Solomonian poetry, insisting on its usefulness to modern literature and incorporating the popular songs of Zakynthos into his poems. In the process, Solomos made vernacular (or demotic) Greek an accepted vehicle for high literary expression. His role in raising demotic Greek to this level is often compared to that of Dante in relation to the Italian language.

Solomos grew up under Venetian rule and originally spoke Italian, but he chose to write his poetry in Greek. Although he learned Greek as a second language, he managed to cultivate it to a very high level and create poetry that became the foundation of the Modern Greek poetic tradition. Indeed, Seferis suggested that Solomos' distance from his Greek heritage played an important role in his emergence as the "national poet" of Greece:

The originator of this literature did not know Greek, but he learned and taught it to the end of his life. The course of the Greek language was born again by Solomos' mind and, perhaps because he came to it from afar, he looked at things with a fresh, sure eye. Paradoxically, the distance from which Solomos participated in all things Greek seems to have functioned as the catalyst for his achievement as the founder of Modern Greek poetry.

However, Solomos was not the only begetter of the Heptanesean School. Andreas Kalvos also contributed a great deal to the new poetics even though, while he was alive, his poetry was attacked by his contemporaries. Kalvos also saw his motherland from afar, but he responded with a nostalgia expressed lyrically through odes. His lyrical ego—opening a special insight into the self-determination of the poetic subject—is apparent in his earliest verses. As a mediator between the Muses and the people, Kalvos assumes the role of personally addressing the gods themselves. Watching his colonized home from afar, his poetry adopts the heroic slogan *Freedom or Death*. Together, the growing self-consciousness of the poetic subject and the heroic choice of freedom even at the cost of death reveal Kalvos' Romantic orientation. If the hope of freedom for the homeland had proved impossible, the alternative solution would have taken its moral weight from the poetic subject's willing embrace of death.

Aristotelis Valaoritis, a politician as well as a poet, was another giant of the Heptanesean School. One of the most distinguished poets of the 19th century his imaginative epic-lyrical poems express his nationalistic ideals through depictions of the freedom fighters' heroic acts during the War of Independence (1821-23). Valaoritis' poetry is more imbued by the events of the war than that of any other poet of the Heptanesean School. In spite of his distance from mainland Greece and his attachment to the distinctive poetry of the Ionian Islands, Valaoritis published his poetry in Athens. Although in his political speeches, and even in the prologues of the many poetry anthologies he compiled, he always used the *Katharevousa* (a conservative literary and official form of Modern Greek based on classical Greek), he was a prominent supporter of the use of demotic Greek in poetry. When Valaoritis arrived in Athens in 1863 the peak of Greek Romanticism had already passed and given way to a poetic decline, as if Greek literature were waiting for something new to appear. Valaoritis' poetry, romantic at its base, and thus intimate in its style with the so-called First Athenian School, nevertheless draws its subject matter from history and cultivates a heroic mood. It attempts to draw Greek poetry away from the kind of Romanticism that focused on sentimental psychosis, as expressed by the last representatives of the First Athenian School. As a point of interest, Valaoritis was also the great-grandfather of Nanos Valaoritis, one of the most distinguished contemporary writers and poets of Greece.

Andreas Laskaratos, a notorious satirical writer and poet from the Ionian island of Cefalonia, is also considered a representative of the Heptanesean School. Laskaratos' satires were so effective that he was excommunicated by the Greek Orthodox Church. His mockery targeted many of the church's most prominent members, including the Homeric scholar and translator Iakovos Polilas and many other notables.

The general characteristics of the poetry of this era were the exclusive use of demotic Greek, the influence of contemporary Italian poetry, an idealistic view of the arts in general, the idolizing of the female figure, strong love for the Greek motherland, the idealization of Eros, a love of nature, a richly imaginative use of hero figures and other heroic imagery, a strong faith in the power of symbols, traditional artistic icons, and religious imagery, a somewhat diffuse love for humanity and beauty, a commitment to both truthfulness and sentimentality, and finally a love of freedom and of the duty to pursue it at all costs.

During the era of the Heptanesean School, the great event of the war for liberation from Turkish occupation (1821-1830) occurred, and this defining event in Modern Greek history strongly influenced the literature of the first years of the newborn free Greece. The first poems after liberation, not only by poets of the Heptanesean School but also by Athenian poets, refer almost without exception to the events of the war but also reflect the Romanticism that had spread from Western Europe to Greece in the early 19th century and influenced most poets of this era, despite certain differences in the reception of Romanticism between the poets of the Heptanesean and the First Athenian School.

The next major development in the history of Modern Greek poetry was the emergence towards the end of the 19th century of the New Athenian School, whose most prominent practitioners include George Drossinis, Kostis Palamas, Konstantinos Theotokis, Lorentzos Mavilis, John Gryparis, Lampros Porphyras, Miltiadis Malakasis, and Kostas Kristallis. Less easily characterizable than the Heptanesean and First Athenian poets, the works of the New Athenian poets express a great variety of moods, interests, and attitudes that flow from the individual conditions in which each of these poets lived and the experiences they had.

The poetry of Miltiadis Malakasis, for example, exhibits a generally pensive mood matched with great lyrical skill and pervasive musicality. Nostalgia dominates in many of his poems, connected to a preoccupation with worlds that have vanished. Much of the substance of his poetry expresses what he saw as the true way of life of the Greek people during the years immediately following the War of Independence.

Lampros Porphyras was a melancholic man who lived an isolated, asocial life by choice. Financially independent, he was also free from the stresses of earning a living. Influenced by Symbolism, he nevertheless developed a particular, personal style characterized by simple language and highly original verse forms. His poetry is also notable for its sweetness of expression and a tone of harmonious musicality.

Zacharias Papantoniou was a remarkably sensitive man, and his timeless poems appeal to all social strata. His love of plants, animals, nature, and, above all, for children was intense, and his famous reading book *High Mountains* is still the best and most comprehensive in the history of Greek readers. In many of his poems and works, he refers to the Roumeli and Karpenissi regions, praising their high mountains and natural beauty, for which he had a powerful longing.

Georgios Souris' poetry is characterized by its enormous fertility and the sheer number of poems he produced. He also wrote in a consistently good-natured way, commenting freely on the people he knew or observed, including the rulers and the kings, but without ever shaming. Often he satirized himself, one famous example being the poem "My Image". Interestingly, his language is mixed. He mainly used demotic Greek, but *Katharevousa* is not absent from his poems, and he fought intensely with Yannis Psycharis and other militant "demoticists" of the early 20th century.

Among the New Athenian poets, John Gryparis' poems were especially influenced by the streams of French Parnassianism and Symbolism. Gryparis is also renowned for his translations of classical Greek tragedies, which formed the basis for the revival of ancient Greek drama in the context of the Delphic festivals organized first by Angelos Sikelianos and later by the National Theater.

The most prominent poet of this era was Kostis Palamas, whose long career spanned several decades and culminated in his being named the National Poet of Greece. His contribution to Modern Greek poetry, inspired by both the neo-Hellenic poetic tradition and contemporary European trends, was immense, and his work varied widely in form and mood as well as in subject matter, which ranged from everyday life events to esoteric views of the Greek psyche, to historical events, and to international issues and trends.

Kostis Palamas wrote a wide variety of poems, long and short, but his most serious works were two epic-lyric collections, *The King's Flute* and *The Dodecalogue of the Gypsy*, works which are read and studied even today, as they still provide insights into today's events and conditions in Greece. As a leading proponent of the Greek literary renewal envisioned by the so-called generation of 1880, Palamas, fully aware of his leading role, undertook, in addition to renewing the interpretation of the Greek literary tradition, the renewal of the literary horizon, which presupposed the emergence of new poets. He embraced newcomers such as John Papadiamantopoulos, Nikos Campas, and George Drossinis, promoting their work through positive reviews, and as a result became the living consciousness of a whole new generation of poets. Drosinis' verses are characterized by lively use of rhythm and rhyme. Elements of European Romanticism still remain despite many other departures from the poetics of the old school, probably reflecting the poet's idealistic outlook.

The dramatic changes in the political landscape at this time raised hopes of a bourgeois renaissance, and it was in this context that Palamas assumed the role of *national poet*, as the optimistic leader of such renaissance and the "bard" who promoted national ideals. In particular, his two great compositions, *The Flute of the King* and *The Dodecalogue of the Gypsy*, reflected national aspirations for territorial expansion and expressed a call for the triumphant rebirth of Hellenism. Clearly, in the poet's mind at least, this kind of patriotic poetry was tantamount to a political act.

Around 1910, while Palamas was still writing *The King's Flute* and *The Dodecalogue of the Gyspy*, Constantine Cavafy emerged in Alexandria, Egypt, as a very different poet, already writing in a mature style, although he did not become well-known in Athens until around 1920. What was unique about this new poet was the prose format he employed, together with his use of traditional language as well as the demotic. Cavafy influenced Greek poetry in an unprecedented way, while his poetry combined the exactness and accuracy of a master craftsman of words with Sappho's sentimentalism. Both poets are laconic, yet they both reflect intensely on love and eroticism.

Although Greek poets love the ancient poetic roots they have inherited, and although they have always drawn from those roots, European trends have influenced Modern Greek poetry to an unprecedented extent. The various poetic movements that have emerged in Europe since the Romantic era have changed the way Greek poets write in fundamental ways, but this should not be viewed through a negative lens. Instead, it should be considered as just one more element that has moulded Modern Greek poetry into the rich vehicle of expression it has become. Undoubtedly, Greek poets have drawn freely from the endless, ancient beauty of their literature and have used it as a vehicle to look deep inside themselves and their culture in the hope of discovering who they are and where they should be heading, but they also live in a cosmos that includes others with divergent points of view and their own ways of delving into the concepts of life and death, the human condition, the aspirations and wishes of people, political upheavals and trends, and human violence against other humans, and all these have become subjects of their writing.

European trends are imbued in each and every line of Modern Greek poetry. Romanticism for example, which steered the development of Greek poetry for more than fifty years in the early 19th century, is abundant in the works of both the Heptanesean School and the First Athenian School. As a movement, Romanticism eschewed all traditional rules and standardized formats of poetry in favour of the spontaneous expression of emotion and imagination, and the free exploration of the absolute, the ideal, and the sentimental. Romanticism was attracted to the paradoxical and the mysterious but also evinced nostalgia for the past and an often melancholic attitude and pessimism towards the present. Imagery and rhythm were of utmost importance, and the first-person perspective became the new norm, while the preferred subjects included personal experiences of nature, god, adventure, Eros, and the struggle for freedom.

Then Parnassianism appeared. This French poetic movement of the middle 19th century valued accuracy and detail and avoided sentimentality and overt passion, but it also invented new rhythmic and verse rules while reviving mythological subjects and concepts from the ancient arts. Inspiration was drawn from classical standards of beauty and ancient literary traditions that respected traditional forms, rhythms, and rhyme schemes on the one hand and on the other from fleeting perceptions and simple daily events. A dynamic satirical attitude was also common. The poets who followed this trend tended to write sonnets using exact syllable counts and concise expression. Many poets of the Athenian School of Poetry, including Kostis Palamas, George Drosinis, Kostas Kristallis and others, followed Parnassianism.

Towards the beginning of the 20th century Symbolism became the dominant trend and influenced many emerging poets of the time. Sometimes also called Neo-romanticism, this movement emphasized lyricism, albeit in a rather subdued form. It gave prominence to the interior world of the poet, using external images as symbols of the poet's psychological condition. In this poetry, reverie and suggestion, melancholy and richly expressive language, convey deep emotional aspirations and wants. Mystical elements are sometimes prominent too, and free verse, with a stress on musicality and suggestive imagery, symbols of psychological conditioning, and subjective experience are integral elements. Traditional poetic forms are not abandoned, but there is a dialogue between old styles and modern innovations. Elements of this dialogue can be found in the poems of Angelos Sikelianos, Constantine Cavafy, Kostas Varnalis, and many other poets who emerged around this time. Symbolism was mixed with elements of Neo-symbolism and Neo-romanticism in the work of poets such as Kostas Karyotakis, Maria Polydouris, Tellos Agras, Napoleon Lapathiotis and others, until George Seferis appeared. His *Strophe*, 1931, marks a decisive turn into the realms of a Modernism that dissolved all traditional forms.

Surrealism, with its departure from realism and introduction of the imagination as the primal force behind creativity, also visited Greece—

and stayed, giving credibility to automatic writing and encouraging complete freedom of word use. It also banished rhyme and verse; the poets' craftsmanship expressed itself instead through unexpected combinations of words and inexplicable colorations of imagery. Thematically, surrealism decreed that people should not live a life trapped in reality but should break these shackles by using their imagination, especially their dreamscapes and subconscious. Automatic writing was popular because it seemed to transcend logic and free writing from any thought-out process, offering a totally new approach to the perception of reality. The two poets who most passionately followed this new form of expression were Nikos Engonopoulos and Andreas Empiricos, but surrealistic elements can also be found in lighter form in the works of Odysseus Elytis and Nikos Gatsos.

The devastating effects on Greece of the Second World War and the civil war that followed—persecutions, oppression, victimization, and maltreatment of people for their political beliefs—turned Greek poetry towards social issues and inequalities. The Greek poetry of those days became a vehicle for expressing people's anger, their protest and rebellion, but it also turned towards concepts that had to do with existential wonder, nostalgia for a simpler past, loneliness, societal decay, and contemplation of death. Some of the important figures who wrote poetry imbued with such elements included Tasos Livaditis, popularly named the *people's poet*, Tasos Varvitsiotis, Nanos Valaoritis, Titos Patrikios, Kiki Dimoula, and Katerina Anghelaki Rooke.

Yet even while various European trends from Romanticism to Surrealism strongly influenced Modern Greek poetry, the unobtrusive spring of classical beauty and myth remained the foundation from which most poets throughout the modern era drew strength and inspiration to create their marvelous poems, and from which they kept discovering new ways to enrich their poetic craftsmanship. The importance of myth is no surprise; Greece has the richest and most beautiful mythology on this earth. The poems of Cavafy, Seferis, and Ritsos, to name only the most famous Modern Greek poets, are saturated with traditional mythological imagery and themes. In Cavafy, "Priam's Night Journey" and "Ithaka" are perhaps the best-known of his poems based on classical mythology. In Seferis, the use of myth is prominent in "Comrades in Hades" and throughout *Strophe* but fades somewhat in *Three Secret Poems*, only to develop still further in *Mythestorema* and *Thrush* as well as in *Logbook II*. In Ritsos, the mythological foundations of his poetry appears most clearly in *Fourth Dimension* and later on in *Agamemnon*,

Orestis, Persephone, Return of Ifigeneia, Helen, and *Phedra,* but is also present in subdued form in *Moonlight Sonnet, Dead House,* and *Small Homeric Poems.* Agellos Sikelianos also uses myth extensively, as do later poets such as Takis Sinopoulos, Miltos Sachtouris, and Titos Patrikios, to name only a few. The classical myth is used mainly as a tool for introspection and self-discovery as well as a method of exploring the pessimistic present as an expression of contemporary melancholy.

Worldwide, Constantine Cavafy is considered the equal of Yeats and Rilke and remains one of the towering figures of poetry of the past 100 years. Although his output was small, he has had an enormous impact on later generations of poets. His reputation was built on two divided currents: his historical poems reclaiming Grecian antiquity and his more personal, erotic poems of memory and desire, passion and loss. Both currents, however, are infused with a tone of irony and disenchantment. Sensuous, erotic, and precise, Cavafy does not so much tell a story as create an atmosphere, sweeping the reader away on a blue Aegean sea of longing. The endurance of his work is in an approach that fuses the immediacy of the Hellenic past and the direct moment of an imagined erotic encounter in a perspective balanced between the ancient and the modern.

The Nobel Prize winner George Seferis wrote this about Cavafy:

> We have to be careful not to be swept away by what we like to see and read because the deceptive old man of the Alexandrian Sea, Cavafy, like Proteus, who always eluded capture by changing his appearance, often changes his style and mood; therefore we can't take at face value the superficial meaning of his words or the dialectic voices he often uses.

Other notable poets of the early 20th century were Agellos Sikelianos with his prolific lyrical gift and Kostas Varnalis, who imbued his leftist views in his poetry. Also during the 1920s, a new group of poets appeared who have come to be known as the *between-the-two-world-wars generation.* Their poetry is marked by the disillusionment that followed the Greco-Turkish War (1919-1922) and its atrocities. The most important figures of this group of poets were Napoleon Paraschos, Tellos Agras, Achilles Lapathiotis, Kostas Karyotakis, and Maria Polydouri. Of these, Kostas Karyotakis was by far the most prominent. His verses are filled with Neo-romantic symbolism and with his disappointment for what he saw as the lack of ideals in the post-war world. Lyrical and ardent, his poems focus on natural imagery, but with traces of expressionism and surrealism. His work has broad appeal and has been translated into more than thirty languages.

Karyotakis is also identified with the Greek "Lost Generation" movement. Most of his contemporaries viewed him in a dim light during his lifetime, though without any obvious reason for their negative views, but after his suicide, the recognition that he was indeed a great poet rapidly took hold, and he has had a significant influence on later Greek poets. Nowadays his poetry is taught in universities not only in Greece but in many other countries. Karyotakis gave existential depth as well as a tragic dimension to the emotional nuances and melancholic tones of the Neo-symbolist and Neo-romantic trends of the time. With a rare clarity of spirit and a penetrating vision, he daringly captures and conveys the post-war climate of dissolution and the sense of impasse of his generation, as well as the traumas of his own inner spiritual struggles. Karyotakis' poetry has no trace of the sentiment, or courtesy that were abundant in earlier poets. Instead, it exudes a sense of futility and loss, and its attitude is both anti-sentimental and anti-democratic. Karyotakis writes poems about the absurd, the insignificant, even the ridiculous, and his tone often amounts to sarcasm.

Another poet of the 1920s, Maria Polydouris, known for her idiomorphic personal life, which was intricately connected to that of Kostas Karyotakis, with whom she fell in love when they both worked for the city of Athens. Polydouris' love for Karyotakis marked her life and her poetry, as well as her reputation, for ever. Her poetry revolves around the two axes of love and death, but it has a spring-like, yet mature, lyricism that expresses a deep sadness, even anguish, with her life. Its often sensational emotional outbursts sometimes cover up certain poetic weaknesses and structural imperfections. As the critic Kostas Stergiopoulos comments, "Maria Polydouris wrote her poems as she did her personal diary. The transmutation took place automatically since expression for her meant the straight transcription of her internal world into a poetic language with all the generalizations and exaggerations her romantic nature dictated."

Polydouris' collected poems were published in 1960, and many of her poems have been set to music by well-known Greek composers. Famous for her amazing radiance and child-like beauty, together with her feminism, her delicate health, her pride and her unreliability, Polydouris in some ways represents an ideal figure for the feminist movement. She was impulsive in her life, but in her poetry both confessional and reflective, and works somewhat like Cavafy's.

The 1930s saw the first appearance of such big names as George Seferis, Odysseus Elytis, both Nobel Prize winners, Yannis Ritsos, Nikos Engonopoulos, Andreas Embirikos, Nikos Gatsos and many more. Neo-romanticism was still in full swing when a poetry collection entitled *Strophe* by the great George Seferis appeared. *Strophe*, which in plain English means *Turn*, is regarded as the key turning point in Modern Greek poetry, the point at which the old models of poetry fully gave way to the new era of Modernism, free verse, and unabashed surrealism. The 1930s generation of poets severed all attachments to traditional verse, with collections published by Seferis (notably *Strophe* and *Sterna*) and Yannis Ritsos (*Tractor* and *Epitaphios*) leading the way. In this revolution, the year 1935 is of particular importance. In that year, the best-known Greek literary magazine, *Nea Grammata*, was founded. Seferis was one of the first contributors, and the magazine also published the first poems by Odysseus Elytis and another important surrealist poet, Andreas Embirikos. Also in 1935, the last collection by the giant of Greek poetry of that era, Kostis Palamas, was released, and that indeed constituted a poetic turn to new formats, moods, and trends. Of course, many of the poets of this generation still followed the symbolism of the previous era, and in the same decade the poets Nikiforos Vrettakos and Nikos Engonopoulos also appeared on the scene.

The poetry of modern Greece draws on a literary tradition and cultural heritage unparalleled by any other nation. As this brief survey of the development of Greek poetry over almost three centuries shows, Modern Greek poetics differentiates itself from all others in more ways than one. A closer look at the work of some of the most important recent poets will make this clear.

George Seferis, a distinguished diplomat as well as a poet, raised the bar for Modern Greek poetry with his first book *Strophe*, which introduced Modernism to Greek readers. As with any other Greek poet, Seferis' poems are enriched with well-known Greek motifs of azure seas, isolated islands, secluded coves, golden sands, and, behind all these, the ancient beauty and glorious past represented by classical topoi, statues, and ancient temples. His adoration of everything Greek is evident throughout his work —the harsh and punitive landscapes, the naked, frugal beauty, the sea's whoosh on the shores of his memories from the land of his childhood, the tall, granite mountains, the ancient traditions and customs, the daily struggle of ordinary folk, and the continuity of the Greek language through the eons.

In Seferis' poetry, the reader discovers a strange interrelation between the art of poetry in general and the particular artistic technique used by this poet. The two appear to coexist, meddle, and interrelate in his poetics, serving and complementing each other. As the poems search and self-reveal, trying to surface, struggling to develop, so does the technique used, and both toil to come to the light, creating concentric circles such as when one tosses a pebble into a body of water. In these circles, the basic characteristics of Seferis' art become evident. The reader also discovers dualities in paired images such as *nostos-thanatos* ("homecoming-death") in the *Thrush* and *myth-history* in *Mythistorema*, an image that also passes over to his three *Log Books*, and most importantly from our perspective, the duality *nostos-algos* (homecoming-pain) in his famous poem "The Return of the Emigré" in which this *nostos* results in a traumatic encounter with reality when the old émigré returns, searching for childhood images that no longer exist, but finds that everything has become small and insignificant. For Seferis, this recognition symbolizes the pain associated with today's harsh reality. Seferis' images regularly transpose the contemporary and the ancient and thus create an unavoidable comparison that sees contemporary Greece as of lesser importance. At the same time, readers cannot but connect the images of ancient rocks, statues, marbles, temples, and so on with the reasons that today's Greeks consider themselves as failing to measure up to their glorious antiquity.

Odysseus Elytis, the other Greek Nobel Prize winner, first appeared in Greek literature with his collection, *Orientations*. He is generally considered the most important Greek poet of modern times, and his career spanned several decades, with numerous further collections that brought him to the foreground of Modern Greek poetry, a position he still enjoys decades after his death. A poet of new ways of expression, Elytis consistently ploughed new roads in the field of poetry in the ways he presented his imagery and ideas. Undoubtedly, he was influenced by contemporary European trends, Surrealism for one, but the reader can also find elements of the Baroque in his poetry, along with Romanticism. His poetry stood against most of the established forms of Greek poetry of the time, and for that reason Elytis was often scolded by his contemporaries for being too radical in expression, yet he acted as a truly free poet, following some forms and creating new ones as he saw fit. It was as if he wanted to teach his fellow poets, as well as today's poetry readers, the "Elytis lesson" in poetry.

Elytis' poetry is imbued with a passionate lyricism and is full of color, feeling, and vivid imagery. His poetry is an act of jubilation that takes the landscape and the poet, still in their paradisiacal forms, on a journey of knowing, suffering, soiling, transforming, transcending, and liberating, again largely through connections with myth. Elytis uses the treasure trove of Greek mythology, together with his own creations, the way a master mythmaker guides the conscience of the landscape, as well as that of the poet himself, to the threshing point of deliverance through the heroic acts and spiritual symbolism that myths represent.

From the first Elytis poem that you read, you will encounter all the elements that will be repeated again and again over the years in this poet's work: the sea, seagulls, waves, the voyage, the song of the traveler, the homecoming, and, above all, Eros. Here the birth of the diaphanous landscape and that of the observer come at the same time, and this transforms Elytis' poetry into a diachronic beauty that his readers all over the globe are lucky to enjoy.

In the 1930s, another new poet with a very different voice rose up among the literary circles of Athens and began to create what became the most prolific output of any Modern Greek poet. This was Yannis Ritsos, the most copious Greek poet of the twentieth century. From his earliest to his last books, his inspiration was undiminished, and his acute eye for detail and exquisite perception never failed throughout his long creative life. Nothing from the greatest to the most minuscule went unnoticed by Yannis Ritsos, and every possibility was exposed and experimented with in his poems. His works incorporate endless infusions of color, melody, jest, catharsis, and infinite tenderness. In particular, his perspective is infused with wonder about everyday events, which he drew with the most eloquent images a poet can muster, rendering his thoughts with love and compassion even for the simplest person.

Ritsos' poetry evolved as though reflecting on the poet's life, from youthful enthusiasm, idealism, and rebelliousness to the mature, pragmatic, and didactic elder who searches for each person's place under the sun, for each hungry man's chair at the table during the most elaborate feast. His poetry stands quite gracefully apart from hatred, as he never resorted to vitriol, not even against a system and a dogma that incarcerated him time and again for his political views.

Ritsos managed to stay above demonizing and persecuting his opponents through the power of his medium, being a believer in the strength of the human spirit as redeemer of all wrongs. He held true to his ethics, proving once and again that no matter how often or how low one is forced down by the oppression of others, no matter from what high position, the invincible human spirit can lift one beyond.

Ritsos' work reflects this reality, repeatedly making references to the ancient myths and symbols within a setting of contemporary issues and Greek dilemmas. He reaches back into ancient tributaries, into myths and symbols, for guidance and for meaning while testifying to the injustices of contemporary Greek life. Drawing strength from the ancient heroes, he discovers the other side of things, the eloquent side of words won by chance, the poetic appeal of the ordinary, the serendipitous answer to every difficult or almost unanswerable question. He discovers, as though in a form of epiphany, the answer to many difficult questions. Most significantly, he attains a perspective from which nothing happens at random and nothing comes to the life of a person or a populace without a specific reason. He therefore recognizes that the duty of every person, and of the populace as a whole, is to know, appreciate, and find solace in the opportunities provided by such meanings. Ritsos belongs to the pantheon of the few great poets of all ages.

During the same period, yet another great poet came to the foreground. Tasos Livaditis, Yannis Ritsos' good friend, followed a similar path. He was also a poet who wrote for the cause of the left but who turned introspective and devoted his verse to social issues and inequalities of the Greek society, a poet who was imprisoned for his political views just like Ritsos, and one who turned out to be the people's poet in more ways than one. Livaditis stands apart from other poets of his time because of the heartrending existential agony his deep understanding produced, initially expressed as a tender, compassionate cry within the boundaries of an optimistic realism but, in the second phase of his creative career, as an introverted search for the meaning of life after the dissolution of his expectations as an artist-fighter for a better future.

It was October when Livaditis said farewell:

> The calendar will show October
> with the wilted leaves and revolutions

His last verses underscored that message:

> Here I've come to the end. Time to go. As you will also go,
> and the ghosts of my life will search for me
> running in the night and leaves will shiver and fall.
> Autumn comes this way. For this, I say to you,
> let us look at life with more compassion, since it was never real.

He never imagined that the ghosts of his life would multiply at such a fast pace so soon after his death. Indeed, the adventurousness of his vision turned out to be a hardship. The rapidly changing fashions in social behaviour, unforeseen by this most suspicious of men, shifted dramatically shortly after his death. Within just one or two years, with the dissolution of the Soviet Union, the so-called socialist dream had collapsed.

Tasos Livaditis is one of the last poets who dreamed of a different Greece and gave all he had to turn that dream into reality. He was one of the last who believed in the collective versus the personal, even if that collective involved dramatic risks, in his case not only exile and persecution but also the adventure of his internal revolution. The person who dreamed of a better world was embittered when his vision became a utopia in the original Greek sense of the term. Yet he never lost his faith in humanity, and although the hardships of his life marked him, he always stood gracefully opposite the descending sun, and in that dusky, red glow he wept alone, but always with optimism for the future. Tragically, Livaditis' life was cut short. He died at the age of 66 and left a nation to mourn its people's poet and reflect on the fact that the world of the committed poet is one of humiliation and exhaustion. It is a world of bitterness and futility, and Tasos Livaditis was persecuted relentlessly and suffered a lot. But how else could he have written such great poems?

The poetry of the 1940s was greatly influenced by the Second World War, first the Italian invasion and then the German occupation. These dire events prompted numerous poets to explore images of destruction, famine, and all the other negative effects that war inflicts on a people. Several important poems of this decade took inspiration from history, either directly like Elytis' "Heroic and Mourning Song for the Lost Second Lieutenant of the Albanian Campaign" or indirectly, through metaphor, like Ritsos' epic *Romiosini*, or through hints, as in Nikos Engonopoulos' "Bolivar".

After the Second World War and the civil war that followed, and as Greece fought tooth and nail to find its footing in the changing world of the 1950s, a large number of new poets appeared who could be called the "after-the-war generation". These poets created work characterized by a concern with social issues and the divisive politics of East and West, the two great power blocs that took control of people's lives, literally and figuratively. The most important Greek poets who explored social and political issues from a leftist perspective—and who were persecuted for

their political affiliations—included Manolis Anagnostakis, Titos Pa-
trikios, and Tasos Livaditis. Others, such as Miltos Sachtouris, Takis
Sinopoulos, and Nikos Karouzos, were prominent unaffiliated voices,
belonging to no particular group. The poetry of Patrikios and Livaditis
has in common a fascination with terrible images of pain and suffering
that incorporated elements of surrealism, while Karouzos' poetry is
more religious or philosophical due to his close connection with the tra-
ditions of the Greek Orthodox Church. Anagnostakis' poetry gripped
readers from its first appearance, thanks to his steadfast attention to the
inequalities and related social issues that became pervasive after the civil
war. His poetry resonates with readers even today. Once asked whether
his work should be called political or not, Anagnostakis answered:

> At times my poetry has been purely political, although
> personally I don't think I'm a political poet. I believe I write
> both erotic and political poetry. These two can be easily
> combined because the times we live in combine them. That is,
> one can't be an erotic poet unless one remembers the political
> context of the times we live in, during which political passions
> have been intensified. There's a political element in my poetry
> as an expression of politics, although it is expressed from
> within an erotic context. I don't know if we understand this
> concept easily. That's why I deny all this about poetry of defeat
> and the like. My poetry isn't poetry of defeat. It's an agony for
> the season, an anxiety about the season. When the season is
> over, poetry ends. You can't always write poetry. I'm not a
> professional poet. I took up poetry as a way of expression
> because I couldn't express myself differently. In other words,
> the life of our times was so pressing, so difficult, that one
> couldn't endure it unless he expressed it in his poetry.
> (Source: *www.nostimonimar.gr/manolis-anagnostakis-erotikos
> -ke-politikos-*)

Another important poet of the same era who derived his thematic
landscape and imagery from the Occupation and the Civil War was
Miltos Sachtouris. Indeed, Sachtouris' work personified the nightmare
of history into an individual experience of incredible intensity. A poet
of passion and anger, he gave us a poetry in which mourning and drama,
indignation and horror, walk hand in hand. This is why some of his best
poems sound like exorcisms, most notably "The Beast", from his best

collection, *With the Face on the Wall*, which was released three years after the end of the Civil War when the poet was still only 33 years old.

A poet of exquisite intensity, Sachtouris wants readers to shiver with the same sensations he lived through during the terrifying or exhilarating experiences from which he drew his poems. His work shows how the personal experiences of any great poet transcend the merely personal and move into the realm of the universal. From his experience of the Occupation and the Civil War, Sachtouris creates his own Underworld, but above it, he sets a sky that represents (although not always) the exaltation that comes from gazing deep into the abyss and then raising the eyes and seeing "how black people are / how crystal are the stars".

Nikiforos Vrettakos, nominated unsuccessfully for the Nobel Prize four times, was also influenced by the Second World War, the resistance, and the civil war that followed liberation from the Germans. His work is full of the atrocities he experienced or witnessed and that played a decisive role in his writing, but it oscillates between optimism and pessimism, between joy and disappointment. Religion is intensely present in his poems, but Vrettakos' greatest assets are always love and strength. He believed that humanity can do anything and overcome any obstacle through love and unity. Always truthful and authentic, Vrettakos wrote poetry collections that glorify love and humanity. Nature and rural life also play an important role in his poems. He adored his home village and spent countless hours gazing at Mount Taygetos, its streams and other natural wonders.

Another poet of the same was Titos Patrikios, whose works influenced Modern Greek literature in an unprecedented way. He wrote poems on a variety of issues and suffered the same fate as Yannis Ritsos and Tasos Livaditis. In an interview, Patrikios has this to say about his work and life:

> Perhaps poetry is the art most written rather than read. Poetry finds you, and when it meets you, be careful not to deny it. These days more than ever, poets are needed because often our superficiality makes life more enjoyable. In poetry, if you are very serious, you become dull. My greatest influences came from the heroes of the books I read when I was a child: Achilles, Odysseus, Jason, even when, at a later time, I learned he wasn't such a good boy. I was also influenced by heroes like Don Quixote and his adventures. A few years ago I realized

that although poetry is autobiographical and relates to personal experiences, it becomes useful only when it gives the reader the power to create his own truth and therefore discover himself.

After the generation of poets whose works were affected by the Second World War, the Resistance and the Civil War, we reach a very different era, in which the generations of the 1970s and 1980s explore new concerns. One of these is Kiki Dimoula, a woman with an exceptional voice and an even more exceptional poetic craft. Her poetic career followed an evolutionary course, with influences from Cavafy at the beginning followed by her characteristic word-morphing style and her personal image-moulding. Dimoula's insistent conceptualizing, clearly existential, expresses an agonizing search for the meaning of perishable human life. The subjects that dominate her poems are absence, decay, loss, loneliness, and the fleeting nature of time. The key elements of Dimoula's writing are her swift and sharp verse, her ironic tone, the use of words from *Katharevousa*, along with the use of technical terms, epithets, slang, and neologisms, a proverbial mood relying on opposite or homonymous words and surprise pairs, her deliberate neglect of syntax, and her repetitions. She uses metaphor, sound cadences, epodes, and contradictory and transcendent elements that include the disorganization of syntax, oxymoron, where the meaning is left pending, and a ubiquitous anthropomorphism that undertakes the task of creating a new, unified creature, thus releasing associations that would otherwise remain captive of expressive compatibility.

Katerina Anghelaki Rook, also a poet of the same era soon followed Dimoula but with exquisitely crafted verse and superb eroticism. The famous line of Mayakovski that "time is something unbelievably long" is refuted by the work of such poets themselves, because no other type of writing can withstand time as much as poetry. Such is the sense of duration and eternity we reap when reading the poetry of Katerina Anghelaki Rook. Undoubtedly, Rook is one of the most important Modern Greek poets. Readers have known this for many years. In reading her poetry, we find that, in verse after verse, she reveals new levels of her world, her experiences, excitement, traumas, and sensations, with true feeling and undeniable immediacy. Rook is a sensual poet, but not just that. Knowing that sensuality is not sufficient in itself, she plumbs it to existential depth without ever losing the *embodiedness* of her poetry. For years, many have characterized her as essentially an erotic poet, but this is not derogatory. Erotic poetry is perhaps the most difficult to write. Rook's eroticism is as intense as the most intense erotic experience, but its extensions and anxieties raise the major and eternal poetic issue: life and death. This is the erotic conversation at its deepest.

A poet with a special vision, yet with just one book of poetry, was Dimitris Liantinis, a philosophy professor at the Kapodistrian University of Athens. Liantinis produced many volumes of prose but published only one book of poetry. His poems have a distinctly heavenly cadence, not surprising since most refer to heavenly bodies: stars, constellations, nebulas, and galaxies. A great lover of ancient Greek culture, Liantinis devoted his life to studying and reinterpreting this rich cultural heritage. He wrote about various subjects but emphasized the need to incorporate the ancient Greek ideas and morals into the Modern Greek education system. He also held strong views on what he saw as the decline of Western culture in general. However, he achieved notoriety in Greece largely because of his strange and unexplained disappearance on the morning of June 1, 1998, at the age of 56 years. His poems dive deep into the human psyche where his thunderous voice tries to awaken what is hidden there but has been lost in everyday trivialities. His voice demands attention and evokes a contemplative desire. Undoubtedly, he was one of the great thinkers of modern Greece.

Seeing modern Greek poetry though the lens of its tradition, its historical foundation, one can't but agree that, in the lyrical manner of Odysseus Elytis or in the melancholy mood of George Seferis, or in the humanism of Yannis Ritsos and Tasos Livaditis, in the existential questioning of Kiki Dimoula and Nikiforos Vrettakos, in the eroticism of Constantine Cavafy and Katerina Anghelaki Rooke, one discovers all the ancient beauty first encountered in Homer and Anacreon and Sappho. Modern Greek poetry still stands alone, as enriched and as gleaming from the same ancient beauty as if the centuries between antiquity and today had never disrupted the invincibility of the Hellenic Pneuma. Indeed, the same Attic sun still shines on the verses of today's poets as it did on those of their ancestors, as eloquent as the Cretan sea waves lapping on their shores, as beautiful as the ones described by Homer and Elytis and Archilochus and Palamas.

Modern Greek poetry speaks to us as if speaking from the ancient days. It remains as potent as the original Greek verses three thousand years ago, as evocative as the brilliant horizons of Santorini, as integral to modern life as Sophocles' writings were to the lives of Athenians in the fifth-century BC. Yet, although there is a big chasm in the chronological chart of Greek poetry, a disruption that took place during the Byzantine years and the years of the Ottoman occupation, today's poetry still stands as unfettered by this gap as it is strong. It finds its base on the same eloquent foundation of the ancients, as if no disruption occurred. This integrity can be attributed to the strength and endurance of the Hellenic language, the unerring tool that every Greek poet has used, a language that is considered one of the richest on earth. This is why, when we read Kostis Palamas' poems, we can't but feel the same awe we experience reading the works of Homer.

IN THEIR OWN WORDS

Nanos Valaoritis nephew of the Heptanesian poet Aristotelis Valaoritis, and an accomplished poet himself with many poetry books and translations in his bibliography lives in Athens and asked in a recent interview about poetry he said:

> The trigger that urged me to write poetry was Cavafy's poetry, which I discovered in my 14th year at a book fair. In him, I found an existential character that was very much who I was as a teenager, contrary to the nationalist historiography in the poetry of Calvos, Solomos, or Palamas. I first appeared in New Grammata in 1939 at the age of 18. However, then came the war and the Occupation, during which half of our home was confiscated by German officers. Imagine, in the other half we secretly organized resistance meetings! Later on, the demon of surrealism came into me because of Embirikos, but also thanks to Elytis and Gatsos. In that time of war, Engonopoulos had published "Bolivar", and Gatsos "Amorgos", if I remember. I wrote at that time romantic-heroic poems that I now reject. But Embirikos remembered one of my poems about a heroic woman, and he made a great impression on him. I continue to write poetry because it is first of all an internal need, but it is shaped differently in each season. I advocate a cultural development: to discover and use our own identity without fear and passion, without any complex of inferiority or pseudo-prejudice.
> (Source: *www.lifo.gr/guide/cultureblogs/bookblog/34513*)

Katerina Gogou another poet of the seventies generation, also speaks about poetry in a very personal way:

> The great love of my life, however, was poetry. What I feared most was to become a poet to lock myself in a room and look at the sea and forget everything else. I was afraid that the wounds of my body would heal, and from blurry memories

and the news by ERT I'd fill out papers and promote opinions. I was afraid that my race would accept and use me. I was afraid that my screaming would become mumbling to put my people to sleep; that I'd learn meter and technical things and lock myself in them so my fans would sing of me. I write to justify myself. I write out of indignation for the evil and from my love for the people and their lives. I felt the great silence; there is no communication from anywhere; my jaws hurt from not talking. And when I started writing, I thought I'd break the pen. I had so much passion for what I wanted to say. I do not know how others write. I was living and writing, as I said in my interview with the newspaper Eleftherotypia"
(Source: *tvxs.gr/news/.../κατερίνα-γώγου-η-οργισμένη-ποι-ήτρια-των-εξαρχεί.*)

Antonis Fostieris also belongs to the poets of the seventies. His poetic language stands out for its clarity and tone of familiarity. It is a dense and talkative language in which the poet formulates an attitude of towards life's events and personal experiences. The main characteristic of his poetry is the combination of emotional and aesthetic elements with philosophical meditation. He is a crafty poet, a great image creator, who exploits the multiple meanings of words. Dense, glossy, glamorous, precise as a clock mechanism—whose tick sounds like a heartbeat— Fostieris' poetry, seemingly clear, with all its sound combinations and ambiguities, is characterized by a playful grace beneath which an agony runs deep, another element that undoubtedly gives his poetry some of its charm.

Kiki Dimoula wrote this about Fostieris:

> Fostieris' language, his tireless defender, managed to escape from the established linguistic ready-made tones in which most of his contemporaries have become victims, and charted a new path with the goal of its own recognition. His language attacks the surly depth of concepts with the wonder of a youth.

George Douatzis, another poet of the seventies generation, has been writing poetry for a long time. A close friend of Tasos Livaditis, he wrote a requiem for Livaditis on the 20th anniversary of his death. Douatzis' poetry, imbued by soft tones and a deeply considered idealism, goes far beyond the dialogue with an imaginary reader but extends dynamically across all contemporary social, cultural, aesthetic, and moral dimensions. His poetry is infused with politics, existentialism, and eroticism. He is obviously tormented by his anger at what is happening in the world and by the dilemma of trying to talk about daily things while at the same time revealing eternal moments in the course of humanity. His poems expose both his social conscience and his love for his homeland and stress the need to abandon introversion and stop the individual from undermining the collective. They underscore the multidimensionality of the crisis that his motherland is experiencing, a crisis that all modern societies experience in their own ways.

When Haris Vlavianos, another poet of the same era was asked why he wrote poems, he answered in the following enigmatic manner:

> Because after the stroke the Sikelianos exclaimed: "I saw the absolute black and it was inexpressibly nice." Because "when the soul ceases to admire, it is defeated" (Fernando Pessoa). Because it is easier to deprive yourself of some words than to waste your time trying to conquer them. Because one of the books that Joyce ordered at a well-known Londoner bookseller in 1914 when he was living in Trieste was Pinocchio's adventures. Because when Bataille was asked how she wrote, she replied: "In the way a woman with moral principles and a hazy past would take her clothes off in an orgy." Because if the passion ended, poetry would be superfluous.
> (Source: *Why I Write,* Agra Editions, Athens, Greece)

When Cloe Koutsoubelis was asked *how* she writes poetry, she said:

> An unknown woman lives in my studio. She wears a black dress that leaves her back naked. I have never seen her face. It is like subletting. Some would talk about occupation or perseverance. However, the woman has settled properly. She spreads on the counter various aromatic soaps she has made in various shapes and colors. She is usually cold and blows her nose. This happens to her, she says, because she crosses cold seasons on continents that have not yet been created. Moreover, she works wonderfully within the gap that is known to be completely clear. The woman is clinically absent.

Sometimes I suspect that I have been trying to have fun for a long time. That's why I'm determined. Once I meet her, I will ask for her name. I'm afraid she will answer "Chloe."

Phaidon Theophilou writes in the introduction to his poetry book, *The Cycle of my Close Cousin:*

> I never got involved with it nor did I ever deal with my personal death. I shall, when it might be possible, when the time comes for my death, and of course if I have enough time, since Epicouros said to his students, "Do not be afraid of death, for when it comes, you will not be here anymore." Talk to me even if it is too late. For the feelings of life that have been distilled. Let it be late. Talk to me about the killer egos which swirl upward. Talk to me about your life from dusk to dusk. No. Just a glass of red wine for me.

Ifigeneia Siafaka, a contemporary poetess reviewing the poetry of Alexandra Baconika, writes:

> It is important to look at how Alexandra Bakonika is put in front of the *female* and, by extension, what are the messages her poetry brings, compensating not only for the stereotypical phallicist positions but also by proposing a different reason against another type of *feminine* erotic poetry, which has as its main features an unprecedented fragility, passive position, emotional fluidity, minimal use of rational mechanisms, and, ultimately, the presentation of an untreated or difficult-to-process psychological world that requires more medicinal attention than contemplative reading.

The following excerpt from interview with another contemporary poet, Tolis Nikiforou, is equally suggestive:

> *Love and Death. The impulses of life. Who manages to triumph?*
> The final winner is always death. Everything wil perish, everything will be lost. But the triumph of life is love in its broadest sense. All artistic creation, of which poetry is one example, is an erotic act. It is a confrontation with the sense of futility and a confirmation of human dignity in the face of

the death that awaits us all.

What is your biggest fear?

The loss of my loved ones, sickness and death.

In an excerpt from your poem "A Child from the Anarchist Collection", you say: "I hide a child inside me, who does not accept that I can laugh when one is crying; inside me exists an inexpressible child who wants to make life using his heart as model." How painful can it be for a person to hide within him the child he once was?

The creator, the artist, the poet maintains in himself a childish look at things, the magic of the discovery of the world. With his primal innocence, he moves into the place of creation which is memory that supersedes its sorrow.

(Source: *https://www.vakxikon.gr/τόλης-νικηφόρου-ζω-ολόψυχα-το-παρόν/*)

When Dina Georgantopoulos was asked to describe her poetry she said:

My poetry is a simple and automatic recording of emotions presented with words. It is written everywhere, on the road, in the subway, at home, and especially in the lonely hours of the journey to my innermost being. Each piece of what I write is there to remind me of the feeling and the moment of reflection, until the pieces were joined on a page that testified to the importance of the pieces to the creation of a complete work to be shared. My poetry consists of exercises on the endurance of my truth, events that marked the time they were born; the experiential narrative of the relationship of thoughts and emotions, recording in a way that does not interfere with any secrets; the desire for the reader to feel the mood to be as transparent as I can be and to read with understanding my secret truths.

(Source: *fractalart.gr/ntina-georgantopoulou*)

George Theoharis has this to say about poetry:

Poetry is the paradigm of the Word that creates the aesthetics of writing as a result of the surprise resulting from the use of the language as a tool.

Poetry transforms human sorrow into a song opposite ravaging time.

Poetry is melancholy with tones. It is the desperate reasoning the afflicted man articulates when he attempts to confront the ultimatum of death, believing that, through the Word, he will annul it.

Poetry is our loving penetration of the other-I and above all to the other-I who stands on the other side of us. It is the ballast which balances the seaways of the ship with which we all travel.

Poetry is a channel of delivering our expectations for something beautiful.

Poetry is the moral of words. It is the poet's consciousness.

Geshemani Sideridis gives this answer to the question of what poetry means to her:

I believe that poetry is the unique and personal view of everyone who understands the things around him. The different way of expressing a feeling, a state, or a concept, an image: to animate in a separate way a smell or to free a sound from the boredom of absolute silence. Perhaps it is the language that is inside you with which you name things. It is the elegant or the subversive or the sharp, we could say, the reason you approach a situation at any given time. Ultimately, it may be the many different versions through which you may approach a truth or a fantasy with colorful eyes. In any case that's the reason why poetry is built artistically.
(Source: *dimitriosgogas.blogspot.com/2014/07/blog-post_5588*
.html)

Ifigeneia Siafaka's views are even more focused on fleeting moments:

Poetry, for me, is the effort of a lively moment (both mentally and physically) that seeks to be spoken, thus transmuting the energy that flows into the body. It is a way to make a symbol of the unspoken and give balance to the poetic subject. Without this first moment of energy, poetry can't exist. This is the quintessence of the poem but also the message that the creator will pass on to the reader. And this is the basis for any further processing. Moreover, because it is a deep and unique relationship of the creator with the illogical element, poetry transcends its creator by commenting on the human condition because it creates a parallel reality that is aesthetically superior. It is the way art can influence the recipient's consciousness and steer it inwardly.

For her part, Sissy Doutsiou defines poetry as "the concern that the spiritual man offers opposite the awe of the world." She continues:

The heart and eyes of the poet coordinate with the emotion that stems from the happiness of Eros, the misery of separation and loss, and the cycle of life and death. The poet caresses the pain, the horror, the deepest desire for any enjoyment and for ecstasy, and his disagreement with the moral code of his time. Poetry has power and the flesh and bones required to shake the body of the reader. It is the artistic work of man's ability to translate mainly his senses while he converses in depth with the unexpected. It constitutes the work of loneliness; the loneliness of the human body and mind which can engrave his artistic work. Poetry as well as theater is a way of life. The poet's prompting to surprise himself constantly with the thematic range of his poetry convinces him of the possibility of an unbeatable romance over social and political happenings. The poet tries to survive the barbarity of his times through his work. It is not a record of personal existential deadlocks, nor an experimentation in form, but a charming spiritual aura that is reinforced by reflection and critical attitude to the danger of the absence of great emotions and intense experiences. Poetry walks, raises objections and embraces enthusiastically the anthology of human life.

Tzoutzi Mantzourani describes poetry in a very particular way:

Silence teaches you to listen. Poetry means to create sounds out of silence there where the words are born and to give life to the silence of the words," Hugo Mujica said. I don't remember when I started to write, but I remember my first poem: I wrote it in the class of Ancient Greek in the first grades of high school, when the teacher gave us an exercise. I was caught by the verb that she gave us, and I composed my first poem. My whole life went on like that. Some event would trigger me, and I would start writing. I still do the same after all this time. Poetry means to endure and to stand, naked, just as you are, whoever you are, in front of the reader and be revealed to him. Let him touch the wounds of your soul and listen to them. If you have even said a little lie, but you haven't stood totally naked before the reader, you haven't written poetry. You can craft lyrics, you may know how to structure sentences, put them in sequence, but you don't write poetry. Poetry is written only when you plunge your pen into the blood of your heart until you drain it. That's the only way.

When Manolis Messinis was asked what poetry meant to him, he replied:

Reality is something else and something more than what is coded in the logic and the language of events. And here is the inner link between the thought and the effort of poetry: its attempt to abolish the power of events and to speak the language that is not the language which is imposed on us and is reinforced and benefited by the events as they occur. And if poetry can't change the world, through poetry, however, we can more readily accept the contradictions of this world: the stars and the sewers, the rose and the thorn, life and death.

Mary Mavronas comments:

I've always written: to trick the winters and lightning. I've turned pieces of my soul into silent words: to feel like I'm somewhere, with an antithesis of freedom on the fingers and with a shiver in the veins, endurance to the early in life defeats, rebellion against earthly attachments. I felt the smell of ancient voyages. Erebus reminded me of my fortitude. Poetry for me means love, soul vibrations, pain that brings birth and death together. Poetry is the return of the whole of existence to its most primitive source.

Likewise, Harris Psarras writes:

Poetry, like all other art forms, makes people's lives bearable. It comforts them in their suffering. It brings them closer to their expectations, the tangible and the unreachable. With the use of its one tool, language, poetry focuses on our sensitivity and our perception, without the need for sensory filters as much as the fine arts and music require. Poetry not only concentrates the meaning of language but also those delicate threads that make up the cocoon of meaning, while it doesn't need the reader's credulity as much as prose. The best poems seem unintended, like the objects of the natural world, and, at the same time, they are as fine as the works of any master craftsman."

(Excerpt from "Calm Voices", *Culture Now*, 30th issue, September 2014)

Eleni Marinakis comments:

Poetry is not cut off from reality; the world around us exists with its everyday life that often finds us unprepared to deal with it. Everything that happens around us always affects us. The crisis of values, of course, is measured based on our own internal measuring tool. The quantity, as we know, does not always refer to quality, yet it's necessary to remove cargo so that we do not sink, and to concentrate closer to perfection, we have to search for the minuscule to get to know ourselves and the world. While looking at things closely, we penetrate them; however, the distance is also necessary to give them their "normal" dimensions, to put them in place, assuming there's a proper place for everything. And because you ask for my own position, if militancy is defined by drums and cries, I am not on the first line.

More straightforwardly, Vaso Kosmidis writes:

The child, the flower, sun, sundown, sunrise, sea, sky, rain, crying, smiles, pictures, these all are poetry and I like to write about their importance in our lives. My thought process is simple and my philosophy simpler, and that undoubtedly I consider poetry."

41

Nektaria Mendrinos, on the other hand, says:

> Poetry is a fundamental necessity, which has the first word when other senses and other ways of expression aren't enough. When in moments of sorrow the tear isn't enough or can't even be liquefied, when in moments of joy laughter continues to sing inside a person, when love's demands overpower the body, when silence isn't enough food for loneliness, nor the senses enough for beauty, then poetry for me becomes its own reason and will to exist.

Asimina Xirogiannis underlines:

> There are thousands of definitions of poetry. Personally, as a creator, I do not care about the primary experience as much as in the way it is filtered inside me. The original stimulus can come from anywhere and can be anything: a person, a verse, a sound, another creator. What is important is how I transform them into art. Poetry is the processing of some of our initial stimuli in order to acquire universality which will relate to the reader."

Similarly Paulina Pampoudis says,

> Poetry is an art form to make a living. (I use the words *make a living* literally.) It is the art of capturing life through hints about the interpretation of the world beyond the recruiting capacity of your consciousness. In a poem, I confess: "I imply more than I can / imagine: I write." Poetry has to convey, at first or second level of reading, directly and alive, something that no art (except music and love) can convey: an extrasensory perception of the visible and invisible world.

In an interview, Ioulita Iliopoulos answered a number of questions about poetry and what the term *good poetry* might mean. She started by defining poetry as "the expression of reason that requires the most persistent internal search but also the greatest use of language—even when it doesn't appear easily. Poetry obeys itself; at least to the self we attribute to it, or else it obeys our personal perception of poetic function and expression. It has special and sometimes secret 'rules.'" Then she was asked:

> *Can we talk about high and low poetry? Ultimately, how is the artistic-spiritual value of a poem determined?*
> I think we can only talk about poetry. The word *poetry* in itself, doesn't tolerate the adjective *low* which you mentioned; something is either poetry or not. Our view of it and our personal concept of expression change from poet to poet, from time to time.
> *What in your opinion is great poetry?*
> The one that astounds our thinking with the power of the concept and the magic of language.*
> (Source: *http://www.alfavita.gr/arthron/tehni/ioylita-iliopoy loy-i-megalyteri-poiisi-einai-ayti-poy-kathilonei-ti-skepsi-mas-me-tin*)

Manolis Aligizakis writes:

I like my poetry to be about longing and desire, about the passage of the seasons, especially the moments when one season turns into another, summer turns into winter, which permeate my verse with a finely tuned eloquence. I wish my poems to be vibrant and radiant, and inspired by a powerful and subtle music to get under the skin of the reader and to revel in the vitality of the sensuous motion of language which makes the reader discover the microcosm and the macrocosm that blend into the simple images of everyday life. I want my poems to remain afraid that the mystery of these simple everyday images may be violated, disturbed, for example, by a phone call from a person buried the day before yesterday or the sacrilegious acts of the cement city, which makes dust of every emotion and refinement or by the hierodules and pimps who turn every ideology into profit. I want my poetry to declare that everything vanish, everything flow through my fingers, everything except the smile that is whole, the smile that cannot be divided or analyzed, the moment that boils and bubbles. I want my poems to remain in the reader's memory and heart long after he puts my book aside.

DIONISIOS SOLOMOS

Dionysios Solomos, (8 April 1798 – 9 February 1857) was from Zakynthos. He's best known for writing the *Hymn to Liberty* of which the first two stanzas, set to music by Nikolaos Mantzaros, became the Greek national anthem. He was the central figure of the Heptanesean School of poetry.

Solomos went to Italy and was initially enrolled at the Lyceum of St. Catherine in Venice, but he had adjustment difficulties because of the school's strict discipline. For that reason, Rossi, his tutor, took Solomos with him to Cremona, where he finished his high-school studies in 1815. In November 1815, Solomos was enrolled at Pavia University's Faculty of Law, from which he graduated in 1817. Given the interest the young poet showed in the flourishing Italian literature and being a perfect speaker of Italian, he started writing poems in Italian.

After 10 years of studies Solomos returned to Zakynthos in 1818 with a solid background in literature. In Zakynthos, which at that time was well known for its flourishing literary culture, the poet acquainted himself with people interested in literature such as Antonios Matesis, Georgios Tertsetis, Dionysios Tagiapieras and Nikolaos Lountzis who became his most well-known friends. They used to gather in each other's homes and amused themselves by making up poems.

The important turning point in the Greek works of Solomos was the *Hymn to Liberty* that was completed in May 1823 – a poem inspired by the Greek revolution 1821. The poem was at first published in 1824 in occupied Mesolongi and afterwards in Paris in 1825 translated into French and later in other languages. This resulted in the poet's fame proliferation outside the Greek borders. Thanks to this poem, Solomos was revered until his death, since the rest of his work was only known to his small circle of admirers. The Hymn to Liberty inaugurated a new phase in the poet's literary work: this is the time when the poet has finally managed to master the language and experimented with more complex forms, opening up to new kinds of inspirations.

After 1847, Solomos started writing in Italian once more. Most works from this period are half-finished poems and prose drafts that maybe the poet was planning to translate into Greek. Serious health problems made their appearance in 1851 and Solomos' character became even more temperamental. He alienated himself from friend and after his third stroke the poet did not leave his house. Solomos died in February 1857 from apoplexy. His fame had reached such heights so when the news about his death became known, everyone mourned. Corfu's theater closed down, the Ionian Parliament's sessions were suspended and mourning was declared. His remains were transferred to Zakynthos in 1865.

FOR A GIRL LIVING IN A MONASTERY

Beautiful girl of the monastery,
here I am. I look for you, I wait for you.
Come out to the gate and hear me sing
the sweetest verse my heart has ever sung.
May the wall allow me to be heard,
may it not feel jealous of me,
and before you leave, may you come close,
so that in kissing you I quench this fire.
Beautiful girl of the monastery, come here
and know I cannot let your virgin state,
oh innocent girl, go to waste.

ANTHOULA

Please fall in love with me, oh Anthoula,
my sweet and golden hope,
just as I fell in love when I first saw you.

Your eyes looked down at the green grass
and sorrow adorned them with two pearls.

You cried, oh Anthoula,
remembering your mother
who left you an orphan in this world.

Ah, yes, my love, be careful of the world's deceit
which with its cunning words abducts all precious girls.

Oh, where will you go alone,
my innocent dove? So many traps await you.
Oh Anthoula, come instead to me!

MEMORY

Stop the melodious chords
of the guitar.
They remind me of my youth
and grieving heart,

my youth that passed
so fast before me
and left behind
not one consoling thought.

The traitor only left
a wretched meditation
that expertly foretells
the hour of my death.

Here is the eye that craves
to see the sun again,
here the mouth that yearns
to take its final breath.

THE DREAM

Listen to my dream, my love,
my goddess of beauty.
I dreamed that one night
I walked out with you.

We sauntered together
in a beautiful garden
and in awe you gazed
at all the gleaming stars.

So I asked them, tell me,
oh stars, are any of you
up there as bright as
the eyes of my love?

Tell me if you've ever seen
such glorious hair,
or such a hand, or such a leg
such otherworldly beauty

which anyone who sees
at once demands to know
how such an angel can exist
on earth here, without wings.

With every kiss that night
you sweetly gave me, oh my love,
a new rose bloomed
in that garden of roses

and bloomed the whole night long
until the dawn light
discovered us together,
our faces pallid now.

My love, this was my dream.
It now depends on you
to keep me in your heart
until my dream becomes reality

YOU DON'T LOVE ME

I asked the wilted
flowers of May,
all answered in one voice:
you do not love me

THE YOUNG BLONDE GIRL

I saw the fair young girl
at evening yesterday
embarking on a sailing ship
destined for a far-off, foreign land.

The wind was blowing
and the snow-white sails
filled like a dove
spreading its wings

Her friends stood round,
some cheerful, some forlorn,
while she bade them goodbye,
waving her handkerchief.

I also stood there on the pier
and gazed at her departing form
until the growing distance
made sight impossible.

After a while I couldn't say
whether I watched
the white sails
or the waves' froth

but once both sails and kerchief
vanished in the water
my friends shed tears
and I wept too.

TO A FRIEND ON HIS DEATH BED

The time has come to leave you,
the Underworld I see.
I want to kiss you here,
I wish to, but cannot.

I can only say goodbye.
never to see you again.
I wish to hug you
but my arms are dead

Take my hand, feel how cold it is.
Take it, feel how faint it is.
I have let go all my hope
and wait for Hades only.

Yes, the time has come to leave you,
here is Hades' face.
I cannot even kiss you,
I let my last breath go.

THE CEMETERY

Oh, mother, I am afraid
the dead may wake.

Be still, my child, the dead
hold tight upon their gravestones.

LETTER TO MR GEORGE DE ROSSI, ENGLAND

When you come, you'll find
only the grave of your father
where I stand now, writing to you
on this first day of May.

We will spread the month of May
over his benevolent breast
since tonight he fell asleep
in the arms of Jesus Christ.

He was serene and motionless
up to his final breath,
as still as he is this moment
now that his soul has fled.

Only for a moment before he left
toward his dwelling in the sky
he gently moved his hand
as if to bless you.

THE UNRECOGNIZABLE GIRL

Who is the girl all dressed in white
and walking down the hillside?

As soon as this girl appeared
the grass grew tender as flowers

and spread its beauty
and swayed its tips, in love,

pleading not to be forgotten,
begging to be stepped upon.

Her lips are as pretty and as red
as the flowers of the rosary

and when dawn turns to daybreak
it sends fresh raindrops to her

and her glorious yellow hair
shines against her breast

and her eyes laugh, reflecting
the light blue of the sky.

Who is the girl who's dressed in white
and walks down the hillside?

ANDREAS KALVOS

Andreas Kalvos was born in April 1792 on the island of Zacynthos, the elder of the two sons of Ioannes Kalvos and Andriane Kalvos. His mother came from an established, landowning family. His younger brother, Nicolaos, was born in 1794. In 1802, when Andreas was ten years old, his father took him and Nicolaos, to Livorno Italy, where his brother was consul for the Ionian Islands and where there was a Greek Community. In Livorno Andreas first studied ancient Greek and Latin literature and history. For a while he lived in Pisa where he worked as a secretary and then he moved to Florence, a centre of intellectual and artistic life of the time.

In 1812 his father died, and Kalvos' finances became deeply strained. However, during that year he also met Ugo Foscolo, the most honoured Italian poet and scholar of the era, and, like Kalvos, a native of Zacynthos. Foscolo gave Kalvos a post as his copyist, and put him to teaching a protégé of his. Under the influence of Foscolo Kalvos took up neoclassicism, archaizing ideals, and political liberalism.

At the end of 1813, because of his *advanced* views, Foscolo withdrew to Zurich in Switzerland and Kalvos remained in Florence, where he again became a teacher. In 1816 Kalvos broke off a love affair he had and went to join Foscolo in Switzerland. That year he also learned that his mother had died a year before, a thing that saddened him deeply, as can be seen in his Ode to Death.

In the end of July 1826 Kalvos decided to travel to Greece himself. He reached Nauplion but was soon disappointed by the rivalries and hatreds of the Greeks and their indifference to himself and his work. For many years he and the poet Dionysios Solomos were both living on Corfu, but the two do not appear to have known each other.

In the end of 1852 Kalvos left Corfu, and returned to Britain. On 5 February 1853 he married Charlotte Augusta Wadams, a woman twenty years younger and they settled at Louth, Lincolnshire, where they ran a school for girls. Kalvos died on 3 November 1869 in Louth. His widow died in 1888. They were buried in the graveyard of St Margaret's church, Keddington, near Louth. In June 1960 the poet George Seferis, who at that time was Greek ambassador to Britain, arranged for Kalvos's remains to be transferred to Zacynthos, where they rest in the church of St Nicolas.

FIRST ODE — THE HOMELAND LOVER

Oh, my beloved homeland
oh, isle superb, Zakynthos,
You have given me
my breath and all
Apollo's golden gifts,

now accept this hymn.
The immortals hate the soul
and thunder it down
upon the heads
of the unthankful,

but I did not forget you
even when misfortune
took me away
to foreign lands
for twenty long years.

However happy or unlucky I,
when the light shines upon
the mountains and the waves,
I see you always
here before my eyes

and as the night enrobes
the heavenly roses
with the blackest *peplos,*
you remain the only joy
in all my dreams.

There, the people thrive,
there, the maidens
of Parnassus dance
and gather tender leaves
to crown the lyre

and the rough waters
of the ocean swiftly swell
and flood and shatter
the Albian deadly rocks
to endless pieces.

The rough Aeolian wind
carried me there
where sunrays of the sweetest freedom
have sustained me,
healed me,

where I admired your temples
and those of the Celts
oh, holy city, what
of the logic you miss?
Which Aphrodite?

The forests of Zakynthos
and her dark mountains
often heard the sound
of Artemis' silver
heavenly arrows

and still these days
the shepherds will respect
her trees and those fresh springs
where Nereids
wander still.

For the first time my body
kissed the Ionian waves
and for the first time
the Ionian Zephyrs caressed
the breast of Kythereia

and when the evening star
is lit within the sky,
then the sea craft sail,
inspired by Eros
and full of singing voices

then the same waves kiss,
the same soft winds caress
the bodies and the breasts,
the beautiful curves
of Zakynthian virgins.

Your climate is fragrant,
oh, my beloved homeland,
and your sea is enriched
with the aroma
of golden citrus.

The king of the immortals
gifted you with soil
that bears sweet grapes
and clouds that sail above,
soft, clean, diaphanous.

The eternal light
rains fruits upon you
in the daytime
and the tears of the night
become your lilies

The snows that rarely fall
never linger on your face
and even the blazing heat
never wilts
your emeralds.

Ever happy you are
and even happier
that you have never
lived beneath the whip
of any enemy or tyrant

Let Fate not bury me
in any foreign land.
Death is sweet
when we are buried
in our homeland

SECOND ODE — TO GLORY

Whoever said that glory
was as purposeless
as those who seek it
and burn myrrh to it,
spoke falsely.

Glory bestows wings
on those who seek it,
directs them
to the rough and
difficult path of virtue.

Whoever accepts
the call of glory
but refuses to follow it
has an impotent soul
and a contemptible heart

He has never shed tears
over the graves
of his friends
nor ever kissed
the soil of his kin.

Oh, Hellas, you have seeded
the fiery desire of glory
in the hearts of your sons
and thus are called
the mother of us all.

As when the lion
emerges from its den
charging and wounding,
killing and scattering alike
brave hunters and multitudes of Arabs,

as in the winter
when the haughty waters
of the rushing creeks flow down,
flood fields and sweep away
both shepherds and their flocks

or when at dawn
the sun bestows its light
across the earth, consumes
innumerable stars
above the high Olympus

three hundred souls
of proud Laconians
glorified Assopos
and the grove
of Marathon.

Like them, I seek the steel.
Who will give me
the thunder of war?
Who will lead me
to the struggle today?

Horrible, hated son
of Asia Minor, Ottoman,
why are you still here?
What is in your mind?
Why not escape your death?

The time has come: leave,
ride your wild
Arabian mare
and with her gallop
to defeat the wind.

The oleander sprouts
on Mount Hymettus,
the holy flower decorates
the desolate ruins
of the Parthenon.

But young men and women
old people too,
Hellenic giants, kiss, cut the branches
and crown
each other's heads

Ride your Arabian mare,
Ottoman, ride away,
escape, while you can,
the Hellenic giants
who chase you down.

See the gleam
of their battle-loving arms,
hear the roar
of those who seek
freedom or death.

Understand and gather here,
children of Hellas,
the time of glory has come.
Let us emulate
our glorious ancestors.

When our swords are sharpened
by the thunderbolts,
when our souls
are warmed by glory
who can defeat the Hellenes?

Why do you tremble,
Ottoman? Ride the mare,
chafe her, for beasts
that thrive in battle
chase you.

For you, oh, Glory,
worthy nations
honour their homeland,
singing hymns
to freedom, to joy.

ARISTOTELIS VALAORITIS

Aristotelis Valaoritis was another representative of the Heptanese School and a politician. He was also the great-grandfather of Nanos Valaoritis, one of the most distinguished contemporary writers of Greece.

He was born in Lefkada in 1824 to a Greek father of Epirotic descent. He completed his school education in Lefkada and Corfu and then he went to France and Italy to study law. He never worked as a lawyer though, but completely devoted himself to poetry. He spent an important part of his life in the small island of Madouri.

At the age of 25 he married the daughter of the Venetian scholar Emilio De Tipaldo, Eloisa. Using simple language he wrote many poems regarding the Greek War of Independence. He was credited as a national poet. Some of his most important works are: Stichourgimata, Mnemosina, Kira Frosini, Athanasios Diakos, O Fotinos, Astrapogiannos.

O Fotinos (or *Der Helle* in German), is a very famous unfinished poem relating the so-called Voukentra revolution of 1357 in Lefkada against the Venetian (Italian) occupation. Valaoritis composed this poem on the privately owned isle of Madouri.

Meanwhile, he got into politics. As a member of the Parliament of the United States of the Ionian Islands he fought for the rights of the Ionian Islands. Once the Ionian Islands were united with Greece he moved to Athens, as a member of the Greek Parliament. His speeches were heavily influenced by his poetic language making his rhetorical skills uniquely remarkable. The last years of his life he developed action towards the integration of Epirus to Greece, a goal not fully achieved until the Balkan Wars.

He died in Lefkada in 1879 of heart failure.

THE LITTLE BLONDE GIRL

I like the sea because we are alike
I like it, I heard you saying to yourself,
for sometimes it is wild , it roars, it sighs,
and sometimes it is playful, full of laughter.
Isn't the sea blonde just like my hair?
Isn't my bosom like its froth?
Don't I have waves and sky —
and a grave in my eyes?
I like the sea because we are alike,
and yet the beasts of the world hide inside it.
But doesn't an insatiate love,
the fiercest flame, hide also in my heart?

So I was glad to see you pouting,
dripping poison in my soul.
I exulted when your spite and jealousy
boiled your breath upon your lips.
Then I put my arms around your neck
and quenched your thirst with kisses,
hid my face beneath your hair
and built a nest within your bosom.

My wild wave, enough, my soul,
I beg you, quench your fury, lie down next to me,
let me become your safe, still harbour,
since what's the value of the sea without a shore?

LAMENT FOR THE YOUTH STEFANOS MESSALAS

Hades was ploughing, ploughing the earth that fears Him,
His rows but gravesites, His seed only poison.
Hades was ploughing with His black ox
which blew hard at each stroke of the merciless goad.
Where the ploughshare passed, it felled the trees,
uprooted homes and wrecked the world,
and you, young lad, what sought you on His path?

In your mother's embraces, in your father's too,
you were raised with kisses, and concern looked after you.
Oh, youth, why do you not remain with us?
You thought to sleep inside the earth was sweet,
you did not know, oh child, a grave needs company,
that in it you are destitute, an orphan.
You will not find your father's bones arrayed
where you'll descend, but you'll lie down in loneliness.
Oh, child, why do you want to leave?

But that young stripling heard us while a thousand
worlds and golden dreams around him seemed to shine.
He smiled back sweetly as if to say "the grave, my father
isn't loneliness but rather life and love."

Hades was ploughing, ploughing, and didn't rest,
but day and night His ploughshare worked,
it took the sprouts and hid them in the soil
and soundlessly, alone, He passed and furrowed.

Oh, father and mother, he is gone, the grave is covered,
bid farewell to your child on his last voyage
with your last kiss and bitter tears.
He'll sail as if he were a bird, and I
wish I were with him, to see my daughter in Hade's abode.

ASTRAPOGIANNOS

Excerpt

The horrible vision of Astrapogiannos' corpse
stutters and shivers in the hands of Lampetis.
The eyes of the dead man roll up, roll down,
three times before they vanish into darkness
and the night takes control of his forehead.
No other mark is left behind, but on his still-warm mouth,
like a moon-ray on the marble of his grave,
a mute smile, dead, shrouded like a corpse.

The white beard of the old fighter lies on the snow.
His warrior opponent returns his sword into its sheath,
takes up his bag with his rye bread
and hoists it to one shoulder.
On the other he puts the dead man's corpse,
then paints his fingers with the red blood frothing from the earth,
and with the corpse across his shoulder
he plunges into the ravine and in his haste he vanishes in smoke.

UPROOTED TREE

Excerpt

Tree, how came you, dead, onto my sandy shore?
Whose hand uprooted you, which power took you
from the mountain slope and threw you in the waves?
For a hundred long years, age had left your branches
calm, unwrinkled, and unbendably
attached to your iron and impenetrable bark,
and the ravine's wild calves sharpened their horns on you.
So tell me, mighty tree, how you lie dead now on my shore?

Free of care the insubordinate soul took wing
as if it were an adept, only sometimes seeking cover
under the pines of the hill or sometimes under the cypresses,
sometimes nesting secretly in far-off, lonely chapels
to search for apparitions. Alone, exhausted
it found refuge there. The dead took them as ghosts
during the night, but it perceived them as flowers
and bestowed its eulogies and sang its songs for them.

KALOGIANNOS

Excerpt

Dedicated to my beloved son John Valaoritis

Don't ask me whence I come or where I'm going
I have no home except
the blackberry's wild and thorny branches
where the wind and rain beat me, the poor bird that I am,
but my home's the ravine and joy is my life
as I fly and perch and stretch my long and carefree wings.

When I thirst a little, the sky-dew quenches me,
and I can eat my fill with a tiny ant.
I wake at dawn and dress myself with
the sun's first rays; I put on the gold-stitched
royal chlamydia and commence my song.

When a proud eagle flies to the clouds
and threatens the world, I see and laugh at it.
I neither hate its fortune nor fear its soulless talons.
It won't come down to feast on me,
such creatures find the world too small against its glory.

People call it emperor and put the crown upon its head.
They fashion it double-headed, and they paint
its image holding in one hand the golden sphere
and on the other a drawn sword…

POEM FOR THE STELE OF OLYMPIA DESTROYED BY A TEMPEST

excerpt

In the depths of the sky the gleaming stars dimmed,
the unshakable mountain stirred before me
and vanished into the hungry mouth of the sea.
I had believed the power of all fortune
never could be strong enough to topple you,
my beloved relic of a forgotten race.
Deathless Leviathan, accept my lament.
        When I gaze on you I cry,
and though you've long been our primeval cornerstone
time has now unlocked you, and your vertebrae
lie scattered on the soil, stepped on by dogs.

Oh, the unimaginable rage and curse of god,
the pitiless thunder that always comes down on you,
the earthquakes and tempests that set themselves against
our best achievements and with sudden power
smash down the greatest of them, one upon the other.

TENDRIL

To the maple tree that gazes down on it
and shelters it with shade
at evening and at dawn
the flowery clematis says:

"Oh, proud tree, whose leaves and
branches rustle in the wind,
do you suppose this earth's too small?
Do you imagine that you fit among the stars and clouds?

Water flows tirelessly by your roots
while you suckle on the mist
and you, the beast, feel jealous of me
because I suckle on the moistened bit?

What do you want of me, my maple tree?
Keep your shade away from me.
I am so small my flowers freeze.
Let the sun come and warm them."

"My little blonde tendril, why are you afraid of me?
You always want to crawl alone
and stay alone the whole night long
and for your pillow to have the earth and stone.

Let your flowers match my strength,
become a queen and I your throne,
steady yourself upon my body
and all flowers will envy you in my embrace."

The wild maple fooled the clematis
and amid its branches it consumed it.
Pity that you traded your blonde virginity
for only a little height more.

Poor and alone in your loneliness
your flowers were my secret joy,
but now that you're entwined above,
the clouds and winds enjoy your fragrance.

THE ROCK AND THE WAVE

Excerpt

Rock, stand aside that I may pass, the brave wave says
to the dark and angry rock that blocks the shore,
stand aside, for in my breast that's dead and cold
the dark north wind has nested and a black storm grows.

I don't have froth for armory nor hollow roar for mist
the bloody rivers I've collected are the world's grim curse
that has empowered me, the judgment of a world grown tired
that says, 'rock you must fall, your time has come.'

When I approached you as a slave, fearful and exhausted,
when as a slave I bathed and cleansed your feet,
you stared upon me proudly and to the world you said,
behold the wretched servitude my froth endured

while I, with all my work and service to your highness,
dug your foundation and day by day consumed your flesh,
for in the wounds I gave your tomb I have constructed,
concealed with seaweed, and buried in the sand.

Bow down, behold your roots amid the ocean's depths!
I have demolished your foundations, you have become a shell.
Stand aside then, rock, that I may raise the slave's foot
and step upon your neck! I've awakened like a lion.

* *Translator's note: In this poem, the rock symbolizes the conquering Turks
and the wave the enslaved Greeks.*

MY LOVE FOR THE HOMELAND

It isn't a migrating bird that daily flits by,
tearing the clouds as it flies in the wind.
It's neither ivy engulfing the rock with its branches
nor is it the lightning that flashes and fades.
It isn't the sea that heedless of earthquake roars for you,
my homeland, but your destruction I feel in my viscera

ANDREAS LASKARATOS

Andreas Laskaratos was born in Lixouri in 1811 at a time when the Ionian Islands passed from the French to the British. His first letters were taught by Neophytos Vamvas at the Castle School. At the age of twenty-one, the deacon of Deladecimas appointed him as a scribe to the Senate in Corfu and wrote him to the Law School of the Ionian University because he intended him as a judge although Laskaratos himself wanted to study medicine.

From Corfu he returned to Cephalonia and worked for some time as a Registrar of the County Court. Then he resigned and went to Pisa and Paris to study law. In 1839 he returned and worked as a lawyer for just three years. But his father's death made him re-engage in law because of some family affairs, though Senate responsible for issues having to do with law and lawyers refused to grant him permission. During this period she travels to Crete to study the Cretan linguistic idiom and folk songs. He also traveled to Athens, Syros, Corinth, Patras, Messolonghi. He was a student of Andreas Kalvos, and he also met Dionysios Solomos, who certainly influenced his subsequent course. He dealt with journalism, poetry, and is best known as a libelist. He was married to Penelope Korgialeniou, a well-known and wealthy family on the island, with whom he acquired two sons and seven daughters.

He published several satirical newspapers such as "Lazy", indiscriminately condemning immorality, injustice, hypocrisy. Many times he dealt with the policies and incompetence of politicians while heavily fought against religious superstitions and beliefs, especially the arbitrariness of the religious authority. On March 2, 1856, the metropolitan of Kefalonia, Spyridon Kontomihalos excommunicated Andreas Laskaratos because of his book "The Mysteries of Kefalonia." He then moved to Zakynthos, but on March 16, 1856 he is also exonerated by his metropolitan Nikolaos Kokkinis.

He died in Argostoli, where he lived after the persecutions he suffered on July 24, 1901, but his work remains timeless. Those who have studied it realize that he was a man who was looking ahead for his time and today, what he had predicted and wished to either change or prevent, are as a rule verified.

IMAGE

Come, beloved image,
come, my wife, accompany me,
stay close forever,
protect me from life's pitfalls.

My only guardian angel,
counsel my steps and keep them safe,
and if I lose my bearings,
come light the way before me

Your light sustains my virtue
and preserves my faithfulness
because I know that you are mine

I feel you in my spirit
and know not how to call you,
whether my wife or my soul!

THE DONKEY'S BIRTHDAY

Congratulations, may your donkey
live a long life and become
just as you wish him to be.

May his ears grow keen to your commands
and tune themselves to every word.
May his frame grow tall and fat
just as you wish it to be.

May your donkey, with God's blessing,
live a long life, and may you
have him always with you
just as you wish him to be.

May your donkey live long
and may you also, so that
you may do your work
just as you wish it to be done.

GIVING

Indeed one can give to others
and not give anything at all,
and wickedness may take
and not lose anything from others.

The same way that on Easter Day
the priest gives light from his big candle
freely, since it costs him nothing,

but if it wasted candle drips,
one after another, three and then four,
common sense would soon instruct
the priest to ask for alms
even were his wife the only
one allowed to share his light
as I do now with this short poem,
so joyous and ironic
which I gladly gift to you

and to everyone who cherishes
these few words of mine
and claims that this was made for me,
and may whoever like these lines do so in health.

Therefore I welcome everyone
and, with the Bishop's blessing
and my mind made up,
I hear, indeed, I order

monks and priests,
single and married women,
nuns and anchorites
young and pretty girls,
old women with undergarments,
all of them, I insist
may claim my gift.

POLITICAL DRUNKENNESS

Political drunkenness has given me my life
and still enthuses me, attracts me, stirs my wonder.
It's drunkenness, my dear, that fires my soul and makes me
ardent for my country, fierce to claim my right by any means
to transfer judges when I please, to hire my people
for all positions, and to expel my enemies.
I yearn to be the leader, call it my mania
but I live just for this, I only want to govern.
Why would I want to live if I can't rule?
Why would I want a homeland if I don't have the reins?
Let my homeland see me govern and let it go to waste,
let it call me its salvation and let it go to Hell,
let my legacy remain and let my homeland be vanquished.

Even nature craves its drunkenness in politics
and if nature wants it, why not I? What do you care,
you teachers of moralism? Do you think the ones
who rule use different measurements?
They all pursue my way, all follow my direction,
and to achieve their glory, push aside all others.

Oh, my reverent religion, oh, please, come help me,
assist me to the throne, come help me, oh come and help
and introduce me to the crowds with palms and joy
that I become a proper Christian, a churchgoer,
to be voted winner in the first and only ballot
for any government position that I choose,
since I now bow before you, my only wish to follow you
and to be worthy of the leadership.

Even nature craves its drunkenness in politics.
It is nature's wish, and what you say I have forgotten.

SPRING

It's here, it has come.
Women, gather round,
let's march to meet it,
let's march to welcome it.

Here comes sweet spring
adorned in flowers,
riding a donkey,
sitting like a man

with herds of braying
donkeys close behind it,
ready all to copulate
ready to be lovers all.

They kick with all four legs
and bellow in their joy,
so wildly alive that you can see
the madness in their eyes

and braying all along
they bellow out spring's beauty
and carry it abroad
for all the world to see

and spring, as it proceeds
and blazons its warm breath,
fills up the entranceway
of every house with heat.

The newly married maiden
feels hot in the cool air
and dresses in her
lightest cotton dress

and walks out to refresh herself
for all to see her passion
and the wind, if it can,
to cool her ardor.

Ah, spring, sweet spring,
companion of the young,
youth's oestrus, comrade
equally to boys and girls

if you run out to the fields
even if you took away your steps
a myriad of followers
you will always find beside you

while all the long-lived men
who can no longer walk the fields
to meet you, stay behind
and envying, blame the young.

Ah spring, let us give
to others their fair share
without losing our good hold
on the reins of your donkey.

Look how the young girls
play and push each other.
Look how they fall and show
their secret lines to men.

Ah spring, stay steady
on the saddle
and hold more tightly
to your donkey's reins.

Oh spring, oh my sweet spring,
companion of the young
youth's oestrus, comrade
equally to boys and girls.

MILTIADIS MALAKASIS

Miltiadis Malakasis, the poet and one of the most important of Modern Greek lyrical poetry, was born in Messolonghi in 1869. He studied at the Athens School of Law, but he never finished, since he devoted himself to poetry from his teenage years. In 1897 he became acquainted with the Greek poet Jean Moréas who had come to Athens at that time, and this acquaintance was decisive for Malakasis' poetry and his subsequent course. Jean Moréas was moved by the talent of the young poet and translated his poems and published it in France.

In 1908 Malakasis married the daughter of the well-known politician and prime minister of Peloponnese, Deligiorgi, first emperor of Moreas. From 1909 to 1915 he settled with his family in Paris and traveled to Constantinople to Munich and elsewhere. In the meantime he had already achieved a few of his poetic aspirations. He had founded along with Konstantinos Hatzopoulos and Lambros Porphyras, the company of the *Ethniki Glossa,* who had systematic efforts for the promotion of demotic language and had published his poems in *Noumas,* the periodical of the demotic language followers. In 1917 he was appointed Dean and then Director of the Parliament Library.

Malakasis enjoyed an early recognition, and in 1924 he was honored with the National Award of Letters. He published for the first time in the magazine *Weekly* during the period from 1885 and he signed his contributions with MM. More systematically, however, he began publishing poems, short stories and articles in *Estia* and other periodicals and newspapers from 1892 onwards.

He died in Athens, Jan. 27, 1943.

PLAYFUL MOON

Playful is the moon tonight
amid the grapevine leaves,
it flows as if you'd truly
like to drink it in a glass.

It plays not just among
the grapevine leaves
but also at her window
reflecting its soft rays.

FATES

Slow, heavy, steps as if from
ancient nights of unknown years,
echoes of steps on cobblestones,
lost steps, long forgotten,
secret laments of plaintive souls,

weak, small bodies, enervated
faces hiding in the darkness,
big eyes, black, shadowy,
groans rising from Hades
ghosts stooping, black-cloaked,

why do you leave your graves
night after night, visible but silent,
only walking with the mute
laments of plaintive souls?

SONG OF SONGS

Come, lean your blonde head
in my yearning arms
I have some songs to sing for you
now that birds don't lull you anymore.
The night, look, passes dressed in black,
all are asleep around us.
Come, my precious, my enchantress,
and let me breathe in your refined aroma,
oh come, and let me sing a song for you again.
Come lean your blonde head
in my embrace
now that birds don't lull you anymore
and only I can sing for you

FIRST VERSES

I like to read your letter over
and cry
and with my eyes lingering on every line
to see you
still warm, still remembering
when we said
we'd be forever one, remembering
the days
we ran with one another to where nightingales sang
seductively
the day that I remember when you said
I feel
an ache here in my heart

before the cough arrived to stop your words

RAIN

It rains outside the window,
black roofs, black streets,
tears that don't flow down the eyes,
silence, heavy, choking words.

Clouds harried by the winds
cry silently and moan
but cannot make my soul a prisoner
with all the secrets they narrate.

Once, inside the window,
back then when you sat next to me,
deep in your shining eyes I saw
the rain's reflection, and the road,

and further off, far from us both,
still in your eyes I saw
the clouds thrown helter skelter
by the ruthless power of the wind.

Rain outside the window,
black roofs, black streets,
tears that don't flow down the eyes,
the silence heavy, choking words,

clouds that now hang low,
heavy with unending rain,
but in your eyes no more reflecting,
no longer hiding other grief.

BEYOND DEATH

Your Fate had written it before your birth:
that your lips would never smile
and your youth pass without laughter,
and thus your joyless life has spent itself

and now when the candles are lighted
your face is sulphur-yellow
and a crooked smile is on your lips
glued to them, shiny, as if not yours at all.

IN FOUR WALLS

I like you falling on me
when in the night, I walk, oh autumn rain,
to freshen my bare forehead
as if my slow steps echo deep in the abyss
and in the waters of the street I then dissolve.

IN THE CONCH

Deep in the conch
I hide the flutes and violins
entrusting my soul
to your fleshless embrace

but your eyes did not reopen
nor your seductive talk resume.
They were palaces with no foundation
in the wide seas.

So I cast the chains and steel
of all my heavy, circular
old concerns
and all my desperation

and as the moments and the hours
of all the time persist
among the wildest tempests
I harvest roses and froth.

Beyond myself
and for the first time
with the gull's open
wings I fly

and I dive with the dolphin
that shone once
in the immenseness
of forgetfulness

deep in the conch
where I hide the flutes and violins.

MORNING STAR

Oh lustful morning star
how you surrender to the day
in the inundation of light
before you blend and freshly
spread the footprints of the night.
And more than the moon you calm
the darkness while you shine in secret
like hope that with a mere caress
defeats the blackest thoughts.
Oh how alike to dreams you are,
double-edged and slowly fading, flickering, alas,
betrayed by night and even
by the day's bright, ruthless light.

LAMBROS PORPHYRAS

Lambros Porphyras was born in Chios, but from his childhood he settled with his family in Syros. Still a high school student when he published the poem Sadness of the Marble in the newspaper Asty. He immediately became popular in the literary circles and aroused Kostis Palamas's interest, while he was closely associated with the magazines *Art* and *Dionysus*. He studied law at the University of Athens, but did not complete his studies. A socialist and a populist, he was a member of the Educational Group and co-authored the statute of the Socialist and Democratic Movement. In 1900 he traveled to Paris where he got in touch with the literary circles there through his association with Jean Moréas.

When Porphyras returned to Greece he settled in Piraeus, where he stayed until his death in 1932, publishing poems in the most important literary magazines of the time. He was recruited twice during the First World War. During his lifetime he published a single poetry collection entitled Shadows, while in 1932, after his brother edited his book Musical Voices it was also published; this was a collection for which he was honored with the Award for Excellence in the Letters and Arts.

He was a very popular poet and was honored with the Medal of the Mayor of Piraeus, Takis Panagiotopoulos, as well as with the Silver Cross of the Knights of the Order. Porphyras belonged to the notorious poets and was influenced by the European symbolists and by the poetry of Dionysios Solomos and Kostis Palamas.

He died in Piraeus on December 3, 1932.

THEATER

I don't know how to say it. But the road at evening
yesterday resembled a theater in the grayish fog,
the stage vaguely discernible in the fading light
and from afar the actors moving upon it like shadows.

The faraway houses, the yards huddled together
and the branches of trees you'd think were old, discolored sets
where untold actors had played out their curious dramas
and you'd have heard at one time moaning, at another happy laughter.

I don't know. They came out and met and sauntered
and performed, and it was sad and pleasant all at once
and, oh my God, as they performed night fell
and, oh my God, it fell and lowered its black curtain.

SMILE

Beautiful woman, your playful laughter rises
like a futile sound that makes no echo
in the haughty heart connected
to those innocent and silent smiles

bestowing joy, or to those other souls
that cover grief with silence,
and those that perish secretly
in ancient yellowed images

and though they hardly smile at all
they yet shine deep in silenced eyes
like dark reflections spreading in the dusk
in the forlornness of the sea

I SAW

I saw a far-off country in my peaceful dream,
a land whose beauty no soul can describe,
that seized my mind and made me leave my meager village
and promised myself I there alone would settle.

A foolish youth I started, spellbound by the beauty
of my dream, and passed through lands hemmed in by water
and others clothed with shining plains and hillsides,
but still the land I longed for receded, always further off.

The passersby I met urged me to settle.
This is a beauteous land, stay here, they said.
Yes, I replied, your land is good, my friends,
but not the one I dream of, which is far away.

Leave me to travel slowly,
alone to pass the plains and mountains.
Perhaps one day I'll reach it but even if I don't,
don't ever ask me, brothers, anywhere to settle.

VOICES OF THE SEA

Drink your wine in the dark tavern by the sea,
now that the autumn rains have started,
drink it with sailors facing you and stooping fishermen,
men whom poverty and angry seas have punished.

Drink your wine so that your soul grows free
and if grim Fate arrives smile upon it
and if new sufferings befall you let them also drink
and when Hades comes, calmly offer Him a drink as well.

WHEN I SAW YOU COMING

When I saw you coming with the other swallows
only then I understood why they all chattered with such joy,
the birds among the leaves, the fairies in the branches,
the butterflies that in the light were born again.

You slowly walked the pathway, and a certain glow
shone on your face, such flowery beauty on the moistened soil
undoubtedly the spring had met you first
and under the almond trees had kissed your lips.

EPIGRAM

Here in the deserted spring
where the shadow
of a beauty was fooled
and fell in its deep depth

for the water nymphs
on the oak tree branch
a wreath of wildflowers
I would wish to hang

And I beg the cane fields
to sing with flutes
the sorrowful words
and saddened echoes

and for the spring that flows
from the rock's schism
to pour like a lekythos
its songful tears

CYPRESSES

I wish the cypresses would furnish me
some few of their unnumbered branches
to build here next to them
my humble and deserted cabin.

I wish that they could give me too
their dry leaves to lie down on in the summertime
where I would sing their morning song
together with them and their whistling.

Then nothing else but, when my life
will end, full of unending joy,
a few more branches I would ask again
to use for my last bed.

ZACHARIAS PAPANTONIOU

Zacharias Papantoniou was a writer, poet, journalist, art critic, an academic, and a supporter of the native language on the linguistic issue. After his high school he studied medicine, which he never finished because he devoted himself to journalism. Since 1893 he collaborated with the Acropolis of Vasilis Gavrielidis and performed as an amateur actor at the Athens Theater. He published his first short story and he contributed to several newspapers.

During the same period he studied painting. In 1897 he was shocked by the Greek defeat and wrote the *War Songs*. Three years later he became editor-in-chief at *Script* until 1905. In 1906 he was journalist at *Chronos* and *Empros*. In 1908 he became the correspondent of the newspaper *Empros* in Paris. Very soon, however, the managing director of the newspaper stopped paying him because of financial problems. He was disappointed and sick, but fortunately he was supported financially by Sotiris Skypis.

During his time in Paris, he sent the *Parisian Letters* which were rated very important. Upon his return from Paris in 1911, he was introduced to Eleftherios Venizelos through Stefanos Granitsas and was appointed prefect. In 1914, as prefect of Messenia, he was awarded a state award for poetry. When he was prefect of Laconia in 1916, he banned the atonement of the priests against Eleftherios Venizelos and was brought to trial. The following year (1917) his father died, although many said he committed suicide.

In 1918, his book *High Mountains* was released and he was appointed director of the National Gallery. This was followed by the publication of his collection *Swallows*, dedicated to the memory of his brother. In the same year the anti-Venizelists prevailed and his book *High Mountains* was burned in Syntagma Square as it was considered anti-national and anti-religious. In 1923 he was awarded the National Award for Excellence of Letters and Arts.

Venizelos returned and his book *High Mountains* was re-established. In 1938 he was elected as a scholar and published the works *Children's Songs, The Gifts*, and others. Upon his election as an Academic he gave a speech with his opening comment on Theotokopoulos in demotic language. For the first time the demotic language was heard in such a Forum.

He died on February 1, 1940, (exactly the same day he was born) on the tram while going to the Academy at the age of 63.

PRAYER OF THE HUMBLE

Lord, evening comes again, and I beseech You.
No soul have I harmed other than my own,
and those who have harmed me are my own beloved.
I have accepted my own share of bitterness
and others' too. Joy deserted me,
yet still I wait, knowing that to hope is sin.
I love the fear of the night like happiness,
though none knock at my door, only the wind.
I seek no glory, humble in everything I've done.
The rain's song heard at dusk I have enjoyed,
to children I have given laughter and petting to the dogs,
the farmers I have welcomed returning from their toil.
Now nothing more have I to give or to retain,
nor do I expect reward: who could hope for that?
Oh Lord, grace me with my death, I pray.
Thank you for the plains and mountains that I've seen

TWILIGHTS

Memories return me
to my humble street
and recall the sad twilight
of lonely Sundays

In the reflection of sunlight
the withered girl
with neither words nor hope
waters a basil pot. ˙

No passersby walk past
nor anyone she knows
as on the balcony she stands
wearing her festive dress.

Before a ruined door,
like Atropos, an ancient sits,
while a boyish shadow lengthens
to a sad bell's chime.

The sun conceals itself
beneath a purple cloud on the horizon
and the cries of the last street vendor
echo like a psalm.

The world stops in that moment,
as the night delays.
How heavy my heart
this Sunday twilight.

THE BOAT'S ASLEEP

Oh, faint wind, stop your breath,
I fear the waves may roughen,
for here in this moonlit harbor
the small boat fell asleep tonight,

its shape reflecting with a crystal clarity
in the sea's diaphanous glass
you'd think the boat was dreaming,
exhausted by high waves and winds.

Let only our imagination fool us
and let the boat moor in diamond isles
and let it, in its dream, dip oars in sunlit skies
and let the world go by with no commotion.

I'm so concerned it might awake,
don't you disturb the dreamy craft.
Go, wind, sleep in the fairies' cave
and boatmen, keep on drinking in the tavern.

IMPATIENT

As soon as the chicken hatched its eggs,
readying its hatchlings to show their heads,
a rushing and impatient one,
still in the shell, declared:
How long am I to be imprisoned here?
I can't wait any longer. Do you
expect me to exhaust my time in here
while I've so many things to do?
A rooster certainly I'm meant to be
with tall plume and golden feathers,
mornings and evenings to adorn
the rosy dawn and announce
from every fence's top, and in the yard
in every place an army of hens I will command.
But the wise old rooster said: Wait, my little one,
until you've managed to escape the egg.

PARROT

As soon as he could say *good evening*
the parrot suddenly announced:
I'm the wisest, I speak Greek,
what am I doing here?

He dresses in his finest green
and to a birds' symposium goes
to share his wisdom there,
and standing in his sternest posture
coughs a bit, then looks afar
and says to them *good evening.*

His words were much admired,
so learned a bird he seemed:
they said: no wiser bird there is
than he who speaks the tongue of men!

Perhaps from India he arrived
with many a book along with him.
He must have talked to many sages
to learn their bookish tongue.

Oh, educated parrot, give us please
the honor of a few more words.
And so the parrot coughs, and coughs
once more, and says *good evening.*

A LITTLE GIRL'S PRAYER

Oh God, who cares for
humble houses like my own,
please grace my tiny window
with a nest of swallows.

You, oh Lord, who guides the stars
with host of faithful angels,
make my small flowerpot
to fill with lovely flowers,

and give me two white doves
to nest here in my tree
that I may offer them, I promise,
wheat seeds and water from my hands.

CYPRESS

I'm the tall tree that follows the line of prayer as it rises
spoken by a tranquil soul

I'm the lance that pierces the red dusk and guards the Invisible
from denial and irony

I'm the black cassock of the monk who hasn't finished
his penance in the festivity of the land

I'm the bell tower in the temple of pain that chimes my silence
for the souls that daily seek solace in vespers and matins

NAPOLEO LAPATHIOTIS

Napoleo Lapathiotis was born on 31 October 1888 in Athens. He was the son of Leonidas Lapathiotis, a Cypriot and an officer of the Greek Army, who reached the rank of second general and became a minister of military after his participation in the movement in Goudi. Lapathiotis' mother was Vasiliki Papadopoulou, a niece of Charilaos Trikoupis . At the age of ten he moved with his family to Nafplio, where he finished school, learned English, French and Italian while attending piano and painting lessons. In 1905 he was enrolled at the Law School of Athens, from which he graduated normally without practicing the profession of lawyer.

That same year, while he was only seventeen years old, he published in the magazine *Noumas* his poem Ecstasy. It was not his first work, since in 1901 at the age of thirteen he had written the rhythmic drama *Nero the Tyrant*. In 1907 he was a founding member of the poetry magazine *Hegeso*, and published sixteen of his poems in ten issues of the magazine until 1908, when the magazine was closed and Lapathiotis began his literary and journalistic collaboration with the newspaper *Evening News* and the magazine *Hellas* edited by S. Potamianou. In the same year he met with Constantinos Christomanos and Angelos Sikelianos

He died in Athens, Jan, 7, 1944.

POET

The drama of your life and art,
so insignificant and yet so deeply thought,
spending your mind's magnificence
in futile, laughable diversions,
playing with words all day and night,
testing how to put them next to one another,
how to mix them and add music to them,
how to enclose your dreams in verse.

Such pain and struggle, such an agony
to mould and turn your sorrow into harmony

and knead it using all your craftiness
just to return it to the people,
truly I don't know of any other drama
more important than your pain

the pain that longs be imprisoned in a cage
its space the alphabet of man.

And after you have played with rhymes
and words like little children in their games

and after you've diminished all your hope
and lost yourself among your memories

as soon as the regrets appear
when the moment comes to bow or not

you lift your cross along with all your treasure
and to Golgotha you stumble to be crucified!

SECRET

Some souls are made of marble
others of pain or smiles
and one is made of rose petals
though I won't reveal who.

My heart would suffer if I exposed you
so I put a lock on my mouth
and though many wise people are around me
no one has managed to guess yet.

Some souls are made of crystals
others are made of tears
and one is made of rose petals
though I won't reveal who.

I've sworn never to disclose even unto death,
but then, who knows, perhaps someday…
Something is burning my lips! Better
to stop this song right now and go no further.

EVENT

My timid eye looks at you
silently, deep into the dark
and faithfully it promises
to love you ever more.

Thin, tall, crazy for caresses,
lonely, working in a store,
one Saturday I took her
and we spent the night as one.

LONGING

Much do I long for rainy autumn
with its large and heavy raindrops
its withering of leaves and sadness of the dusk
that once intoxicated me.

The heat of summer burns me
with its high noon sun
and its clear diaphanous skies
while my heart craves the pure north wind
and hail to fall among dry leaves.

Then I shall stoop silently
like the sundown
sweetly to recall, who knows…
the last summer, like a far-off violin
that dives like a whisper in my heart.

IN THE TAVERN

Now that the violin is heard and we have had a lot to drink
and by a crazy love we're joined together
in warm camaraderie, bring us another round
that I may dive deep and lose myself in dreams,
my last friend.

If the wine stops flowing and if you also leave
and if the violin stops its sweet hoarse singing
deep in the void of my heart, immense like the sky,
the hoarseness of my death song I shall hear again.

WINTER LANDSCAPE

The grotesque full moon like a slab of ice,
motionless, standing in the middle of sea,

and a big silent reef, as exposed as my palm
with an old, sad, tragically small cane stick

and a shadow-something, that I don't know
what I've lost, returns, unable to becalm

that lost trio frozen and fully lit
in a silent vigil in the night, in the cold

TIREDNESS

I'm so tired of those oft repeated words,
the ones I'll say and those that you and they will say,
and of the verse's call and futile lyricism,
that my soul can't hope for anything but only
for the harbor and the fateful call that one day
chimes my eternal reckoning.

Only then, redeemed from earthly history
forever following the endless movement of the world
and the unceasing light that flows along its dizzying path,
the Great Song that I've never written
my last song, like a glorious torch,
will finally be sung.

GEORGE SOURIS

George Souris was born in 1853 in Syros. His family was wealthy and his father wanted to turn him into a priest. When his family went bankrupt, his father sent him to work for the sausage store of his uncle in Russia. Souris, however, began secretly writing his lyrics and after two months he left. When he came to Athens he was enrolled at the School of Philosophy of the University of Athens. However, he failed to get a degree after Professor Simtello failed him in the lesson of Metrics while others said in Latin, which cost him much as is discovered in his vengeful verses. In order to earn his living expenses, he gave lessons and also worked as a journalist.

As Spyros Melas pointed, Souris had rich spiritual qualifications and a wealth of knowledge which consequently turned him into an excellent journalist who satirized events of his times. His first satirical lyrics were published in the magazines "Asmodaios", "Don't Disappear", and "Rampayas".

On April 2, 1883, at the age of 30, he released the first issue of his newspaper, which George Drosinis baptized "Romios": a rhythmic weekly satirical newspaper. In August of that year he went through exams at the University, but he was rejected although praised, as he satirized, in "Romios", which was issued until 17 November 1918 just before Souris' death. In 1900, at the Municipal Theater of Athens,

Aristophanes' "Clouds" was successfully presented in a rhythmical performance. Souris also wrote several comedic comedies, which satirized the wrongs his times.

He died in Athens, in 1919.

MY IMAGE

Two yards in height
and rough looks too
beard and hair
here and there

forehead enormous
somewhat wide
the superb point
of a great poet

two eyes black
with no evil
filled by longing
and idiocy too

long nostrils
divided in two
and straight chin
resembling Jesus'

deep mouth like a well
flowing hair
that could fill
a mattress on its own

face as wild
as it is wrinkled
pale and cold
and almost dead

no human color
ever suits it
dyed in vain

loose teeth decayed
filled cavities
a miser's looks
no good for anything

OLD AGE

White hair on the head
is thought a bad omen
as if the Fate's curse
insults my old age

Anywhere I set my foot
everywhere I walk
Hades surely follows
yet slowly enough.

Dogs that encircle
this decaying body,
you too have had your bread
my foe and friend both underline

and so I run, a ghost at night
away from the active world
and each grave that I find open
seems like it opens for me.

AND YET

And yet still here
I've grown old
in the struggle of life
and I despise my age
and wish and need
only to be young again.

LAZINESS

I do not care to work today
for laziness has defeated me again
and I sit upon my mattress
and feel my body's heaviness
as if the whole wide earth
cannot contain me
nor ever can the sky.

I perceive the good as evil
and glance down once
and then towards the sky.
Despite this stupid world I live in,
I wish I could just once
live fully and never die.

TO MY SHADOW

Oh crazy shadow, why do you follow me?
Why can't you let me walk alone?
Why don't you disappear?
Why must you always be my close companion?

Sometimes I see you bent and other times you're straight,
sometimes tall as a staff and other times a midget,
sometimes walking ahead of me and other times behind.
I find you again each time I seem to miss you.

Lacking eyes you still grab everything I take.
Sometimes you lead me but other times I you,
I mean to say, you act just like I do,
my second self, my likeness in my shape.

Oh crazy shadow, why do you still follow me?
Why don't you disappear at last?
We meet too often at my house and in the street
and truthfully you frighten me, I must admit.

HEROES

Amid the missiles and explosions
in their prime of youth they fell,
daring and courageous, bodies
unfittingly buried in foreign lands.

No one knows their graves,
no one goes to mourn them,
nor burn incense for them,
and no one ever made a wreath.

Nameless heroes in unknown graves,
no one ever wrote their names
or ever kissed the soil. No cross was ever
placed there nor ever candle lit.

One day a young girl's tears
will flow over graves that
have become the world's cenotaphs
and beacons of victory for their mothers.

SOME INK

Some ink and paper and a few verses
are the only present I can give you,
but I am glad my miser Fate has granted me this gift
for otherwise I never could salute you.

Nothing from my hand have you received
except some badly crafted verses
which someday, who knows, you may find
that others envy, or give hope to you.

And if the happiness that I've implored for you
could one fine morning come before you,
it would reveal what my poor verses hide—
that any greater joy your heart could never hope for.

TO MY WIFE

My dear wife, I don't have to say
how much I've always loved you.
If sometimes we contend and row
in turbulence and turmoil living,
it's because I like upheaval
and long for rougher seas.

Love without some bitterness
lacks sweetness, gives no joy,
so keep your stern composure,
leave me my troubled mind,
and know that now and then
too calm a sea brings vertigo.

Dear wife, though I don't tell you,
you know how much I love you,
your laughter but your anger too,
and if another woman turn my eye,
know that my heart and, yes, my ugliness
belong to you for ever and some more.

JOHN POLEMIS

He was born in Athens in 1862. His father came from Andros, while his mother was from Athens, both families, however, had roots in the Byzantine years. He started writing poetry at 13. Polemis soon developed friendly ties with George Souris, the Cretan poet Emmanuel Stratoudakis and Dimitrios Kambouroglou. When he finished high school he joined the youth club "Muses".

He studied law in Athens and for two years aesthetics and history of art in Paris. His first poems, following tradition of the times, were written in katharevousa. He worked for the Ministry of Education as the General Secretary of the School of Fine Arts, while he was founding member and first president of the Society of Greek Theater Writers. His poetry is characterized by sensitivity and benevolence, elements that have also characterized his whole life. John Polemis joined the New Athenian School opposed to exaggeration and extreme romanticism, while at the same time he established (like Palamas, Drosinis) the demotic language in poetry. He was a low-key poet, sentimental, melodic lyrical and dramatic.

His work, which had an unprecedented popular appeal, was by its melodic verse, simplicity and effortless symbolism. Many of his poems have been set in music. In 1918 he was honored with the Award for Excellence in Letters for his contribution to the Greek letters. John Polemis also wrote dramas, poems for children, a few short stories, and edited poetic anthologies. He was often criticized by his contemporaries and critics for his low-tone style, his intense sensationalism, lack of poetic depth and thematic originality.

He died of bronchopneumonia in Athens, 28th of May 1924.

MOTHERLAND

What is our motherland? Perhaps the plains
and snow-capped mountain peaks?
Is it perhaps the golden sun that shines upon her
or is it night's innumerable bright stars?

Is it perhaps each of her shallow shores
and all her counties with their villages,
each landscape, every isle that distantly appears
on each one of her many seas?

Is it perhaps her ruined monuments,
the ancient temples crumbling in the sun,
yet decorated by her art's immortal glory
that echoes everywhere you turn?

All these are our motherland. These and those
and what we have deep in our hearts
which unseen, like a sunray, shines
and calls inside us: Let us march, my boys!

ANIMALS

I'll never harm
poor animals.
Do they not hurt
just like I do?

I'll always caress
and I'll protect them.
I'll never leave them
hungry in the streets.

Even when I see them
hurt by others
I'll still with courage
go to them

caress them
heal their pain
and comfort them,
doing all I can.

WATERED DOWN WINE (excerpt)

All that he had, lands, houses, wife, and children, lost
and nothing left, nor any word to comfort him,
or soothe his thoughts or kindle hope, he waits,
his patience like a rock upon his chest.

Time, like a ghost, drags its slow feet along,
nor does he know the logic or the reason.
His days are spent in taverns, wine in hand,
his misery to forget, a futile effort.

WASTED YEARS

I wish the years I lived not loving you
could be restored to me,
years unrecalled as if unknown,
the years I lived without you.

River that flowed over rocks,
river that never moistened grass,
water that the earth sucked into its dark depths
where each trace vanished.

I wish I could relive the wasted years
to love you ceaselessly with no end
to bestow on you my first love endlessly
from birth till my last breath.

I've graced you with half of my life,
and wish I had innumerable lives
to give you, to love you as I should,
to repossess my wasted years and you.

THE NIGHTS I'M AWAKE

Two sparkling sapphires, two sweet little eyes
have wounded me
and achingly I stay awake in thought
and night-long contemplation.

The moist night dissipates
as if ascending smoke,
dawn comes, light grows, moon
fades, but still I keep my vigil.

While stars embrace and kiss
and, I would add, do admirably,
I keep still awake
and those sweet eyes still rest.

Whose are they? Do not ask me more
beautiful maiden,
go to your mirror and see them there,
smiling at you.

DON'T CRY

Don't cry, don't ever say that nothing's left for you.
The passing tempest on the mountain peak is left for you,
the rosy dawn, the warm day far off in the sea,
the olive groves among the plains, the city's loud commotion.

The lonely and deserted seashore too is left for you,
where in the evening await the rocks and quay
and houses and the old fisherman who slowly oars.
Don't cry. All our lives remain to us

and every evening life surrounds you
in the soothing breeze and the night's sighs
and the serene and peaceful beauty of our lives,
that too will stay eternally with you.

CARYATIDS

Before the Caryatids, maidens made of marble,
we stood admiring them for hours.
Your eyes revealed a certain sadness
for the stolen one, missing from all the others

in foreign lands, in darkness at the world's end.
Yet I observed them accurate in number
and thought the stolen one had been restored,
but I was counting you, my love, among the others.

POPLAR

Remember our poplar? Playful in the breeze
it kept us safe from the incendiary sun
as joyfully it swayed its graceful top
and whispered pleasantly its subtle pleasures
spreading its laughter to the yards and grapevines

when it was answering your ever-happy laughter.

I passed it yesterday. Oh, what the years can do!
Neglect and loneliness reigned all around,
but that gigantic poplar knew my pain
and with a soft, sad whisper told it
to the wind and to the sun's insufferable heat

when it was answering only to my tears.

WITH SONGS

Those heroes charged with songs upon their lips,
speared down, laid out the bodies of barbarians,
their lives but a song that day,
their victory another song that will remain forever.

These heroes also charged with songs,
speared down and fell upon the soil of martyrs,
their lives but a song this day,
their memory another song that will remain forever.

LORENTZOS MAVILIS

Lorenzzos Mavilis was born in Ithaca in 1860 though he had Spanish origin. His grandfather was consul general of Spain in Corfu, where his family had settled. In fact, he spent most of his life there. In 1880 he decided to go to Germany to study philology and philosophy. His studies continued for fourteen years and was influenced by Nietzsche's theories, and the *Critique of Pure Logic* by the rational Immanuel Kant. He also dealt with the Sanskrit philosophical texts and translated excerpts from the Indian epic Mahabharata. During his stay in Germany he delved in the composition of lyric poems (mainly sonnets) and chess puzzles published in German papers and magazines.

In 1887 he participated in the chess tournament in Frankfurt. Two years later he took part in the chess tournament of the capital of southern Silesia, Breslau, with the pseudonym Sillibam. In 1896, Mavilis participated in the revolution of Crete, fighting with the rebels in the Cretan mountains. And in 1897 during the Greek-Turkish war he gathered seventy volunteers and went to fight in Epirus where he was injured in the hand. The expense of the campaign of volunteers was covered by him.

In 1909 he became an enthusiastic preacher of the uprising and in 1910 he was elected as a Member of the Parliament representing Corfu. In 1911, defending the demotic language as a representative and member of the Revolutionary Assembly of Corfu in the Greek

Parliament, he said, addressing the katharevousa lovers: "There is no vulgar language, there are vulgar people, and there are many vulgar people speaking the katharevousa."

He died in Pamvotida, November 1912.

BEAUTY

In somber intersections, slaves to a wage
work in the incandescent sunlight,
hawkers and cursed laborers,
all jobs from masonry to selling fruit.

They've just one thirst that stays unquenched
when you walk by them, maiden,
your eyes as innocent as doves,
one thirst that stops all other yearnings that they have.

Far away from flowery orchards
deserted by the work's sweet pull,
one only care they nourish

peacefully, in holy hope,
they gaze at you and whisper, sighing,
God bless, sweet girl, and God protect you.

CRETE

Lovely gold-green siren,
eyes full of love, lips lustful,
hair like flowing sunrays,
breasts firm, but body dressed in scales,

you sing this song amid the sea's
rose fog and in the wide and sunny
kingdom of the wind
far carried by the breath of earth.

"My kiss is like Amaltheia's milk
that nourished Gods.
Come enjoy it with

my chaste embrace, life's refugees,
and my holy gifts I give you:
death, eternity, and freedom."

KISS

Like golden sails my dreams sail slowly
on the lustful seas of fantasy
and glide to where you've gone,
where your two eyes laugh and cry

where you shine, beloved lily,
girl of unblemished beauty,
and tuneful songs join your enchantment
that breathes from unkissed lips.

My saddened heart rejoices when
in night's cool darkness, tempest passed,
you come to bloom, my little flower,

in the lonely orchard of the world.
My soul that never learned to kiss
then knows immaculate ecstasy.

SILVER CUP

Crystal, diaphanous, filled
with red wine that shines purple,
a glass opposite you, a humble glass
but full of feeling and of endless love,

it longs for you, it touches you
and slowly pours its contents out
and empty to its bottom now
it craves the warm touch of your hand

and you stand calm and unaffected,
a silver cup, rich in its history,
rich with your proud regard,

you've been used to being loved,
and in the saddened revelry of life
you hide well what you're made of.

ÜBERMENSCH

Raise the slab of mystery,
unafraid of the snake's bite,
ceaselessly searching for the truth
and look, they say, how consoling

it is to count all the arrows of pain
and vigilantly enumerate the wounds
inflicted by each arrow shot
from Fate's pitiless, keen bow

and if you find that pain's the only truth,
then from your courageous chest
throw off the shame of orphanhood

and in the sweetness of your strength and beauty
and with a proud delirious cry
become your God, defeat your Fate.

IDOLS

Oh, my joyless joy, my humble verse
my secret precious pride,
you all rise up from the same dough,
you haven't come to life by chance,

you don't sing senseless, pointless songs
like those of scatterbrained lovers
nor do you belong in drawers
or go searching for your value

but you belong to souls and little bodies
of my aches and longings that
reward you with their bitterness.

Yes, our joys are idols and our truth is grief
but why should I concern myself when
if I just look at you my grief turns into honey.

ÜBERMENSCH'S HOPE

With gifts from Mars, the Übermensch's hope
lights fires in our hearts
till longing becomes flesh
and the oak bends down before the mushroom

and you, symbol of bravery, unerring
shield of freedom, are degraded
by the weak and crafty merchants
like the worms that eat the fallen lion's carcass.

Gone is the beast with its proud talons
that frightened earth and sky, gone are
the walls painted by gunpowder and blood,

but if these verses could survive
and live as you have lived, they'd sing
for you and shatter those who ravaged you.

ROMOS FILYRAS

His real name was John B. Economopoulos. He was born in Derveni near Corinth in 1888 and died in the Dromokaition Asylum on September 9, 1942. He was educated at home by his father, who was an educator.

At the age of 14 Romos settled in Athens, where he worked for various newspapers. He went through many tribulations and transitions throughout his healthy life, then, as a consequence of an aphrodisiac disease, in 1920, he crossed the borders of logic, utopia and drama, only to succumb to madness.

In 1927, he was admitted to the Psychiatric Hospital, where he did not stop writing, sometimes well-crafted poems and sometimes completely mischievous poems. He would write his poems on paper in the psychiatric hospital and he gave them profusely to the guests. His goal was to never get out of there.

He died on September 1942.

IN HADES

One day we'll go down to the darkness
and even if we haven't drunk the whole glass
even if we haven't strayed from virtue's path,
our bodies all will perish in the grave.
Our latest love will feel as ardent as the first,
such passion in the celebration
of our lives that our youth will rekindle
and the fire of our blood will reignite.

Only the girls will reflect on all
the joys that passed and that will come.
They'll stand before us as in a parade
and when like angels they will fill
the sky's great void, our thoughts
won't know which one of all the joys
adorned our youth the most with golden light.

GIVING OURSELVES

If we gave ourselves to youth
and wholly loved each living soul,
if we weren't the last nor yet the first
to do this, yet our ardor is expressed in it

and over the wild darkness of the abyss
and far away from life's commotion:
we won't pave the traitor's path
nor leave such footprints on the soil.

And if our belief in the illusion of another life
didn't sweeten the sadness of our souls,
if non-existence cannot fool us,
we, the worldly and unearthly too,
shall say we've lived to fight
in life and death on equal terms.

THE POET

I had fallen in the depths of the black
hopelessness of the nightmare catalyst
in the heat of summer, the sad and sorrowful
deathly low note of the dreamscape

I had neglected my fate in my slumber
for years. Yet verse and rhythm were never absent
and I had climbed up to where the fount existed
where science said *I had it* and for this I climbed.

Because I had lost *the regular,*
the inspirer of dreams, the world's prophet,
the spontaneous poet who leans on clouds

the great, the holy rhythm interpreter.

AMBUSH

I'd always wait by the sea
like other times, like yesterday, like years ago,
phoenix to spring from the ashes again,
a lily among the coldest snow.
To see my reflection in an image
by the shore, longing for the unknown
that comes like the numbness of a sick man
yet slides down to the cane field.

Smoke that rises from the far-away chimney,
a boat arriving without a captain,
without hair waving in the air,
a dream of love, the first and last.

UNKNOWN GIRL

I wish the one I loved saw me tonight
the one I've never met nor ever seen,
the one I've cherished reverently in my heart
like a warming ray of sun that shines on me.

Tonight when my heart stirs, eyes shine,
and blood ignites within me and my soul rejoices
and my thoughts rise to infinity in the silver
moonlight, a foggy fire engulfs my ecstasy.

I WISH I COULD BE

A bird that sings
with the wind of youth
on a simple branch
with flowers of my first love

but the song turned
soon to mourning.
I wasn't meant to be
what I've for ever dreamed of.

INSPIRATION

Nothing matters in the world but inspiration
alone it sings a lullaby to bitter pain
and rescues us from time's relentless pace.

To see you, to take the beauties that you have
and melt them in my verse's flowing stream,
to nourish them, to multiply, one grand idea
sprinkled with inspiration's myrrh.

PORTRAIT

In the street where people run incuriously
indifferent to beauty, you sauntered
looking as if the breeze was raising you,
as if you never hated anyone.

Your step was soft, a revelation,
your face snow-white, a lily,
and as your shining glance alighted on me
that tranquil smile appeared.

Like the priest of some fantastic faith
or someone painted by Velasquez's holy brush
an Andalusian lord
you peeked out from behind the sea of people.

Once I'd met you in a noisy street,
a serene ghost, fleshless, holy,
you stayed on in my soul like
an ethereal idol and I your fanciful believer.

JOHN GRYPARIS

John Gryparis was born in Sifnos, but spent his childhood and early
school years in Constantinople. His father was a teacher and bookstore
owner. He graduated from the Great School of Genos and in 1888 he
was enrolled in the University of Athens to study literature. In 1892, his
collection Sundowns, written in demotic language was rejected by the
Philadelphia Competition Committee. In the same year, he returned to
Athens for five years, where he worked as a teacher and edited, along
with Alexandra Papadopoulos, the journal Philological Echo. In the two
years he collaborated in Philological Echo, Gryparis succeeded in
working with names such as Palamas, Psycharis, Eftaliotis and others,
turning the formerly unimportant magazine into a serious tool that
worked for the cause of the demotic language. He was also a co-founder,
along with Kostas Hatzopoulos and Yannis Kamboussis, of the
important literary magazine Art, which was pioneering in informing
international forums about the literary movements of Greece and greatly
influenced the renewal of the Greek spiritual and artistic landscape of
his times.

In 1897, while the Armenian massacre by the Turkish authorities
took place, Gryparis returned to Athens where he finally received his
degree in literature. From 1897 until 1911 he worked as a teacher in
secondary education in a few Aegean islands, in Amfissa and Aegio, and
in 1911 he married and left on a scholarship to Europe (Italy, Germany,

France) until 1914. Upon his return he served as school principal in Gythio and the Messolonghi (1914-1917), General Inspector of Secondary Education in Chalkida (1917-1920), editor of the magazine Illustrated Greece (1925) and director of the National Theater (1930-1936). Gryparis also wrote poetry and prose; his unique poetry is written in demotic language in the collection *Scarabs and Terracots*, in which he collected his earlier poems published in literary journals and newspapers. He was honored with the Award for Excellence of Letters and Arts.

He died in Athens, March, 1942.

SOLEMN PROMISE

I became a pilgrim
to repay my solemn promise
and then you came to walk
along with me and barefoot too
but half way there your strength failed

and I took you in my arms
and carried you until
I made out, facing me,
the holy door and temple
far up the mountain side

and tired as I was,
my eyes now almost failing me
with you still in my arms
and let you rest by the church door
which I'll never enter.

BEAUTIFUL ISLAND

The island of my longing fires me up
when I conceive it sailing on the waves,
bows slicing through the sea, the ropes
among its puffed sails creaking in the wind.

The route it started it will never change.
Neither forward nor backward shall it go,
but like a straight-bowed ship in thought,
without me, it sails in the Aegean.

Without me! When amid my joy
like a bride with her coronals
the ship took off and won't return

and standing on the summit of a rock
where ill luck guided me, I see it passing
and desperately extend my arms to hold it.

FOOLISH JOY

With naked feet among the flowers
and wild hair playing with the breeze
the foolish joy flies among the songs
a fragrant child, a soothing mistral.

A butterfly with silky fluff
spreads her bright wings
and airy golden locks
that flash with noontime heat.

Her heart cannot conceal her joy
but when she cries: *what lacks?*
an ancient echo answers
from the hard dry rocks: *your sorrow!*
I'm old and know that only when you suffer
do you learn to know the truth of joy

CLOUD OF SORROW

Why does our joy, our little joy,
to sadness only lead us?
A cloud of sorrow covers us
and we lean our heads aside.

Sweet sister, now I perish,
compassion only saves me now.
The storks, gray-feathered, fly away
and take with them the swallows.

Why does our joy, our little joy,
to sadness only lead us?
Another winter we have spent
in darkness in a foreign land.

MY LIGHT

Across the sky the bright moon
gleams from side to side
in the deserted air the dawn
turns off night's other lights.

But where the new day's rosy flush
glows in the morning twilight
one tiny star close by shines flickeringly,
alone and unknown to the rest.

And I said: take such goodness
far from me; one that near another shines
misplaces its own brightness.

Better alone, and better lonely
in an unfamiliar corner of the world,
my little light shines well enough for me.

SEPARATION

After the wild whirl of love
such separation brought me
sadness vaster even than
the sea that lay between us

but in my heart I hold the sea
so when the wave sings by the shore
its endless grievance will evoke
a saddened hymn, an antiphon

a mourning psalm, a sob
that crying with the sea
from end to end engulfs the shore

in tears, till at the end
our longing sinks into the sands
and turns my sorrow into songs.

LAST VOYAGE

Rusted ship, as your rabbets strangely creak,
you think your planks will gradually give way,
and you imagine sailing in the mouth of the abyss,
your unhealed wounds beseeching for more time.

Mermaid-like, your gaze upon harbor's door,
you hide the unconquered soul within your aging body
and dream of far-off voyages in seas and endless oceans,
your soul enthralled by endless ardor.

Oh true, so true, and if your Fate decrees
you're meant to vanish in the ocean's depth,
better than to idle peacefully at shore
is to chart a route to unknown, far horizons.

TELLOS AGRAS

Tellos Agras (his real name Evaggelos Ioannou) was born in Kalambaka in 1899. The same year his family moved to Athens and from 1906 to Lavrion, where the poet finished the Primary School. In 1916 he graduated from high school and was enrolled at the Law School of the University of Athens, where he received his degree in 1923. In 1924 he worked at the Ministry of Agriculture and Tourism. In 1927 he was appointed to the National Library, where he remained until his death.

His writing work began in 1907 when he was a subscriber to the magazine *The Growing of Children* and from 1911 he began to write regularly in the subscription column of the journal with the nickname Tellos Agras. In May 1923, when he graduated from Law, he wrote the *Farewell* autobiography. He collaborated with other magazines, such as the *Lyra*, the *Altar*, and the *Youth*.

In 1918 he was awarded the Sevastopoulos Award, and he won the First Prize of the literary magazine *Esperia* in their short story contest in London. In 1921 he gave a lecture on Cavafy in the Hellenic Conservatory Hall. That same year he translated *Strophes* of the French-speaking Greek poet Jean Moreas.

Tellos Agras wrote mainly poetry and criticism of literature. He also often wrote in the magazine *Nea Estia*, which he served as editor-in-chief for a while. In 1934, his poetry collection *The Bucolic and the Praises* was published, followed in 1939 by the second one, entitled *Daily*.

It was awarded the First State Poetry Prize in 1940.

His poems were set in music by a few music composers.

On October 11, 1944, he was injured by a stray bullet in his ankle during a shoot-out between the security forces and EAM. He was transferred to the Evaggelismos hospital, where he eventually died in November from septicemia.

LAST NIGHT IN MY DREAM

Last night in my dream I saw
our newly born Christ
as cows blew on him
their hot breath.

His forehead was like the sun
though the manger was so poor
and each of the magic gleams
shone brighter than daylight.

The Magi leaned over his feet
and the star up high above
looked like a crown ready to place
upon the hair of Virgin Mary.

Shepherds and shepherd girls
knelt reverently before him,
blonde angels stood
and sang Hosannas round him.

Yet of the angels and the Magi
I never felt more envious
than of his mother's lips
and her warm, her so warm kiss.

CARRIAGE IN THE RAIN

For hours alone the carriage
under rain awaits
not troubled by the torrents,
but tyrannized
by the unfamiliar neighborhood
that doesn't want it.

The little horses close to one another
stand waiting
beneath one canvas in this place,
the sorrowful nothing
they might through time befriend
remains.

There are no blinds or alleyways
nor deep-shaded ivies.
Nothing remains except
the line of
streetlamps with their two wings,
crossed and bronzed.

The lintels and the cornerstones
have fallen,
the airy passageways, the narrow galleries
and frightened memories
have vanished like discreet
good ladies.

Take my empty life
take my poor soul
take me, your companion,
and we go
as you have vowed,
to yesteryear

ON WORKING DAYS

Poor neighborhoods, abandoned corners
where deserted hearts, encased in frost,
that on a Sunday numb with cold
and sad music stand and sing for us,

tiny faces shining timidly,
lips sealed by sadness,
lips never tasting a warm kiss
except the farewell kiss,

pale begging hands,
unworthy souls in supplication,
shadowed, blinded eyes
oh, saddened urgings of mortality!

You too enrobed your death,
unfortunate, poor, graceful rose,
instead of sparkling with rosy joy,
you seemed a saint in tribulation,
your stem bent, kneeling,
praying the daily Epitaphios.

Poor neighborhoods, abandoned corners
built for pitch black frost
built for the unburied souls,
the daily souls, lonely
for the remains and Sundays
of my soul, you, secret motherland

of my soul, frigid and resembling
a tray with cross and gold confection
and in its middle the holy candle
keeping vigil in the requiem of Love.

ROSES OF A DAY

Roses of Saint George's Day
in the girlish hands of a young boy,
and you hold the unexpected gift,
your roses, in the middle of the road.

Much worked and thrice engraved,
multi-pleated, many-leaved, full-bloomed,
the light breeze stumbles onto them
and opens them for a deceptive browsing!

The neighborhood in spring, the day like a painting,
I felt so lucky to gaze upon such beauty,
such rosy blooms, my mouth a rosebud too,
my lips kissing all the sinful flowers.

Yet how can roses match with you, unless
you too have a rose between your lips?
And if you ever tasted the freshness of a drink
you also had a pair of lips like roses.

Never have my eyes in front of yours
betrayed me as these roses did,
since you were one of them, the same together,
and you too grew along with them.

I knew the reason, guessed correctly,
why you wandered back and forth along the street,
your agile legs ready to run fast
the flexible knees that played a pair
in the street and on the opposite high-up balcony,
oh, tender love of my sixteenth year.

PAN

Quiet! Don't you sometimes hear from deep in the orchard
the Gods of agriculture weeping their green holiday
as flutes sing sweetly to each other?

(in the cisterns the face of autumn still reflecting)

The clear skies didn't fool me yesterday
I saw Him trying to find his way among the grapevines
His moulted skin shimmering on His back.
He stopped: up high, the moon, malicious, shone.

He tuned His ear to listen to the softly blowing breeze.
His eyes and ears searched for vanished echoes
in that still hour when the night turns numb and frozen

and straight to his lips He brought his reed,

discordant yet so sweet, hatred mixed with laughter,
exotic tune drawing evil from the vines
fast tune dispersing unknown shivers

and yet the dead leaves stood and danced.

KOSTAS HATZOPOULOS

Konstantinos Hatzopoulos was born in May 1868 in Agrinio. He attended the high school in Messolonghi and after his graduation he attended the Law School of the University of Athens. He returned as a lawyer to Agrinio. Having solved the means for his livelihood, due to the large estate he inherited from his mother's family, he moved to Athens where he settled and devoted himself to literature.

Kostis Palamas, who was impressed by Hatzopoulos' literary talent, remembering their common school years in Messolonghi, wrote: "...I looked at him from my house, a teenager going to the street, well-dressed, elegant, all in white. Who would have guessed it that years later we were meant to meet in Athens."

Kostas Hatzopoulos appeared in literature at an early age in 1884, publishing his poem "Come, oh, Blonde" in the journal *Weekly*. He wrote in Demotic language and in the struggle that was raging at the time between the conservatives (using the katharevousa) and the demoticists, he helped with the publication of the short-lived but avant-garde magazine *Art*, published between 1897 and 1899.

In 1900 Kostas Hatzopoulos left for Germany. He studied in Munich, Dresden and Leipzig, and he delved in the literature and poetry of the northern peoples which influenced his work a lot. In 1914, with the outbreak of World War I, Kostas Hatzopoulos returned to Greece and began publishing the short stories and novels he had written from time to time in Greece and Germany.

In 1917 he worked in a censorship service. In 1920, while traveling by boat to Italy, he died on board from food poisoning and was buried in the Brindisi Cemetery. His bones were transferred many years later to the First Cemetery of Athens.

CHRISTMAS IN THE VILLAGE

In the foggy evening
the light snow falls
in the deserted dale,
a white sheet on the earth.

You cannot hear a bird's chirp
nor any young lamb's bleat
as if upon the earth the snow is spreading
the terrible silence of the dead.

Then suddenly we hear the sweetest
chime of bells upon the mountain
as if from high above it falls
and spreads across the night.

It echoes so delightfully
amid the breadth of silent nature
that all the town awakens sweetly
to celebrate the holy day.

LET THE BOAT SAIL FREE

Free the boat to the whims of the waves.
Leave control to the wind, let rudder and sail
expand their wings. No end has the world.
Unknown shores endlessly invite us
where life can freshly start, so let the wind
bring us where it wishes when it likes.
Let the fields change to forest and to rocks
that tower above as we go by. Let smoke
rise from the huts whether nature brings the sun
or tempest from on high. Don't ever hope
to commandeer your sails. Go freely with
the waves wherever wind and current lead.
Do you ever know truly what you seek?
Have you ever caught what you have hunted?
Don't you reap the evil while you spread the good?
Don't you stumble on the question that you ask?
What you've longed for, thinking that it smiles at you,
have you prepared the way yourself and won?

Let the waves break just as they wish,
let dizziness guide the blind heart,
and if the tempest roars and clouds approach,
know sunshine somewhere laughs along a shore,
and if the sad tears flood your soul
somewhere a secret joy always awaits for you.

I DON'T LOOK FOR A FOREIGNER

I don't look for a foreigner nor seek a secret
nor do I ask for any favor.
Something has been taken from my soul,
something they have taken.

There weren't any fairies
nor were they hands.
It was a night when the foggy stars
played with the shore

and the wind rose up from the north
and darkness came suddenly.
Oh, my sister, together we weep
for the lost treasure.

The moon opens the waves
and shows a secret path.
Something is taken from my soul
something they have taken.

WHEN SPRING COMES

When spring comes
and the birds return
when the flowers bloom
as in the past
I'll wait for you

and when again
the summer returns
with the mistral
as in the past
I'll wait for you

but when autumn arrives
with its rain
and cloudy skies
I'll come to find you.
I won't wait.

YOU PASSED BY

You passed by and in your hair you had
roses and light and in your hand
white lilies and wheatears from the fields
and seeing you I said summer
has returned again

but on arriving you spread wheatears
on the water and roses in the air
and with the lily you stood pale
like an autumn day.

BLURRY EVENING

The evening comes, blear
and sad and faint,
my pain's but your caress
since you believe I hurt

it tells your legend
softly to the evening
and cries as it narrates
like the echo of a song

or like a bell that breaks
with a slow, soft weeping
as it calls me to the street
and I call you too.

IVY

Oh ivy, crawling, you engulf the house
in your flowerless, scentless leaves
and craft a mournful dome around its door
as if the foggy night has come to squat by its front step

where no birds perch nor sunshine caresses
and not a whisper issues from your breath
and dawn and dusk pass joylessly across you
as if we both live sorrowful and bitter lives

and now that fall has ruined the poplar's leaves
and the honeysuckle that always cheered you
as it bloomed beside you has departed
and only my sadness still fully leaved,

oh, dark, dense ivy, a butterfly as dark as you
seeks beauty from a hidden sunray and flies
among your joyless leaves to drink its sorrow
dripping from the wet and barren clouds,

as if you've spread your branches over me
just as one day you'll spread your silent moment
one morning when the cloudless dawn will shine
its white light over your closed eyes.

SLENDER BIRCH TREES

Dawn passes through the forest and stirs
the slender silvery birch trees
and the seven-layered sunrays play with the maples
while green-gold leaves bathe by the spring.

Among the branches black birds and thrushes hurl
their sweet songs through the light and air
while, you would think, the fir trees must forget
their sadness when they see the sunlit lake.

Oh, dawn, is it you I feel in my viscera
as if your fresh leaves sprouted in my chest
or, you, beautiful eyes, that have hidden
inside you all my joy which you spend here?

And if it's you, smile at me, smile and my flute
will spread your freshened joy onto the dawn,
and if for it you cut wild roses so unevenly
lean down before me, sweet, and gild the space around.

THIN HANDS

Oh, la triste histoire!

~Verlaine

The thin hands that move
in the motionless darkness,
for which secret spell
might the bats search?

Hoarfrost has covered all the roses
and wild roses in the ravines
oh, thin hands that move
in the motionless darkness!

Is your soul longing again
for the wild roses' fragrance?
or for the weeping stories
the nightingales sing in the night?
Hoarfrost has covered all the roses
and the wild roses in the ravines.

GEORGE VIZYENOS

George Vizyenos was born in Vizi of Eastern Thrace, son of a very poor family. At age 10, his grandparents sent him to Constantinople to his uncle to learn sewing. He stayed there until the age of 18. Under the protection of the Cypriot merchant, Giago Georgiadis and later the Archbishop of Cyprus he moved and settled in Cyprus where he studied at the Theological School of Halki, without the obligation to be sanctified. In 1873 he published his first poetry collection *First Poems*.

Among his teachers was also the poet Ilias Tandalidis, who foresaw in Vizyenos elements of particular talent and intelligence, and introduced him to the rich man Georgios Zarifis. In 1874 he enrolled at the Athens School of Philosophy, but at the expense of Zarifis, he went to Gothenburg, Germany where he studied philology and philosophy between 1875-1878.

His studies in Germany greatly expanded his creative world and brought him into contact with romanticism and classicism that focused into the internal world of man.

In 1883 he published his first major short story, "Between Piraeus and Neapolis." He also published the short stories "Who Killed my Brother" and "My Mother's Sin." In 1884, due to the death of his patron, Zarifis, he was forced to return to Athens and worked as a high school teacher.

A year later he was elected as a lecturer at the chair of the History of

Philosophy of the University of Athens. In 1892 he was infected with frenal disease and ended up on April 14, 1892 in the Dromokaition Psychiatric Hospital. There he survived immersed in his delusional passion for the 14 year old Betina Fravasilis, his pupil at the Athens Conservatoire, whom he wished to marry, and after four years of imprisonment in the Asylum he died on April 15, 1896, at the age of 47.

ASYLUM VERSE

Grief in my heart
floods my life like a wave.
I drag my heavy feet
slowly to the grave

since I lost the joy
that I had once
all in an hour
in this land where everything
has changed

and since I started weeping,
my blonde and blue
light of my eyes,
the rhythm of the world
has changed too.

Grief in my heart
floods my life like a wave
as I drag my heavy feet
slowly to the grave.

With the holy cross
in my embrace,
I kiss the holy cross
and from her grave
her golden voice calls me
come fall asleep next
to your blonde boy.

COUPLETS

I decided never to fall in love, I wished
to shield my heart and keep it safe.

But grow mature if you can and when you mature
it won't be difficult to make me love you.

The highest grace cannot be hidden in another,
but shows when innocence adorns her beauty.

I hoped that I could have a small place in your soul
but you ignored me when I stood in line with people.

Since you have recognized your error, correct it
or become the game and joke of all the world.

If I dislike your error and not some other person's,
remember that we always reap just what we sow.

Oh, let me be, and let my peace go undisturbed,
my heart cannot be yours to tear to pieces.

PARABLE

The morning star can never shine
as you when you appear, joy-giving lass

nor does the green clover have as much
as you have freshness on your sweetened lips

nor do the flowers of narcissus have
such fragrance as your lightest breath

nor does the bird know how to sing such
sweet songs as your inventive lips.

One only it can't learn—to sing *I love you*—
and for this, I dare to say, another soul may die.

SONG

Like the inexhaustible spring
that babbles in the ravine
my tears flow silently
endlessly down the road.

They tumble, softening the stones,
they plough through marble,
making deep furrows where
shrubs flower and bloom.

Your heart alone can never
bend, nor will it soften,
and in its hardness
a grain of love will never bloom.

BOY BY THE RIVER

The river flows like crystal
and the boy looks into it and smiles.
What harm can it ever do,
this clear pure water as it flows?

Two lilies flow with the current
and here and there they cross.
The boy imagines that they signal
as if to tell him something.

Here and there they wander
as the water pushes them.
What do they signal to the boy?
What do they want to say?

On the branch of an oak tree he climbs
thinking to hear the lilies speak,
but suddenly the thin branch breaks
and carried him into the water

and as the light leaves his eyes
one reddish light shines over
till the yellow lilies fall like
a cross over his forehead.

Which boy that goes near a river
cannot clearly see
the harm it can do
the clear pure water as it flows?

THRACIAN SONG

Religion, my boys
started in Thrace,
to be precise, Pieria,

and from the breeze of Thrace
Greece took the spark
of all her ancient glory

and carried it
to ancient Athens
and ever first Eleusis

and darkness was lighted
and there appeared great Zeus
with his long beard.

For the sake of this,
we should bring back the light
to the beloved homeland

ANEMONE

A boulder on the hill
alone can see
the creek that flows
before it sings its song.

The anemone that blooms
rooted firmly on the rock
attempts to grasp
the meaning of the song

and down it bends to hear,
leaving its rocky anchor
to know what song is sung
by that fast-flowing creek?

It sings of an embrace
that waits with open arms
to hold a lover ardently
at night on a golden shore.

If only, said the flower,
that embrace were mine,
and leaning further down
to touch the rapid current

as it leaned enough to see
the water in its speed
stripped it of its petals
and down the stream it went.

Now without petals
the stem stands in loneliness.
Ah, why, ah, why did that anemone
deserted its anchor in the rock?

DEBT

Whoever challenges his luck
and with no rudder sails the seas
will meet a tempest and
be cast away and drown.

Whoever builds a nest
on an unstable rock
before he even settles in it
the rock will tumble, burying him.

Whoever stumbles and attempts
to stand again by trusting
other's kindness will be pushed
down never to stand up again.

Blessed is the one who takes no risks
and stays secure in his own house
who never needs to beg the foreigner
nor even to depend on his own countrymen.

KOSTAS KRYSTALLIS

Kostas Krystallis was born in Syrrako, Epirus, in 1868, where he lived until the age of twelve. His father, Dimitris Krystallis, was a trader of livestock products based in Ioannina. His mother was Ioanna Psallidas and he had four other siblings while he was first-born. He attended the elementary school of his village. In 1880 he was enrolled at the Zosimaia School of Ioannina. In the same year his mother died. He attended the four classes of the Zosimaia Greek School and the first grade of High School, and in 1885 he failed to pass his grade. His health interferes with his schooling which he abandons. Other biographers claim that he was employed at his father's shop.

In 1887 he published the poem "Shadows of Hades," referring to episodes of the Revolution of 1821. Because of this he was persecuted by the Turkish authorities and he went to Athens (January 1889), while the Turkish courts sentenced him in absentia to a 25-year exile in Baghdad. In Athens he changed his family name to Krystallis. In Athens he initially worked at the Fexi's printing and at the same time he published poems. In 1891 he was recruited by John Damvergis as editor in the "Weekly" magazine, but his collaboration ended in the same year due to disagreements with the magazine's management. He was then appointed as an employee of the railways of Peloponnese. His difficult life conditions resulted in tuberculosis. He moved to Corfu, hoping that his health would be improved there, but it worsened and eventually he died on April 22, 1894, in Arta at his sister's house.

EMBROIDERING THE KERCHIEF

excerpt

By the seashore the blonde girl sits
embroidering a golden-threaded kerchief
for her groom, a present at her wedding.
The sea and islands she embroiders on it,
the endless sky with myriad brilliant stars,
the fields of blazing flowers on the earth
a mountain of enormous height
with dawn advancing from behind its peak
and at its top a strip of rosy-colored sky
and clearest waters, silvery and diaphanous,
along the mountain's sides, in its ravines,
dark schisms from millennia of erosion,
she embroiders, with green and silky thread
and flocks of sheep in each wide plain
and shepherds from afar so vivid
one could hear their flutes and rural songs
the bleating of lambs and hymns of trees...

SONG OF THE HARVEST

Song that blackbirds sing along the creeks
and on the mountain sides the partridges
and in ravines the nightingales
and in the grapevine groves the lissome girls
where prettiest Golfo sings this to the grapevine:
my well-pruned vine with your big leaves,
I'll come to harvest your red ripened fruit
to make my immortal wine full of aroma
and in my cool cellar I will store and hide it
counting the years and months
until spring comes and a warm summer
when my love returns from foreign lands
and I'll go down the yard to hold his horse
I'll hug and kiss his eyes and lips
I'll offer him my wine from this grapevine
so he forgets the pain of foreign lands.

GATHERING OF THE GRAPES

excerpt

The grapevine blooms and spreads its vines
over the bulrushes and cypress branches
in riverbeds and in crevasses full of rocks
it spreads its fragrance with every stirring
of the air, as on the hillsides, mountains and the plains
great swarms of bees rouse from their hives
to drink the vine's ethereal smells
and forage on its pistils full of nectar
and spread the news in buzzing eulogies.

Girls of the village start their day, following
nature's wisdom to their orchards and their groves,
on mountains and plains, with baskets, joyful
and with songs. The gathering and harvesting begin,
and the countryside awakens to their sweat
and girlish scents and every grapevine row
as if arising from the earth brings forth new chthonian fairies…

SONG OF THE FOREIGN LAND

excerpt

May you be cursed, oh foreign land, with your grief.
I'll climb uphill to reach the mountain top
and find a flowery branch, deep-rooted rock
and cool fresh spring to give me its thick shade.
There I'll drink my fill and deeply breathe
quietly I'll recall my grief in foreign lands
and tell my suffering and release all my aches.

Come open, wounded heart and bitter lips,
begin to smile again and sing a happy song…

MARIA'S APRON

excerpt

Maria was washing her clothes in the river,
her beauty shining, her body sparkling too
beneath her lines of silver buttons and her necklaces,
her snow-white legs clear in the crystal waters
as if they could be roses made of milk.
The hunters and their servants saunter by,
and some declare her sun-born and others see a nymph.
A golden eagle flies above her and dazzled by
her beauty plunges down toward the riverbed
and grasps the maiden's apron. Maria's left
alone to mourn her apron's loss, embroidered
with the flowers of the earth, stars of the sky...

KOSTAS KARYOTAKIS

Kostas Karyotakis is considered one of the most representative Greek poets of the 1920s and one of the first poets who used iconoclastic themes in Greece. His poetry, lyrical and romantic, conveys a great deal of nature, imagery and traces of expressionism and surrealism and it has been translated in more than thirty languages. He also belongs to the Greek Lost Generation movement. His works are taught in universities both in Hellas and abroad.

Karyotakis was born in Tripoli, Greece. As a child he was timid, prone to disease an easy target of viruses and always frightened. This turned him more into himself and he spent his time trying to discover the world through reading and writing which he started in early age. Although he was a very sensitive reserved young man he started publishing poetry in various magazines for children in 1912. While they lived in Chania he fell in love with a young girl, Anna Skordili who not only rejected him but soon after the poet's advance she got married, a fact that sent the poet into melancholy. After receiving his degree from the Athens School of Law and Political Sciences, in 1917, he did not pursue a career as a lawyer. Karyotakis became a clerk in the Prefecture of Thessaloniki.

In February 1919 he published his first collection of poetry, *The Pain of Men and Things*, which was largely ignored or badly criticized by the critics. In 1922 while he worked for Prefecture of Attica he met a young

217

poetess, Maria Polydouri, a colleague who fell in love with him. Kostas Karyotakis rejected her advances and even when she proposed to him he told her in his poetic way that he had syphilis which before 1945 was considered a chronic illness with no proven cure for it, yet a disease that turned the sufferer into a social outcast. In 1924 Karyotakis traveled abroad, visiting Italy and Germany. In December 1927 he published his last collection of poetry: Elegy and Satires. In February 1928, Karyotakis was transferred to Patras and soon after he was sent to Preveza. He lived in Preveza only for 33 days, until his suicide on July 21, 1928. His angst of life in Preveza is felt in the poem Preveza which he wrote shortly before his suicide. After smoking for a few hours, and drink cherry juice, he left 75 drachmas as a gratuity, while the cost of the drink was 5 drachmas, he went to the nearby seashore called Agios Spyridon, and there, under a eucalyptus tree, he shot himself through the heart. His suicide letter was found in his pocket.

DEATHS

There're people who carry
their bad luck inside them

Little hands holding roses
hands warm from the joy of kisses
little hands holding roses
and knocking at the door of death

my beloved eyes that thirsted for something
you have remained thirsty glances
my beloved eyes that thirsted for something
you have remained closed windows

oh, lips that had much to say
your words chose your grave
oh, lips that had much to say
you didn't mention of the grief I write.

Beloved eyes, little hands, lips narrate to me
the momentary pain, the pain of a place
beloved eyes, little hands, lips narrate to me
the pain of things and that of man

SPRING

This the way I see the gardens

A new sadness talks to me tonight in the garden
an almond tree drives its smiling blossom
deep down to the bog's thick water, and
memory of my youth battles the sick acacia

cold breeze awakes in the broken container
every rose is dead in the flowerpot-coffin
the cypress, endless martyrdom, star bound
uplifts its darkness thirsting for air

and they go, a sorrowful procession the pepper tree
treeline dragging along their green hair.
Two palms raise their arms in desperation
the garden is a melancholic place.

SMILE

Although she never learned of it she cried
perhaps because she had to cry
perhaps because misfortune always comes.

Tonight the dusk is just a dream
the ravine remains enchanted
the rain stopped and the tired girl
lied onto the moist cloverfield

her parted lips two cherries
this way as deeply she breaths
her breasts ascent and descent
as if the most crisp April rose.

Sunrays flash through the clouds
and hide in her eyes, the lemon tree
drips moist onto her body

two diamonds stop onto her cheeks
you think she may be crying
as she smiles to the faraway sun.

RETURN

Smile of the Gods, Bay of Saronikos, always great
blessing of our ship's route
we could hear the roar of the high seas as easily as
the calmness of your depth

under the morning dew like a dove with its body's
nonchalance: Athens
shivers and revels like a nymph that longs
for the faraway sun.

Because the sky shines, blonde mane of Pegasus,
Fate of the Parthenon

glass that Zeus keeps upside-down that the dream-light
is poured liked a flood

prodigal son, I return to you swaying like a flower
in the breeze

earth, sky and you, oh sea of Attica, to whom I owe all
my Songs!

BALLAD

For the inglorious poets of the eons

Hated by people and gods
lords fallen from glory, they wilt bitterly
like Verlaire, the only wealth
left to them is rhyme: rich and silvery.
Hugo with "Punishment" gets drunk in
the fearsome revenge of the Olympians
and I shall write a sorrowful ballad
for the inglorious poets.

If Poe lived in misfortune
and if Baudelaire lived as if dead
they were graced with immortality
however no one talks about
the writers of unworthy verse
and Erebus has covered them with a heavy blanket.
But I make this holy offer:
a ballad for the inglorious poets.

Contempt of the world a curse on them
who walk along pale and erect
dedicated to their tragic self-deception
while far away their glory awaits
virginal thought, joyous and deep.
But knowing that all forget them
I nostalgically lament the sorrowful
ballad of the inglorious poets

and sometime in a future day
I want them to say: *who was the one*
who wrote this poor ballad
for the inglorious poets?

JOY

Hope the flower opposite the bulrush
smiles like my love for the verdure
cypress plays tenderly with the rays
graves become fragrant wedding chambers

pulse of the forest gallop of a doe
next to where we two were laid
wild lilies dripped their souls
a bloody rose my joy's bloom.

I see the breeze playing with your hair
your eyes are deep as I find
the path of my life this April

I no longer fear for the anemone
which wilts in the love of life
and I charge to drink the nectar of your lips.

PRECURSOR

You took your eyes and walked away
no one remembers where you've gone
and you wonder where your last tear
may fall and who will accept it

ah, the weight of such struggle overpowers you
and you seek support stretching your arm
you stop awhile whirling around, you hide your face
in your hands, then you restart.

How you can carry on, oh sister soul, seeking forgiveness
giving back love for each of your wounds?
And how you can carry on since all your paths
have been shut over the earth?

Look, the self-deception of the world dances around you
lips lock and offerings are raised up high and laugh
you die and from the start, as if you've gone already —
everyone forgets of you.

I salute you! You've experienced life only in your dreams
for this you deserve a suitable end, beautiful soul
your apotheosis has arrived and it becomes
your first and last joy.

SONG

I walked all around your house (the moth flew
around the lamp until it met its sweet death) though
you didn't come out that I'd burn into the flame of your eyes.

Alas, the fragrance of the body and of the soul
will be spoiled by contamination one night
even more alas that I won't be the spoiler.

WHEN WE GO DOWN THE STEPS

When we descent the steps of death what will we say
to the shadows who will welcome us
the stern, familiar, vague friends
with a smile on their invisible lips?

Here at least we're alone
one day passes the next one comes
and we still retain in our eyes
something that gives color to everything.

But down there what can we say where can we go
we'll be forced to look at each other
with severed arms at the elbows
motionless like the faces of icons.

If one comes to knock onto our gravestone
he will imagine how we lived
if he brings along a rose and drops it
it will become sand dropped on the ground

and if ever we stand onto our toes
we'll see the villa of Posillipo
and the terrain of Paradise, oh Lord
where your fans play cricket.

YOUR LETTERS

I kept your letters, my first love,
in the priceless box of my heart
your letters smell of youth
making my senior joy bloom

your letters talk to me a lot
with their crooked lines and mistakes
they shiver, cry and laugh, they narrate
games of jealousy and coldness

you sprayed perfume and your letters
won't be erased by the passing time
wish our first dreams weren't
erased by your heartlessness

oh my only love, your letters
white boats carry my thoughts down
where the word of Death can't be
wiped out from your letters-graves.

MARIA POLYDOURIS

Maria Polydouris was the daughter of the teacher philologist Eugene Polydouris and Kiriaki Markatou a woman of early feministic views. She graduated from high-school in Kalamata. She appeared in the letters at the age of fourteen with the prose poem *Pain of a Mother* which related the death of a seaman who was washed out at the beach.

In 1921 she was transferred to the Prefecture of Attica and at the same time she was enrolled in the Law department of the University of Athens. While working at the Prefecture of Attica she met the poet and colleague Kostas Karyotakis. A mutual strong attraction joined them that lasted for a short while although it marked their lives to their end. They met January 1922 for the first time. Maria was 20 years old while he was 26. She had published a few poems up to that day and Karyotakis had two books of poetry already published which won him the respect of a few critics and other poets of that era.

The summer of 1922 Karyotakis was diagnosed with syphilis an unhealable chronic disease which was considered a stigma. At once he informed his beloved Maria and asked her to go their separate ways. Maria instead of accepting his suggestion proposed marriage to him even if they did have any children however Karyotakis couldn't accept her sacrifice.

The summer of 1926 Polydouris left for Paris. She studied to become a seamstress yet she never started that job because she was diagnosed with tuberculosis in 1928 and she return to Athens and was hospitalized at the *Sotiria* where all tuberculosis patients were sent. While there her beloved Kostas Karyotakis took his life. Her first collection *The Thrills that Vanish* was published that year and soon after her *Echo in the Void*. At the end tuberculosis won over her and on the 29th of April, at dawn she let her last breath under the influence of morphine which a friend provided for her.

SADNESS OF THE DUSK

The roses of the dusk bloomed again tonight
golden, rosy, and purple
they faded tonight shedding their leaves
as I viewed them every evening
and every time I drank their fragrant dew
I got intoxicated by their blooms
their soft and last breath
I consumed each joy to its best.
Yet upon gazing the dusk tonight, I thought
of our love, that someday it might end
and when the roses of the dusk bloomed
golden, rosy, and purple
as they faded tonight shedding their leaves
this evening I got saddened.

ONE NIGHT AT THE TRAIN STATION

The train station is a sad place
soon after the train leaves.
Moments earlier it was stopped here
on the rails with the passengers
coming and going in haste
laughing without any reason
and the ones who stay behind
don't have their previous faces.
The emptiness of the rails, the silence
of the station that lost its train
and the ones who stay behind scatter
with decisive steps as if following
their Fate. Something of theirs
leaves them every time and they stay
at the station closing their blurry eyes
before they courageously turn back
with their backs even more stooped.
Cursed let it be the separation
yet even with you I shall fall in love
because the *hello* was sweet
and the hand waved in the air
and the handkerchief was whiter
than a bud, a light in the distance
that I hadn't seen before
your vision serene and beautiful.
Cursed separation:
my lips tremble calling your name.

AT THIS TIME

This time, like no other, I think of you
lonely soul, stranger passerby.
Friends and lovers were around you (am I right
or your eyes were saddened?)

Not even one lover or a friend
who in an hour such as this hour
would shake your hand. (Can I protect
your legacy from the false fame?)

No one stood close to you, no one was there
even one you might dare call your friend
your Fate's provocation, your shriek
in the silent loneliness that scares you.

Hideously alone, with the chiton
of your dream permanently ripped
you marched to a famous country
that vanished in the deep heart of infinity

MY SONGS WERE ONLY WRITTEN FOR HIM

Why do I need to accept the Muse's projection?
That I tighten my heart and accept
new loves, beliefs and joys
as if it was my Fate's doing and so exceptional?

Time has passed since the rayed spark of my eye
shone onto the holy and the mortal.
Oh, I haven't kept the senseless lyre of passion
since my songs were only written for Him.

And I sang the grief of my pure soul
along with the sad joy of tears
and all the joy of my song was nothing but his voice
that I'd hear one evening in front of his humble dwelling.

And as sometime I read my joy in his eyes
what more valuable opinion can I state?
At our separation like swallows the verse brought
to him the message: even from faraway twice I love him.

And now my voice leaves not any grieving echo
as it's covered by the darkness of the night
yet everyone is afraid and I still believe
that I've reached the heavy gate of Hades.

For why would I accept the call of Muse when
my trust in gods and people shuttered inside me?
A senseless Lyre of passion doesn't suit me
since my songs were only written for Him.

DOUBT

The young man you expected
won't come tonight.
What would you had told him? Why?
Let futility vanish
sever the unfortunate sprout.

Don't let the endless
cunning desire
fool your heart
a secret sadness flows
over this spring evening.

Yet you don't listen to advice
enchantment has strong hold on you
he'll never come tonight
and tomorrow will turn
even more painful.

Absence will shine
light into his darkened eyes;
with reserved ardor
a secret grief
will kiss his awkward hands

that I shall see spread
timid in victory
sweet as if they can
the caressing waves that pull me
like a pebble into the depth

DESTINY

My soul, child of the prodigal grief, which calm
day you expect to come and take you along?
You won't relive your dreams under the sun
your fire will be put out and only grace will stay with you.

you'll patiently wait on your golden throne
like a rich ornament, like a pale pearl.
Look, the ghost of night goes by with its triumphant sword
like a mystery of the darkened underworld.

Raise your proud arms and pray
to become one of its many dark secrets
that hope won't touch you, like the rays don't touch

the sunless abyss and the foreign lands that welcome you.
And only through your thoughts sometimes
you'll recall the beautiful things you've desired and missed.

PRIDE

I waited for you, until the stars of dawn
appeared in the firmament
their fire dried up all my tears
and the cold hill of Lycavittos didn't hear me
when silently I cried for the dream that died in my heart.

But now that thoughts brought you back to me
I shall wait for the star again
to tell it, holding back a tear that has appeared
in my eyes, that like a joy I held you in my embrace
warm and gleaming, my complete grief.

YOU WON'T RETURN

You won't return anymore to grace me with
something from the gifts the beautiful life
has graced you: perhaps a flower? The life
that fills your heart and body with such beauty.

You won't return anymore to take my hands
that froze as if an enemy's hands?
Joined with yours, calm pair of hands
that need doesn't come near them any longer.

You won't return! And the days pass by slowly
and as you go away my familiar fate
comes close to me, alone
for so long with the secret grief.

Don't you ever think that perhaps, truly,
in sad moment I'll direct myself
to the fateful end that awaits me
and never to return?

FORGETFULLNESS

With my loving heart I got to know you, wild forest.
I drank your secret fragrance in the kiss of the wind.
I waited to pass through you in the moonlit night
when the airy ghost went through your branches.

I got to know you during my erotic nights, wrinkled
sea as if the forehead of contemplation, my thought
went over you like a caress and your bloomed edge
with the fragrant seaweed would always invite me.

My erotic nights got to know you my beautiful flowers
diaphanous, shaded, colorful like lighted signs.
The heavy dew, a kiss and golden fluff
appeared on your eyelids tightly shut in darkness.

Now, bestowed onto the light of denial and altered,
you show me that I may lose my mind's path.
Are you truly what I knew well? My beloved
flowers, the silvery sea, thick forest full of pines?

FOR KARIOTAKIS

The young men who arrived to the deserted island
one night counted themselves and found you missing.
They looked each other in the eyes and no wonder
they shook their heads in sadness.

They recalled many nights that from your loneliness
a sign of fire you would send and they knew
the sad welcome of the abyss lighting the roads
and for this they stayed in their familiar places

they grieved, as if fatefully and sorrowfully
they hanged from the "rock" of danger
and when you said goodbye, you, the forever desperate
they sang a few verses of a traditional dirge.

The young men arrive to the island every year
and they search for the elegy of life in your vacant spot.
They maintain two tears in their eyes for you
and for the new Epoch you have established.

KOSTIS PALAMAS

Kostis Palamas was the Greek poet who wrote the words to the Olympic Hymn. He was a central figure of the Greek literary generation of the 1880s and one of the cofounders of the so-called New Athenian School along with Georgios Drosinis, Nikos Kampas, Ioanis Polemis.

Born in Patras, he received his primary and secondary education in Mesolonghi. In the 1880s, he worked as a journalist. He published his first collection of verses, *Songs of My Fatherland*, in 1886. He held an administrative post at the University of Athens between 1897 and 1926, and died during the German occupation of Greece during World War II. His funeral was a major event of the Greek resistance: the funerary poem composed and recited by fellow poet Angelos Sikelianos roused the mourners and culminated in an angry demonstration of a 100,000 people against Nazi occupation.

Palamas wrote the lyrics to the *Olympic Hymn*, composed by Spyridon Samaras. It was first performed at the 1896 Summer Olympics, the first modern Olympic Games. The *Hymn* was then shelved as each host city from then until the 1960 Winter Olympics commissioned an original piece for its edition of the Games, but the version by Samaras and Palamas was declared the official Olympic Anthem in 1958 and has been performed at each edition of the Games since the 1960 Winter Olympics.

He has been informally called the national poet of Greece and was closely associated with the struggle to rid Modern Greece of the purist language. His most important poem, *The Twelve Lays of the Gypsy* (1907), is a poetical and philosophical journey. His Gypsy is a free-thinking, intellectual rebel, a Greek Gypsy in a post-classical, post-Byzantine Greek world, an explorer of work, love, art, country, history, religion and science, keenly aware of his roots and of the contradictions between his classical and Christian heritages.

ORPHIC HYMN

Beyond the minds of the thoughtless
functionary and orphic hymnist
I bring back the hymn
of an ancient light worship
as my thoughts run to it now

a river stashed away

the people's buzzing but a surprise
to the rhythm of my guitar
that during the night I start to climb
the difficult to reach mountain top

first I wish to hail the Apollonian light
while down where people live
sleep and darkness still prevail

HUMILITY

My pride to stand before you
naked: down with my pride

I bring you my soul, a tender flower
I bring you my thought, my orphanhood
I bring you my love, my poverty
I've come to be caught in the net of your lust

I bring you the mirror that reflects
all the sunsets and all the stars
as you wish them, as your desire longs
to smash it to pieces with your golden hands

to the lands of immenseness: dreamy
voyages, wishes for a safe trip
but instead of these I want to be
the earth on which you'll step
with your beloved tender soles

HEDONISM

A fleshless string of beads made of songs
I haven't given you today
with the spells and games of a charmer
I'll cloy you, my love

naked and like a vine I'll climb
to taste your body that devours me
with my fingers I'll conflagrate
the tender hairs of your mound

enrapturing wine and milk that soothes
to sleep I'll bring to moisten you
with all my body drop by drop

and on your white sculptured legs
two vases that drive me crazy
my honey like a maniac, at last, I'll ejaculate

TWO EYES

The oil of my lamp burnt out
and I keep vigil. What a night!
No star, only a ghost with two
eyes nailed at the edge of my bed

the world has vanished sucked into
the mouth of the dark Abyss
only two eyes exist over the void
two eyes that fill nothingness

only two eyes that lit the darkness
all are asleep, vanish, disappear
only two awaken eyes gaze me, they don't
go to sleep: their eyelids will never close

GOLDEN RIVER

My glance runs free, vanishes
through the waves and clouds up high
only to stop where the sky
touches the sea and talks

the asleep shore blows the breeze lightly
a bird turns white the sky becomes black
the night arrives only the west turns rosy
the day resembles a smiling corpse

and when the west's joy departs
we'll gaze the moon in our lake
creating a wide river of gold

that time, my fresh love, I'll say to you
deep in our hearts, sea filled with passion,
this golden river is our Love

BORN TO THE SUN

The joy was great at the Olympus
the Gods parceled the earth
while the light giver was absent
to be forgotten without an heir
but the light giver came and
signaled to the sea that stirred fertility
and the island of the Sun was born

and it was the most beautiful
where craftsmen lived
who were like supermen
and they created many statues
as beautiful as Gods
and full of life like people

GODS

And the first man saw
the sun's ascent for the first time
and he heard the music
responding to it sweetly

thousands of words
thousand compliments
offered to the spring of day

and everything, what a miracle,
the hymns and everything
spread to the four corners of the earth
and the eons gave them flesh

and turned them into
gods of light
monsters of harmony

IMAGINATION

Come, oh maiden, imagination
and you too ringleader thought
bring all the tireless workers
fairies of the rhythm

and bring the depth of lust
the heights of vision

and bring the flowers
made of gold and marble
the gleaming words
to build a palace and erect
the idol of the Sun inside it

and make it exquisitely great
adorable like a sunray

THE EXILED MAIDEN

Thousands of years will pass until you, oh glory
will return to the unknown spade of the farmer
that lifted the slab of your grave and you rose
and saw the unrecognizable world and the different Hellas
the east and barbarous lands are foreign to you
which you didn't like and you turned to the west.

Return, come back to your motherland
who you might be, a power, a queen, a dream, a shadow
goddess of beauty or spring of virtue, oh Nike,
come back, oh, come to your motherland, come back.

SCENT OF A ROSE

This year's heavy winter tired me a lot
it found me old and without fire
and often I felt as if ready to fall
on the snowed up pathway

yet I found courage in the laughter of March yesterday
as I walked along the ancient paths
and when I smelled the first scent of a rose
tears flowed down my eyes

GEORGE SEFERIS

George Seferis was born in Smyrna, Asia Minor, in 1900. He attended school in Smyrna and finished his high school studies in Athens. When his family moved to Paris in 1918, Seferis studied law at the University of Paris and became interested in literature. He returned to Athens in 1925 and was admitted to the Royal Greek Ministry of Foreign Affairs in the following year. This was the beginning of a long and successful diplomatic career, during which he held posts in England (1931-1934) and Albania (1936-1938).

During the Second World War, Seferis accompanied the Free Greek Government in exile to Crete, Egypt, South Africa, and Italy, and returned to liberated Athens in 1944. He continued to serve in the Ministry of Foreign Affairs and held diplomatic posts in Ankara (1948-1950) and London (1951-1953). He was appointed minister to Lebanon, Syria, Jordan, and Iraq (1953-1956), and was Royal Greek Ambassador to the United Kingdom from 1957 to 1961, the last post before his retirement in Athens. Seferis received many honors and prizes, among them honorary doctoral degrees from the universities of Cambridge (1960), Oxford (1964), Salonika (1964), and Princeton (1965).

His wide travels provide the backdrop and color for much of Seferis's writing, which is filled with the themes of alienation, wandering, and death. George Seferis's early poetry consists of *Strophe*, 1931, a group of rhymed Lyrics strongly influenced by the Symbolists, and *The Cistern*

1932, conveying an image of man's most deeply felt being which lies hidden from, and ignored by, the everyday world. His mature poetry, in which one senses an awareness of the presence of the past and particularly of Greece's great past as related to her present, begins with *Mythistorema*, 1935, a series of twenty-four short poems which translate the Odyssean myths into modern idiom. In his *Book of Exercises*, 1940, *Logbook I*, 1940, *Logbook II*, 1944, *Thrush*, 1947, and *Logbook III*, 1955, Seferis is preoccupied with the themes he developed in *Mythistorema*, using Homer's Odyssey as his symbolic source; however, in *The King of Asine* (*in Logbook I*), considered by many critics his finest poem, the source is a single reference in the *Iliad* to this all-but-forgotten king. The recent book of poetry, *Three Secret Poems*, 1966, consists of twenty-eight short lyric pieces verging on the surrealistic.

He died during the dictatorship years, a government he dishonored just some months before his death. His funeral turned into one of the largest public demonstrations against the military junta.

STROPHE

Moment, sent by a hand
that I had so much loved
you reached me almost at dusk
like a black dove.

The road shone before me
soft breath of sleep
at the end of a secret feast
moment, grain of sand,

that you alone kept
the tragic clepsydra whole
silent, as though it had seen Hydra
in the heavenly orchard.

DENIAL

On the secluded seashore
white like a dove
we thirsted at noon
but the water was brackish.

On the golden sand
we wrote her name;
when the sea breeze blew
the writing vanished.

With what heart, with what spirit
what desire and what passion
we led our life; what a mistake!
so we changed it.

EROTIKOS LOGOS

I

Fateful rose, you looked for ways to wound us
but you bend like the secret to be redeemed
and the command you chose to give us was beautiful
and your smile was like a ready sword.

The accent of your circle brought the world to life
the path of a deep thought emerged from your thorn
our ardor dawned sweet and naked to possess you
the world was as easy as a simple heartbeat.

V

Where did the double-edged day that had changed everything
          go?
Won't there be a navigable river for us?
Won't there be a sky dripping the morning dew
for the soul that the lotus benumbed and nourished?

On the stone of patience we long for the miracle
that opens the heavens and everything becomes possible
we long for the angel as in the ancient drama
when the open roses of twilight

vanish…scarlet rose of the wind and fate
you remained only in memory, a heavy rhythm
rose of the night you passed purple undulation
of the undulating sea…The world is simple.

EROTIKOS LOGOS II

The secrets of the sea are forgotten on the shore
the darkness of the depth is forgotten on the surf;
suddenly the memory corals shine purple...
Oh do not stir it...carefully listen to its soft

momentum...you touched the tree with the apples
the arm stretched out, the thread points the way and leads
    you...
Oh dark shivering in the root and on the leaves
were it just you that would bring the forgotten dawn!

May the lilies bloom again on the plain of separation
may the days mature the embrace of heavens
may only those eyes gleam in the sun glare
let the pure soul be written like a song for the flute.

Was it the night that closed its eyes? Ash remains
as though from a bow's string a muffled sound
ash and vertigo on the black seashore
and a dense fluttering enclosed in the surmise.

Rose of the wind, you knew but took us unknown
when thought built bridges so that
two fingers would entangle and two fates would go by
to be spilled into the low and becalmed light.

MYTHISTOREMA

I

The angel,
we had waited for him for three years, concentrated
    closely examining
the pines, the seashore, the stars.
Joining the blade of the plough or the ship's keel
once again we searched to discover the first sperm
so that the ancient drama might recommence.

We went back to our homes broken hearted
with incapable limbs, with mouths ravaged
    by the taste of rust and salinity.
When we woke, we traveled to the north, strangers
driven into the mist by the perfect wings
of swans that wounded us.
During winter nights the strong eastern wind
    maddened us
in the summers we got lost in the agony of day
    that couldn't die.
We brought back
these petroglyphs of a humble art.

II

One more well inside a cave.
At other times it was easy for us to draw up idols and
    ornaments
to please some friends who were still loyal to us.
Now the ropes are broken; only the grooves on the
    well's lip
remind us of our past happiness
the fingers on the well's lip, as the poet put it.
The fingers feel the coolness of the stone, a little
that the body's heat prevails over it
and the cave gambles its soul and loses it
every moment, filled by silence, without a drop of water.

III

Remember the baths
where you were murdered

I woke up having in my hands this marble head
that exhausts my elbows and I don't know where
    to lean it.
It was falling in the dream as I was coming out of the dream
thus our lives joined and it will be very difficult for us to
    separate again.

I gaze it in the eyes; neither open nor closed
I speak to the mouth that keeps trying to speak
I touch the cheeks that have gone through the skin.
I don't have any other strength;
my hands disappear and come back near me
mutilated.

IV

Argonauts

And the soul
if it is to know itself
must look
into its own soul
the stranger and the enemy, we have seen him in the mirror.
They were good boys, the comrades, they didn't complain
about the tiredness or the thirst or the frost
they had the behaviour of the trees and the waves
that accept the wind and the rain
that accept the night and the sun
without changing in the middle of change.

They were good boys, for days on
they sweated at the oars with lowered eyes
breathing in rhythm
and their blood reddened a submissive skin.
Sometimes they sang, with lowered eyes
when we passed by the deserted island with the prickly pear trees
toward the west, beyond the cape of the dogs
that bark.
If it is to know itself, they said
it must look into its own soul, they said
and the oars struck the gold of the sea
in the sunset.
We passed by many capes, many islands, the sea
that brings another sea, gulls and seals.
Sometimes grieving women wept
lamenting their lost children
and others angrily sought Alexander the Great
and glories lost in the depths of Asia.

We moored on shores filled with night fragrances
with bird chirpings, with waters that left on our hands
memory of a great happiness.
But the voyages did not end.

Their souls became one with the oars and the oarlocks
with the solemn face of the prow
with the rudder's wake
with the water that shattered their image.
The comrades died one by one
with lowered eyes. Their oars
point to the place where they sleep on the shore.

No one remembers them. Justice.

V

We didn't know them
        deep inside it was hope that said
we had met them in early childhood.
Perhaps we had seen them twice and then they went to the ships
cargoes of coal, cargoes of crops and our friends
vanished beyond the ocean forever.
Daybreak finds us beside the tired lamp
drawing on paper, awkwardly, painfully
ships, mermaids or conches;
at dusk we go down the river
because it shows us the way to the sea
and we spend our nights in cellars smelling of tar.

Our friends have left us
perhaps we never saw them, perhaps
we encountered them when sleep
still brought us very close to the breathing wave
perhaps we search for them because we search for the other life,
beyond the statues.

VI

Maurice Ravel

The orchard with its fountains in the rain
you will only see from behind the fogged up glass
of the lower window. Your room
will be lit by the fireplace flames
and sometimes the distant lightning will reveal
the wrinkles on your face my old Friend.

The orchard with its fountain that in your hand was
a rhythm of the other life beyond the broken
statues and the tragic columns
and a dance amid the oleanders
close to the new quarries
a fogged up glass would have cut it off from your days.
You won't breathe; the soil and the sap of the trees
will spring from your memory to strike
this window that is struck by the rain
of the outside world.

VII

South Wind

Westward the sea joins the mountain range.
From our left the south wind blows and maddens us
the kind of wind that strips the bones off the flesh.
Our home among the pines and the carob trees.
Large windows. Large tables
where we've been writing the letters destined for you
for so many months and dropping them
into our separation so that it may get filled up.

Star of dawn, when you lowered your eyes
our hours were sweeter than oil
over the wound, more joyful than cool water
to our palate, more peaceful than the plumes of the swan.
You held our lives in your palm.
After the bitter bread of exile
if we stand before a white wall at night
your voice nears us like a hope of fire
and again this wind sharpens
a razor against our nerves.

Each of us writes to you the same things
and each turns silent before the other
gazing, each of us, the same world separately
the light and darkness on the mountain range
and you.

Who will lift this sorrow from our hearts?
Last night heavy rain and today again
the cloudy sky weighs down on us. Our thoughts
like the pine needles of yesterday's downpour
gathered up and useless by our front door
as though to build a tower that collapses.

Among these decimated villages
over this cape, open to the south wind
with the mountain range before us hiding you
who would estimate for us the sentence to oblivion?
Who will accept our offering at the end of this autumn?

VIII

But what are they after, our souls, traveling
on the decks of decayed ships
crowded with pallid women and crying babies
incapable of forgetting themselves either with the flying fish
or the stars pointed by the tips of the masts?
Rubbed by gramophone records
unwillingly dedicated to inexistent pilgrimages
murmuring broken thoughts from foreign languages?

But what are they after, our souls, traveling
on rotten ships
from harbour to harbour?

Shifting broken stones, breathing
the coolness of pine with greater difficulty each day
swimming in the waters of this sea
and that sea
without a sense of touch
without people
in a homeland that is no longer ours
nor yours.

We knew that the islands were beautiful
somewhere, perhaps around here, where we grope
a bit lower or slightly higher
a very tiny space.

IX

The harbour is old I can't wait any longer
neither for the friend who left for the island with the pines
nor for the friend who left for the island with the plane trees
nor for the friend who left for the open sea.
I caress the rusted cannons, I caress the oars
that my body will be reborn and decide.
The sails only give off the smell
of the salinity from another storm.

If I decided to remain alone, I seek
the solitude, not this kind of waiting,
nor the shattering of my soul on the horizon
nor these lines, these colours, this silence.

Stars of the night return me to the anticipation
of Odysseus for the dead among the asphodels.
When we moored over here among the asphodels
        we hoped to find
the glen that saw the wounded Adonis.

X

Our homeland is closed in, all mountains
that day and night have the low sky as their roof.
We have no rivers, no water wells, no springs
only a few cisterns, even them empty, that echo
        and which we worship.
A stagnant hollow sound, same as our loneliness
same as our love, same as our bodies.
It seems strange that once we managed to build
our houses, huts and our sheepfolds.
And our marriages, the fresh coronals and our fingers
become inexplicable enigmas to our souls.
How were our children born, how did they grow strong?

Our homeland is closed in. Two black Symplegades
enclose it. When we go down
to the harbours on Sunday to breathe freely
we see lit in the sunset
the broken ships from voyages that never ended
bodies that no longer know how to love.

XI

Sometimes your blood froze like the moon;
in the inexhaustible night your blood
spread its white wings over
the black rocks, the shapes of trees and
the houses
with a bit of light from our childhood years.

XII

Bottle in the sea

Three rocks, a few burnt up pines, a lonely chapel
and a bit higher
the same landscape is repeated
three rusted rocks in the shape of a gate
a few black and yellow burnt up pines
and a square little house, buried in whitewash
and still higher, many times over
the same landscape reappears level after level
to the horizon, to the sky at sundown.

Here we moored the ship to splice the broken oars
to drink some water and to sleep.
The sea that embittered us is deep and unexplored
and unfolds a boundless serenity.
Here among the pebbles we found a coin
and we threw the dice for it.
The youngest won it and disappeared.

We sailed away again with our broken oars.

XIII

Hydra

Dolphins, banners and cannon shots.
The sea once so bitter for your soul
carried the many-coloured and glittering ships
it swayed, rolled and pitched them, totally blue with white wings
once so bitter for your soul
now full of colours in the sun.

White sails and sunlight and the wet oars
struck the stilled waters with a rhythm of drums.

Your eyes, gazing, would be beautiful
your arms, extending, would shine
your lips, would be alive, as they used to be
before such miracle;
you searched for it
        what did you search for in front of the ashes
or in the rain, in the fog, in the wind
even when the lights were dimmed
and the city was sinking and from the stone pavement
the Nazarene showed you his heart
what did you search for? Why don't you come?
What did you search for?

XVI

His name is Orestes

On the track, again on the track, on the track,
how many laps, how many blood circles, how many
black rows, the people who watch me
who were watching me in the chariot when
I raised my arm glorious, and they cried joyfully.

The horses' froth strikes me, when are the horses going to tire?
The axle creaks, burns, when is the axle going to catch fire?
When are the reins going to break, when will the hooves
tread on the ground with all their breadth
on the soft grass, among the poppies where
you'd pick a daisy in the spring?
Your eyes were lovely though you didn't know where to look
I didn't know where to look either, I, without a country
I who fights over here, how many more laps?

And I feel my knees giving way over the axle
over the wheels, over the wild track
knees give way easily when the gods wish it
none can escape, what can you do with your strength, you can't
escape the sea that cradled you and which you seek
at this hour of struggle, among the horse panting
with the canes that sing in the autumn to a Lydian
        rhythm
the sea that you can't find no matter how you run
how you run around before the black, bored Eumenides,
unforgiven

XVIII

I regret that I let a broad river pass through
my fingers
without drinking a single drop.
Now I sink into the stone.
A small pine in the red soil
I have no other company.
Whatever I loved vanished along with the houses
that were new last summer
and crumbled with the wind of autumn.

EPIPHANY 1937

The flowering sea and the mountains in the waning
    moon
the great rock near the cactus pear trees and the asphodels
the water pitcher that wouldn't go dry at the end of the day
and the empty bed near the cypresses and your hair
golden, the stars of the Swan and that star, Aldebaran.
I got hold of my life, I got hold of my life traveling
among yellow trees in the slanting rain
in silent slopes loaded with beech-tree leaves
no fire on their peaks; it's getting dark.
I got hold of my life; a line on your left hand
on your knee a scar, perhaps they still exist
in the sand of last summer, perhaps
they're still there where the north wind blew and I hear
the unfamiliar voice around the frozen lake.
The faces I see don't ask questions nor does the woman
stooping as she walks breastfeeding her baby.
I climb the mountains; bruised ravines; the snow
    covered
plain, up to the far end the snow-covered plain, they ask nothing
nor does the time enslaved in silent chapels, nor
do the hands outstretched to beg, nor the roads.
I got hold of my life whispering in the boundless silence
I no longer know how to speak nor how to think; whispers
like the cypress' breath that night
like the human voice of the night sea on pebbles
like the memory of your voice saying 'happiness'.
I close my eyes searching for the secret encounter of waters
under the ice , the smile of the sea, the closed water wells
groping with my veins those veins
    that escape me
there, where the water lilies end and this man
who saunters as though blind on the snow of silence.
I got hold of my life, with him, searching for the water
    that touches you

heavy drops on the green leaves, on your face
in the vacant garden, drops on the motionless cistern
discovering a dead swan with its snow-white wings
living trees and your eyes fixated.
This road has no end, doesn't change, no matter
        how hard you try
to recall your childhood years, the ones who left
        those
who got lost in their sleep, the pelagic graves
no matter how hard you ask the bodies you loved to stoop
under the hardened branches of the plane trees there
where the naked sunray stood
and a dog leaped and your heart shuddered
the road has no change; I got hold of my life.
        The snow
and the frozen water in the horses' hoof-marks.

ODYSSEUS ELYTIS

Descendant of an old family of Lesbos, he was born in Heraclion on the island of Crete, in 1911. Sometime later his family settled permanently in Athens where the poet finished his secondary school and studied at the Law School of the Athens University. His first appearance as a poet in the magazine *Nea Grammata* was saluted as an important event and the new style he introduced succeeded in prevailing and effectively contributing to the poetical reform of Greek poetry.

Upon the outbreak of the war he served in the rank of Second Lieutenant, first at the Headquarters of the 1st Army Corps and then at the 24th Regiment, on the first line. During the German occupation and later, after Greece was liberated, he kept very active, publishing successive collections of poetry and writing essays concerning contemporary poetry and art issues. He served as Programme Director of the Greek National Radio Foundation, Member of the National Theatre's Administrative Council, President of the Administrative Council of the Greek Radio and Television Service as well as Member of the Consultative Committee of the Greek National Tourist's Organisation. In 1960 he was awarded the First State Poetry Prize, in 1965 the Order of the Phoenix Brigade and in 1975 he was proclaimed Doctor Honoris Causa of the Philosophical School of the Thessaloniki University and Honorary Citizen of the Town of Mytilene.

During the years 1948-1952 and 1969-1972 he settled in Paris.

279

There, he attended philology and literature lessons in the Sorbonne and got acquainted with the pioneers of the world's avant-garde Breton, Tzara, Ungaretti, Matisse, Picasso, Chagall, Giacometti. In 1948 he was the representative of Greece at the *International Meetings of Geneva*, in 1949 at the Founding Congress of the *International Art Critics Union* in Paris and in 1962 at the *Incontro Romano della Cultura* in Rome.

Elytis' poetry has marked, through an active presence of over forty years, a broad spectrum. He devoted himself exclusively to today's Hellenism, of which he attempted to build up the mythology and the institutions. His main endeavour has been to rid his people's conscience from unjustifiable remorses and to complement natural elements through ethical powers. A parallel way concerning technique resulted in introducing the *inner architecture*, which is clearly perceptible in a great many works of his; mainly in the *Axion Esti - It Is Worthy*. This work, thanks to its setting to music by Mikis Theodorakis, was to be widely spread among all Greeks and grew to be a kind of the people's new gospel.

FOR THE AEGEAN

I

Eros
the archipelago
and the bow of its froths
and the seagulls of its dreams
on its highest mast the sailor waves
a song

Eros
its song
and the horizons of its journey
and the echo of its nostalgia
on her wettest rock his fiancée awaits
a ship

Eros
its ship
and the nonchalance of its summer winds
and the jib of its hope
on its lightest undulation an island rocks
the homecoming.

II

Games of the water
in the shadowy passages
they speak of dawn with their kisses
where the horizon
begins —

and the echo of wild doves
vibrates in their cave
glaucous waking in the spring
of day
sun —

the mistral bestows the sail
unto the sea
the caressing of hair
to its carefree dream
freshness —

wave in the light
rebirths the eyes
on which Life sails toward
the gazing
life —

SUN THE FIRST

I

I don't know the night horrible anonymity of death
a fleet of stars moor in the inlet of my soul
that you, guarding Hesperus, may shine next to the sky
light breeze of an island dreaming of me
pronouncing the dawn from its high rocks
my two eyes sail you in an embrace with the star
of my true heart: I don't know the night anymore

I don't know the name of a world that denies me
clearly I read the ostracons the leaves the stars
hatred is superfluous to me in the roads of the sky
unless it is the dream looking at me again
in tears that I pass through the sea of immortality
oh Hesperus, under the contour of your golden fire
the night which is only night I don't know anymore.

VARIATIONS ON A SUNBEAM

RED

The mouth which is daemon word crater
food of the poppy blood of anguish
which is the great cumin of spring
your mouth speaks with four hundred roses
it beats the trees overwhelms the whole earth
pours the first shiver into the body.

Great fragrance of the finger multiplies my passion
my open eye hurts on the thorns
it isn't as much the fountain that desires the two fowl-breasts
as the buzzing of a wasp on naked hips.

Give me the scar of amaranth the spells
of the girl who spins
the *goodbye* the *I'm coming* the *I'll give you*
caves of health will drink it to the sun's health
the world will be either the loss or the double voyage
here in the wind's sheet there in the infinity's gaze.

Cane tulip cheek of concern
cool offspring of fire
I'll throw May on his back I'll squeeze him in my arms
I'll beat May I'll consume him.

SONG HEROIC AND ELEGIAC FOR THE LOST SECOND LEUTENANT OF THE ALBANIAN CAMPAIGN

A

There where the sun used to dwell
where time was opening with the eyes of a virgin
as the wind was snowing from the nudging almond tree
and horse riders were lit on the peaks of grass

there where the hoof of a splendid maple tree struck
and high up a flag flapped earth and water
where weapons never burdened backs
but all the tiredness of the sky
the whole world shone like a drop of water
in the morning, by the feet of the mountain

now, as if from God's sigh a shadow spreads

now the stooping agony with bony hands
takes and wipes on itself one by one the flowers
waters stop in the ravines
where in the famine of joy the songs recline
Monks of rocks with cold hair
silently break the bread of desolation.

Winter cuts up to the bone. Something evil
will be ignited. The horse-mountain's hair goes wild.

Up high vultures share the sky's crumbs.

AXION ESTI — THE PASSION

B

They gave me the language of the Hellenes;
a humble house on the shores of Homer.
My only concern my language on the shores of Homer.
Two-branded breams there and perches
    wind blasted verbs
green currents mixed with the azure
    which I saw aflame in my viscera
sponges, jellyfish
    with the first words of the Sirens
rosy shells with the first black shivers.
    My only concern my language with the first black shivers.
Pomegranates there, quinces
    gods with dark complexion, uncles and cousins
pouring olive oil in the huge storage jars
    and fragrance from the ravine sweet smelling
osier and bulrush
    broom and ginger root
with the first chirpings of the finches,
    sweet psalmodies with the very first Glory to You.
My only concern my language, with the very first Glory to You.
    Laurels there and palm branches
censer and incense burning
    blessing the sabers and the muzzleloaders.
On the ground spread with vine leaves
    smell of burnt meat, eggs cracking
and Christ is Risen
    with the first firings of the Hellenes.
Secret loves with the first words of the Hymn.
    My only concern my language, with the first words of the Hymn.

C

You never gave me wealth
always devastated by the races of Continents
    and always praised by their arrogance!
The North took the grapevine
    and the South took the Wheat Ear
buying out the direction of the wind
    and profanely cashing in the trees' wealth
two or three times.
    But I knew nothing
other than the thyme in the sun's pin
    and I felt nothing
but the water drop on my unshaven beard
    yet I laid my rough cheek on the stone's rougher
century after century.
    I slept on the concern of my tomorrow
like the soldier by his rifle.
    And I searched for the compassion of the night
like an ascetic his God.
    Out of my sweat they created a diamond
and secretly they replaced
    the virgin of my glance.
They weighted my joy and they found it light, they said,
    and they stepped on it like an insect.
They stepped on my joy and encased it in stone
    and lastly they left me the stone
a horrible likeness of me.
    They strike it with a heavy axe, they bore it with a sharpened scalpel
they carve my stone with a bitter chisel.
    And as time erodes the matter, the prophesy emerges
clearly out of my face:

FEAR THE WRATH OF THE DEAD
AND THE STATUES OF THE ROCKS

LACONIC

The grief of death inflamed me so much that my glow returned to the sun

which sends me now to the perfect syntax of stone and ether.

Then, he whom I sought, I am.

Oh, linen summer, wise autumn,

minimal winter,

life contributes its olive leaf mite

and in the night of fools it confirms again with a small cricket the law-fulness

of the Unhoped-for.

LITTLE GREEN SEA

Little green sea thirteen years of age
how I would like to adopt you
and send you to school in Ionia
to learn of mandarin and absinthe.
Little green sea thirteen years of age
in the little tower of the lighthouse at high noon
to turn the sun and hear
how destiny becomes undone and how
from hill to hill our distant
relatives still communicate
holding the air like statues.
Little green sea thirteen years of age
with the white collar and your ribbon
enter Smyrna through the window
to copy for me the reflections on the ceiling
and from the *God Have Mercy* and the *Glory to You*
and with a little north wind and little levanter
wave by wave come back.
Little green sea thirteen years of age
I would secretly sleep with you
and find deep in your embrace
bits of stones the gods' words
bits of stones quotations of Heraclitus.

THE MONOGRAM

I

Fate will turn elsewhere the lines
of the palm, like a key keeper
time momentarily will consent.

How else, since men love each other.

The sky will re-enact in our viscera
and innocence will strike the world
with the sharpness of the black of death.

II

I mourn the sun and I mourn the years that will come
without us and I sing the others that have passed
if this is true

the bodies spoken to and boats that hummed sweetly
guitars flickering underwater
the *believe me* and the *don't*
once in the air once in the music

the two small animals, our hands
that longed to climb secretly one on the other
the flowerpot with the dewdrops in the open yard gates
and the pieces of seas coming together
above the dry rocks, behind the stone walls
the anemone that sat on your palm
and the mauve trembled thrice for three days above the waterfalls

If these are true I sing
the wooden beam and the square weaving
on the wall, the Mermaid with the unbraided hair
the cat that watched us in the darkness

Boy with the incense and the red cross
the hour evening comes on the rock's inaccessibility
I mourn the garment I touched and the world came to me

MARINA

Give me mint and basil
        and verbena to smell
and with these I would kiss you
        what first would I recall

The fountain with the doves
        the Archangel's sword
the orchard with the stars
        and the well so deep

The nights that I took you to a stroll
        to the sky's other side
and I stared at you rising
        like the sister of the Morning Star

Marina my green star
        Marina light of the Morning Star
Marina my wild dove
        and lily of the summer.

OF THE LITTLE NORTH WIND

To the little north wind I sent word
　　to be a good little boy
not to strike the door shutters
　　nor the little window

Because in the house where I keep vigil
　　my true love is dying
and through my tears I can see
　　that she's hardly breathing

Grievance overtakes me
　　because in this world
I have lost all summers
　　and I've reached the winter

Like the ship that opened up
　　its sails and moved on
I see that seashores vanish
　　and the world gets smaller

Farewell orchards farewell ravines
　　farewell kisses and farewell embraces
farewell capes and blonde seashores
　　farewell eternal vows.

THE SEA CLOVER

Once in a thousand years
    the spirits of the sea
in the darkened seaweed
    in the green pebbles
they plant it and it grows
    before the sunrise
they chant their charms and
    the clover of the sea rises

And whoever finds it does not die
    and whoever finds it does not die

Once in a thousand years
    nightingales sing differently
they don't laugh nor they cry
    they only say they only say:
once in a thousand years
    love becomes eternal
wish it to be your luck wish it to be your luck
    and this year will bring you success

And from the places of the sky
    it will bring your love

The three leaved sea clover
    whoever finds it, send it to me
whoever finds it, send it to me
    the three leaved sea clover.

EROS AND PSYCHE

The life of others strikes me like
a wild black sea. Whatever you believe in the night
God changes. Softly the houses go
some reach down to the quay with their lights on
the soul of the dead (as they say) goes

ah, what can you be that they call you *soul*
that neither the wind in its passing gave you
matter, nor ever took any feather from you
what balsam or what poison you pour so that

in ancient times the courteous Diotima
singing inwardly was able to alter
man's mind and the flow of Swabia's waters*
that those in love can be both here and there

of two stars and one single destiny

the earth seems to be unsuspecting
thought it's not. Satiate with diamonds and coal
it still knows to speak from where truth comes
with subterranean drums or springs of great clarity
it comes to confirm for you. Which? What?

The only thing you believe in and God doesn't change
is something that nevertheless exists
undeciphered within the Futile and the Nothing.

*Because from being Zeus' child
and fighting in the claws of Harpy
he reverently signed as: Scardanelli.*

CONSTANTINE CAVAFY

Cavafy was born on April, 1863. Son of a family of merchants, he had eight older siblings all of whom died before him. Two of his brothers were painters, and another wrote poems in English and French; a cousin of his translated Shakespeare.

His father died in 1870 leaving the family in difficult financial position. Cavafy's mother moved the family to England, where the two eldest sons took over their father's business however their inexperience caused the ruin of the family fortunes and they returned to Alexandria. But the few years that Cavafy spent in England shaped his poetic sensibility and he became so comfortable with the second language that he wrote his first poems in English.

After the brief time he spent in England he moved with his mother to Constantinople where he lived with his grandfather; his stay here was brief and he arrived in Alexandria in 1879. After working for short periods for the Alexandrian Newspaper and the Egyptian Stock Exchange, at the age of twenty-nine Cavafy took up an appointment as a special clerk in the Irrigation Service of the Ministry of public works, a position he held for the next thirty years.

Constantine Cavafy had a very small circle of people around him. For much of his adult life he lived alone. Influential relationships included his twenty-year acquaintance with E.M. Forster. Cavafy remained virtually unknown in Greece until late in his career. He was introduced to the mainland Greek literary circles through a favorable review written by the Greek writer Xenopoulos in 1903; however, he got little recognition since his writing style was different from the mainstream Greek poetry of the time. Some twenty years later, after the war of 1919-1923 between Greece and Turkey, a new generation of poets such as Karyotakis would find some inspiration in Cavafy's work.

However today he's considered one of the most influential poets of modern Greece and along with Palamas, Kalvos, Seferis, Elytis, Egonopoulos and Ritsos he was instrumental in the revival and recognition of Greek poetry both in Greece and abroad. His first published poem was printed for the magazine Hesperos in 1886. He also published articles and philosophical diatribes in newspapers and magazines of Leipsia, Constantinople, Alexandria and Athens.

In 1926, the military government of Pangalos, after a submission by G. Haritakis, awarded him the "Silver Medal of Phoenix". The same year the periodical Alexandrian Art was launched under his guidance.

Cavafy's poems have been translated into just about all the European languages. He died of cancer of the larynx on April 29, 1933, on his seventieth birthday, in Alexandria.

VOICES

Ideal and beloved voices
of the dead or those who
for us are lost like the dead

at times they talk in our dreams
at times our minds hear them when in thought

and with their sound, for a moment, echoes
return from the first poetry of our lives —
like distant music, at night, that slowly fades away.

THERMOPYLAE

Honor to those who in their lives
are committed to guard Thermopylae
never swerving from duty
just and exact in all their actions
but tolerant too, and compassionate
gallant when rich and when
they are poor, again a little gallant
again assisting as much as they can
always speaking the truth
but without hatred for those who lie

and more honor is due to them
when they foresee (and many do foresee)
that Ephialtis will appear in the end
and the Medes will break through at last.

DESIRES

Like beautiful bodies of the dead that haven't grown old
that were locked, in tears, in the gleaming mausoleum
with roses at their heads and jasmines by their legs —
the way desires that have passed look
when not fulfilled; without any of them having enjoyed
a single night of lust or a single shining morning.

CANDLES

The days of the future stand in front of us
like a line of lit candles —
golden, warm and lively little candles

the days of the past remain behind
a sorrowful line of burned out candles
the closest ones are still smoking
cold candles, melted, and drooping

I don't want to look at them, their shape saddens me
and it saddens me to remember their previous light
I look ahead at my lit candles

I don't want to look back and see in horror
how fast the dark line lengthens
how quickly the burned out candles multiply.

THE HORSES OF ACHILLES

When they saw Patroklos dead
who was so brave and strong and young
the horses of Achilles began to cry
     their immortal nature was outraged
at the sight of this work of death.
They reared up and tossed their long manes
     they stamped the ground with their hooves and mourned
Patroklos whom they felt was soulless — devastated —
lifeless flesh now — his spirit gone —
     defenseless — without breath —
returned from life to the great Nothing

     Zeus saw the tears of the immortal
horses and felt sad. He said, "At the wedding of Peleus
I shouldn't have acted so mindlessly
     it would have been better if we had not given you away
my unhappy horses! What need did you have to be
down there among miserable humans, playthings of fate
     you whom death cannot ambush who will never grow old
you are still tormented by disaster. People
have entangled you in their suffering."— But
     for the endless calamity of death
those two noble animals shed their tears.

THE CITY

You said: "I'll go to another land to another sea;
I'll find another city better than this one.
Every effort I make is ill-fated, doomed;
and my heart — like a dead thing — lies buried.
How long will my mind continue to wither like this?
Everywhere I turn my eyes, wherever they happen to fall
I see the black ruins of my life, here
where I've squandered, wasted and ruined so many years."

New lands you'll not find, you'll not find other seas
the city will follow you. You'll return to the same streets
you'll age in the same neighborhoods; and in these
same houses you'll turn gray. You'll always
arrive in the same city. Don't even hope to escape it
there is no ship for you, no road out of town.
As you have wasted your life here, in this small corner
you've wasted it in the whole world.

FINALITIES

Amid the fears and suspicions
with unsettled mind and frightened eyes
we melt away and we plan how to act
in order to avoid the certain
danger that threatens us so gravely.
And yet we are mistaken, the danger is not in our way;
the messages were false
(we neither heard them, nor fully understood them).
Another catastrophe that we never imagined,
sudden, torrential falls on us
and unprepared — there is not enough time — it takes us away.

THE IDES OF MARCH

Beware of grandeur, oh soul.
And if you can't overcome your ambitions
pursue them with hesitant precaution
and the more you go forward, the more
inquiring and careful you must be.

And when you reach your zenith, as a Caesar at last
when you take on the role of such a famous man
then most of all be careful when you go out on the street
like any famous master with your entourage
if by chance some Artemidoros approaches
out of the crowd, bringing you a letter
and says in a hurry "Read this at once
these are serious matters that concern you"
don't fail to stop; don't fail to postpone
every speech or task; don't fail to turn away
the various people who greet you and bow to you
(you can see them later); let even the Senate wait
for you must consider at once
the serious writings of Artemidoros

THE WINDOWS

In these dark rooms where I spend
leaden days I go up and down
looking for the windows. — To open
one would be a great consolation. —
But they are nowhere to be found or I can't
find them. And perhaps it is better that I don't.
Perhaps their light will be a new tyranny.
Who knows what it will reveal?

.

ITHAKA

When you start on your way to Ithaka
pray that your journey will be long
full of adventures, full of knowledge.
Do not fear The Lestrygonyans
the Cyclopes or the angry Poseidon
you will never run into them
if your thoughts are kept high, if a clear
excitement moves your body and your spirit.
You will never meet the Lestrygonians
or the Cyclops or the angry Poseidon
unless you carry them in your soul
unless your soul raises them before you.

Pray that the way is long.
Let the summer mornings be many
when you will enter with such pleasure, such joy,
harbors you have never seen before
may you stop at Phoenician markets
to buy their fine merchandise
mother-of-pearl and coral, amber and ebony
and pleasurable perfumes of every kind
as many as you can get
and may you visit a lot of Egyptian cities
to learn and go on learning from their scholars.

Always maintain Ithaka in your mind
your arrival there is your destiny
but don't hurry the trip at all
let it last for many years
and when you reach the island and you are old
rich with all you have gained on the way
do not expect any further riches from Ithaka

Ithaca gave you the beautiful voyage
without her you would never have started your journey
she has nothing else to give you

and if you find Ithaca poor, Ithaka has not tricked you
you've become such a wise person, with so much experience
you've already understood what Ithakas mean.

AS MUCH AS YOU CAN

And if you can't lead your life the way you want it
at least try this
as much as you can: do not degrade it
in a crowded relationship with the world
in too many things and too much talk.

Do not degrade it by showing it around
dragging it along and exposing it
to the daily nonsense
of relationships and associations
until it is strange to you and a burden.

COME BACK

Come back often and take me
beloved sensation, come back and take me —
when the memory in my body awakens
and the old desire again runs through my blood
when the lips and the skin remember
and the hands feel as if they were touching again

come back often and take me at night
when the lips and the skin remember...

TROJANS

Our efforts are like those of the unfortunate
like the efforts of the Trojans.
We succeed a bit, we regain
our confidence and we start feeling
brave and having high hopes.

But always something comes up and stops us
Achilles appears in front of us in the trench
and with loud shouts frightens us back —

Our efforts are like those of the Trojans.
We think that with resolution and boldness
we can reverse the downhill course of fate
and we stand outside ready to fight.

But when the great crisis comes
our boldness and resolution vanish
our soul is shaken, paralyzed
and we run around the walls
trying to save ourselves by running away

and yet our fall is certain. High up
on the walls, the dirge has already started
mourning memories and auras of our days
Priamos and Ekavi weep bitterly for us.

VERY SELDOM

He is an old man worn out and hunched
maimed by the years and his own excesses
walking slowly he crosses the narrow street
and yet as he enters his house and hides
his old age and his terrible condition, he contemplates
the share he still has of youth.

Ephebes recite his verses now
his visions flash through their lively eyes
their healthy, lustful minds
their firm, well-shaped bodies
are stirred by the way he expressed beauty.

MORNING SEA

Let me stand here, let me look
at nature for a while
the yellow shore, the intense blue
of the morning sea, the clear sky; all
grand and beautifully radiant.

Let me stand here and let me pretend
that I see these things (I really saw them
for a moment when I first stood here)
and not what I do see, even here, my fantasies
my memories, my visions of carnal delight.

FAR AWAY

I would like to tell you a memory
but it seems nearly erased as though nothing remains —
because it lies far away in my youthful years

skin that was made of jasmine…
that day in August — was it August? — the night
I barely remember the eyes: they were, I think, blue
ah yes, blue, a sapphire blue

WALLS

Without much thought without pity without shame
they've built these high, thick walls around me

and now I sit here in despair
I think of nothing else: this fate consumes my mind

because I had so many things to do outside
ah, why didn't I notice when they built the walls?

But I never heard the builders or any sound at all.
Imperceptibly they shut me off from the world.

SINCE NINE O'CLOCK

Twelve thirty. Time has gone by quickly
since nine o'clock when I lit the lamp
and sat down here. I sat without reading
and without speaking. Whom would I speak to
alone in this house?

The vision of my youthful body
has come and visited me since nine o'clock
when I lit the lamp and has recalled
closed rooms full of fragrance
and lost carnal pleasure — what bold pleasure!
And it also brought before my eyes
roads that are now unrecognizable
taverns full of action that have closed
and theaters and coffee bars that no longer exist.

The vision of my youthful body
also brought me sad memories
family mourning, separations
feelings about loved ones, emotions
of the dead so little appreciated.

Half past twelve. How time has gone by.
Half past twelve. How the years went by.

IONIAN

Although we broke their statues
and drove them out of their temples
the gods didn't die out at all because of that
"oh land of Ionia, it's you they still love
it's you their souls still remember
when dawn comes on you of an August morning
the vigor of their lives goes through your atmosphere
and at times the ethereal figure of a youth
obscure, with quick steps
passes over your hills.

HE SWEARS

Quite often he swears to start a better life
but when the night comes with its own advisories
with its compromises and with its promises
when the night comes with its own power
over the body that craves and seeks
to the same dark joy, forlorn, he returns.

YANNIS RITSOS

Yannis Ritsos was born in Monemvasia, Greece, in 1909 to a well-heeled family of land owners. He did his early schooling in the region and finished high school in Gythion and in 1925 he moved to Athens where he started working in typing and copying legal documents. A year later he returned to his hometown with the first signs of tuberculosis, where he spent his time writing and drawing.

In 1927 he went back to Athens and spent the following three years in a tuberculosis sanatorium. During these three years he started publishing poetry and he studied Marxism, committing himself to furthering the ideals of communism.

Ritsos spent the following six years between 1931 and 1937 in Athens, where he worked as an actor and dancer in theatrical groups. He published his first poetry book Tractor, referring to the working class in 1934 and in 1935 his second book Pyramids; a year later his famous Epitaphios was published in an edition of ten thousand copies although some of them were publicly burned by the military government.

For six months between 1937 and 1938 he stays in the Parnitha sanatorium and during the German occupation he remains in Athens spending his time writing fervidly. Early in 1945 he joined the National Liberation forces of Greece and contributed theatrical works to the people's Theatre of Macedonia. After the Varkiza agreement of disarmament he returned to Athens and he worked as an editor for the publisher Govotsis. In 1948 the poet is arrested and sent to exile on Limnos and then to Makronissos and later one to Saint Eustratios.

In 1954 he married Filitsa Georgiadis, a doctor on the island of Samos and their daughter Ery was born in 1955. From this point on, his work began appearing in Greece regularly and his Moonlight Sonata won him the National Prize for Poetry. Three volumes of his poems were released between 1955 and 1967 when he was suddenly arrested by the colonels' junta and sent to exile on Yiaros and then Leros, and his poetry is again banned. In 1968, he was hospitalized in Athens and then sent into exile to his wife's home in Samos where he stayed for a year and a half before he goes back to Athens for an operation; after the operation he stayed in Athens and published his poetry in the magazine Nea Keimena although his work was still officially banned.

In 1972 he was awarded the Grand Prize for Poetry at the Knokke-le-Zout Biennale. After the dictatorship Ritsos was a free man at last, and devoted all his time to his work. In 1975, he was awarded with an honorary doctorate from University of Thessaloniki and the Alfred de Vigny Poetry Prize in France. In 1976, and he was awarded the International Poetry Prize of Etna Taormina of Sicily and in 1977 the Lenin Prize for Poetry. He died in 1990 at the age of 81.

FEAR OF LIFE

Stony day
stony sun
stony silence

the horses died on the mountain
the trees died in the whitewash
you didn't die

sound of their distant hooves
sound of the old panting
in the petrified noon

and the fear that perhaps you wouldn't die
and the fear of water trickling
fear, water, breath – life

MYTH

At night we lighted the oil lamps
and took the roads asking the passers-by

she wore a dress we said
in the color of dreams didn't you see her?
She wore two light blue earrings

no one had seen her, only in the cabin at the end of the village
the old woman the lumberjack's mother pointed her finger
and showed us the river behind the trees

down to where two light blue stars flickered

ONE DEAD

He said: the light with the enlarged eyes
with the enlarged arm hairs
with the magnified voices of builders on the opposite
construction site with the blinding sea
between their naked ribs is terrible

you have to get saddled with a mountain – he said –
that you may pass standing through the sun's responsibility

however down in the basement – he said –
are the large empty barrels like coffins of your ancestors
there is the conciliatory shadow
and the oil stains on the floor
and the roots of the tree that pushes through the wall
its contorted fingers

The security of death – he said

there you hear the distant words of vineyards and seeds
you taste the silence and the moisture
you get used to being dead

and he was truly dead without being accustomed to it
when the long days came with flags
when light knocked on his door
no one opened

he was dead without being used to it

INVITATION

Come to the luminous beaches – he murmured to himself –
here where the colors celebrate – look –
here where the royal family never passed
with their closed carriages and official emissaries

come – it's not good if they see you – he said –
I am the deserter of the night
I am the burglar of darkness
I have filled my shirt and my pockets with sun

come – it burns my hands and my chest
come let me give it to you

and I have something to tell you
that even I cannot hear

ADMISSION

Defeated by the light- blue
with his head leaning on the knees of silence
dead tired of life
dead tired of youth
sunken inside his fire
and the seaweed stirring in his armpit –

the wave of day didn't find resistance
not even on a pebble of his thought

as he was ready for love
and for death

THE HILL

Someone had a lot of dead people
he dug the ground he buried them himself
stone by stone earth on earth
he built a hill
on top of the hill
he built his cabin facing the sun

after that he opened pathways
he planted trees
carefully geometrically thoughtfully
his eye was always smiling
his hand wasn't trembling
the hill

There on Sunday afternoons mothers climb
pushing their baby carriages
the workers of the neighborhood in clean shirts
go there to sunbathe and breath some fresh air
at twilight pairs in love saunter
and learn to read the stars
under the trees a child plays harmonica
the pop vendor yells about his lemonade

on the hill they all know
that they are closer to the sky

but no one knows how the hill was built
no one knows how many sleep in the hills' bowels

THE MEANING OF SIMPLICITY

I hide behind simple things that you may find me
if you don't find me you will find these things
you will touch what my hand touched
the traces of our hands will join

the August moon shines in the kitchen
like a tin-plated saucepan (it turns like that because I tell you
this)
it lights the empty house and the kneeling silence of the house –
silence stays always kneeling

each word is an exit
for an encounter often postponed
and then the word is true since it insists on the encounter

DUTY

One star gleams in the twilight like a lit
keyhole
you glue your eye on it – you look inside – you see everything

the world is fully illuminated behind the locked door

you need to open it

PERHAPS SOMEDAY

I want to show you these rosy clouds in the night
but you can't see. It is night – what can you see?

So I can see through your eyes, he said
that I won't be alone that you won't be alone and truly
there is nothing to the direction I pointed

only stars crowded together in the night tired
like people on a picnic who come back on a truck
regretful sleepy nobody singing
with wilted wildflowers in their sweaty palms

but I shall insist in seeing and showing you, he said
because if you don't see it is as if I didn't see –
I shall insist at least not seeing with your eyes –
and perhaps someday from different directions we shall meet

FINAL AGREEMENT

When the rain struck the window with one of its fingers
the window opened toward the inside. Deep inside
an unknown person, a sound – your voice?

Your voice distrusted your ear
the other day the sun went down the fields like a descent of farmers
with scythes and pitchforks
you went out to the road yelling
not knowing about what you were yelling
stopping for a moment with a smile under your voice
as if under the rosy fully illuminated umbrella of a woman
sauntering along the railing of the park

there suddenly you recognized that this was your true voice
agreeing with all the unsuspecting voices floating in the air

RACECOURSE

Racecourse during the night the lights the music
the glittering cars along the whole length of the avenue

When the neighborhood lights go out
when the last music note falls like a dry leaf
the racecourse facade becomes
like a huge taken-out denture. Then
the bronze instruments sleep in their cases
animals heard wailing over the city
the tiger in her cage concentrates on her shadow
the animal tamer takes off his uniform and smokes his cigarette
and the neighborhood moment by moment is lit
as the eyes of the lions glitter behind the iron bars

TRANSFORMATION

This which you call serenity or discipline, kindness or apathy
this which you call a closed mouth with clenched teeth
showing the sweet silence of a mouth hiding the clenched
    teeth
is just the metals' fortitude under the useful
    hammer
under the formidable hammer – because you know
that from the amorphous you pass to the formed

AFTERNOON

Afternoon full of fallen plaster, black stones, dry
    thorns
the afternoon has a difficult color of old footsteps stopped
    halfway
of old storage jars buried in the yard and over them tiredness
    and grass

Two people killed, five killed, twelve – so many so many
each hour has its own killed. Behind the windows
stand the ones who are missing and the pitcher with water they
    didn't drink

and this star that fell on the edge of the evening
is like the severed ear that can't hear the crickets
that can't hear our excuses – it disdains
in hearing our songs – alone, alone
alone, detached from others, indifferent to condemnation or
    justification

SUDDENLY

Silent night, silent and you had stopped
waiting, almost quiet
and suddenly on your face so intensely you felt
the touch of the absent. He will come. Then
you heard the window shutters hitting each other
wings came up and a bit farther down the sea
drowning in its own voice

UNDERSTANDING

Sunday. Buttons shine on coats
like small laughter. The bus is gone
some cheerful voices – strange
that you can hear and you answer. Under the pine trees
a worker is trying to learn harmonica. A woman
said good morning to someone – so simple and natural
      good morning
that you would like to learn how to play harmonica under
      the pine trees

Neither division nor subtraction. To be able to look outside
yourself – warmth and serenity. Not to be
'just yourself' but 'you too'. A small addition
a small act of practical arithmetic easily understood
that even a child can do successfully playing with his
      fingers in the light
or playing this harmonica so the woman can hear it

CONCLUSION

This window is alone
this star is alone
like a forgotten cigarette on the table –
it smokes, it smokes lonely in the light- blue

I am also alone, he said
I light my cigarette, I smoke
I smoke and think I am not alone

MINIATURE

The woman stands up before the table; her sorrowful
        hands
slice thin pieces of lemon for the tea
like yellow wheels for a very small carriage
of a child's fairytale. The young army officer opposite her
sunken deep in the old armchair. He doesn't look at her.
He lights his cigarette. His hand having the match trembles
lighting up his tender chin and the little hand of the teacup.
        The clock
stops its heartbeat momentarily. Something has been postponed.
The moment passed. It is late. Let us have our tea.
So then is it possible for death to come on such a small carriage?
To pass by and go away? So that this small carriage with
the yellow small wheels left behind alone stopped
for years in a side street with shut-off lampposts and
then a short song some mist and then nothing?

WAITING

Night falls late in the neighborhood. We can't sleep
we wait for daybreak. We wait
for the sun to strike like a hammer the tin roofs of the sheds
to strike our foreheads, our hearts
to turn into sound that can be heard – a different sound
because silence is filled by gunshots from unknown points

WOMEN

Women are very distant. Their bed-sheets smell of goodnight.
They place the bread on the table that we won't miss them
then we understand that we did something wrong.
We get up from the chair saying:
"You are very tired today" or "don't worry, let me light the lamp."

When we light the match she turns slowly going to
the kitchen with an inexplicable concentration. Her back
is a sad little mountain loaded with many dead –
the family dead her dead and your death

You hear her footsteps creaking on the old floor planks
you hear the plates crying in the plate rack and then the train
is heard carrying soldiers to the front lines.

THANK YOU

You won't say thank you to me
as you don't say thank you to your heartbeats
which carve the face of your life

but I shall say thank you to you
because I know what I owe you

this thank you is my song

TASOS LIVADITIS

Tasos Livaditis was born in Athens April 20, 1922. He was enrolled in the Law School of the University of Athens. German occupation interrupted his studies and his involvement with the Resistance and the political party EPON. His father, bankrupt by this time died during the occupation years and while the poet was exiled in Makronisos his mother also died. In 1946 he got married to Maria Stoupa, the valuable companion of his life and they had a daughter, Vassiliki. That same year he made his first literary appearance with the publication of his poem *The Hatzidimitri Song* in *Elefthera Grammata*. In 1947 he coordinated the release of the literary magazine *Themelio*. In 1952 his poetry books *Battle at the Edge of the Night* and *This Star is for all of us* were noticed. Three years later he was taken by the police because of his book *It Blows in the Crossroads of the World* but he was acquitted. His book *Women with Equine Eyes*, 1958, was a landmark in his literary career and his turn into the introverted and existential poetry of his middle life. In 1961 he went on a country tour along with Mikis Theodorakis who presented his poems set in music. The same year he collaborated with Kosta Kotzias in the writing of the script and the poems for the Alekos Alexandrakis film *Neighbourhood of Dreams* which was the turning point of Greek cinema but which was censored by the police. In 1986 he published his book *Violets for a Season* which is considered his swan song. He died in Athens, October 30th 1988 of an abdominal aneurism. The rest of his hand written poems were published after his death in a book titled *Autumn Handwritings.*

He was the recipient of the First Poetry Prize in the World Youth Poetry Festival of Warsaw 1953, the First Poetry Prize of the City of Athens, 1957; the second National Literary Prize for poetry 1976; the First National Literary prize for poetry 1979.

SIMPLE TALK

I would like to speak
in a simple way
as one unbuttons his shirt
and reveals an old wound
like your elbow that feels cold
you look
and discover there's a hole in your garment
as a comrade sits on a rock and mends
his undershirt.
To speak of whether I may come back one day
carrying a dirty mess-tin full of exile
having in my pockets two tightly held fists

to speak
in a simple way —
but for a moment let me put down my crutches.

Once we dreamed of becoming great poets
we talked of the sun
now our heart pierces us
like a nail in our boot.
When once we said: sky, now we say: courage.
We aren't poets anymore
only comrades
with big scars and even bigger dreams.
The wind that screams just outside our tent
the barb wire fastened on the belly of the night
a broken oil lamp
the oil drips

Thomas' face in the gauzes
probably red and swollen from the rifle butt hits
a smell of smoke and dirty feet.
Elias says: the weather will change
Dimitris is silent
and Nikolas
struggles to fill the holes of the tent

with a piece of boiled potato.
Someone coughs. We are cold.
The footsteps of the patrol are heard.
Tonight we decided to write you a letter, mother
that perhaps we may hear the rain
drip on your worn out clogs
that perhaps we may see your smile
hanging from your chin over our thirst.
They feed us rotten potatoes: do not worry
they curse us and they hit us: please love us
perhaps we may never return — but you keep lighting
the lamp, mother, others will return.
Now you probably gather the white cloths of the exile from
the cloths-line
you stitch the patch of your concern on our socks
you know, mother, we'll never use the gloves
you knitted for us
we gave them to a comrade who was taken away
to be court marshalled
we also gave him a can of food and a piece of
our palm
he tied the edge of his sack with a string
he tossed the sack on his shoulder
and we saw him climbing the hill
with his thin legs scissoring the opposite
sky into pieces.
Every morning they count us
every evening we count the leftover plates
the leftover grief in our eyes
as the rain throws the dice with the policemen
while night falls and the whistles start rumbling.
Now we want to put our hands in our armpits
to look whether a star gleams in the sky
to remember that face
against the opening of the door
but we can't remember
we have no time to remember

we don't have time but to stand tall
and die.
My beloved
perhaps I feel cold when it rains
perhaps I caress the crumbs of memory
in my pockets
my palms that once held you are still hot
but I can't return.
How can I deny the piece of hardened bread that twenty of us
shared
how can I deny my mother who expects from me
a cup of sage tea
how can I deny our child to who we promised a piece
of the sky
how can I deny Nikolas —
who was singing while they aimed to execute him.
If I return we won't have a lamp to light, we won't
know where to place our dream.
We'll sit silently
and when I shall look at you
the holed boot of the comrade I denied
will cover my eyes like a cloud.
Do love me.
And when I return
holding my heart like a big bundle
we'll sit on the worn out steps.
I don't like my calloused hands anymore — I'll say.

You'll smile and hold them in your palms tightly
a star will chime in the moistened sky
perhaps
I'll cry.
Today we opened our day
like a sack forgotten by the years.
We searched to find the socks you wore, comrade
your hands
your life that ended.

Grief threw a handful of nails
into our eyes.
Then we washed the cookhouse
we started the fire
and two of us shared a cigarette
under the ragged clouds.
Here our lives are egg shells under
their feet
with death so ever close
and how can you sing
from a patch on the hole of your elbow
with the name of the dead comrade
like a fork piercing your tongue?
It's enough that we speak
in a simple way
as one is hungry in a simple way
as one loves
as we die
in a simple way.

THE DEFEATED

He kneeled and laid his forehead on the floor. It was the difficult time. When he got up his embarrassed face that we all knew well had stayed there on the planks like an useless upside turned helmet.

The same man returned home without face — like God.

PIGSTY

Things have changed; these days they don't kill, they only
point at you with the finger and it's enough. Then they make
a circle that always becomes smaller, they slowly get closer
you retreat back against the wall until in desperation you, alone,
open a hole to hide in it.

When the circle is cleared in its place stands another in every
respect lovable man.

THE SIXTH DAY

It was the sixth day of creation; mother was dressed in black; she wore her good hat with the veil "God shouldn't had done this to us" she said; at the far end pale workers put together the big stage of the circus

"come back home, it's late", "which home?" I asked and hugged the lamp-post of the street

my young cousin was almost dead when I pushed her behind the closet, "I love you" she'd say but I had already undressed her — like a whore — when we buried her, I stayed there forever, behind the closet, half eaten by the mice

and it was the sixth day of creation

pulleys grunted as they lifted the first clock up to the roof of the station

I sat by the side of the street, so sorry, that even the blind could see me.

SECRET GATE

Wings stirred under the furniture and at the end of the hall
the dark mirror often made the children sick because they
didn't want to grow up

mother cried and beg me to come down though it was my fate
to walk on the ceiling: my own battle, mother, where I was
the only dead

for this I knew the subterranean secret gate to the sky.

THE MUSICIAN

    Often during the night, without noticing it, I'd arrive to another city
where there would be no other but an old man who dreamed that some-
day
he'd become a musician and now half naked he sat in the rain — on top
of his knees with his coat he was covering an old, imaginary violin,
"do you hear it?" he says to me "yes" I say to him "I have
always heard it"
    while at the far end of the road the statue narrated the true voyage
to the birds.

THE VISITOR'S LETTER

    Suddenly on an autumn day he left; on the table he had left
a letter "don't send me away" it read and spoke of a deep inhabitable
emotion; in the house all the lights were turned on that I wouldn't
understand that perhaps he had never come while next to the letter
he had left the mystery of his death, already covered by cobwebs
"how you found me?" he said to me "I never existed", "for this"
I said and it was as if we were born and raised in a carriage that run
over the shiver of the roads
    yet I still couldn't fight against this façade of the house
its ravaged walls dived deeper than my blood in the darkness
of the night

THE NAILS

Sometimes, at a special time, I think of narrating all the details:
for example how this incurable disease started on the opposite wall
or about that woman in the park whose body was nailed on the bench
and I say this without exaggeration; the nails protruded from her cloths
like small buttons while her purse with her identity card floated down
the creek that we couldn't find out anything about her and as I
went up to the loft they allotted to me for the night I discovered they
had all moved and only hay was left behind because they always had
the fear of comedown and there were moments when everyone
anticipated the inescapable and when the night fell serenely they
quietened down because the others were going back and forth
in the hallway to look behind the door at the far end

for this I've stayed on the sidelines hoping to rediscover that
lost soul

DAILY USE

Of course all these were somehow vague perhaps even inexplicable
for the ones who raise their glass emphatically over the table without
seeing who holds it until slowly the everyday use makes us mortal
thus I always tried to look elsewhere when the doorbell rang and when
everything was quietened: where is the host, why is he hiding?

I leaned on the table that I wouldn't fall; then bowing my head
I opened the door and followed my path

and at night, dinner time, in horror I listened to them narrating
their stories that in a way silenced the dark, remote outside — there
where we had lived

THE ONE WHO COULD SEE

   He had a mysterious expression almost worrisome as he looked
for days on at that same spot in the room; therefore I stopped by the stairs
and tried to catch his attention and when he rang the doorbell and
entered he was so miserable the lamp walked ahead of him on
its own "but you don't see him, he lives with us" he said; the others
talked and laughed loudly (because of their fear of course) and only
the boy sat at the edge of the room and also looked at the same point
sadly
   and I thought what makes us old is, perhaps, the same childhood
that pushes us away that, after all, we won't understand

PROPERTY

Those of course had left but their death had remained here and it
fluttered inside the rooms and I had to raise my arm to protect my eyes
in order to pass through. For this reason I saw nothing of the world

only sometimes when I was very sad my dead mother smiled and
looked over my shoulder the child standing behind us (even though
it was so inattentive that we had grown) then I would lean on the chair
and sit there seeing the black shade of the trees descending because
the only thing one has in the world is someplace to lean and cry
for the game that remained unfinished

SHADOWS ON THE WALL

How did I truly dare to believe that I could escape, I, who
was just a man, temporary dwelling of fear and behind the peplos
the gods stood silently perhaps even they were in fear "what
do you dream off?" I would often ask and at dusk the owl was
heard far away while someone cried outside the door because
the lives we'll never live are here and they push us aside like the
big shadow of beggars on the wall while they stretch their arms
further, thin and uncertain, as if you couldn't know which is
their true existence

RETURN

In reality I knew that suddenly something unforeseen would had cancelled everything and when I heard them talking I felt as if I hadn't grown at all so indifferent they were (and I had to protect that and there wasn't any safe place anywhere) and as I walked into the street I, as desolate as ever, stretched my arm to no one because who knows whether someone would be there waiting; then the doorbell rang "why you returned?" I asked him; he was an old childhood friend "I still have something to finish" he said and all night long I heard him sobbing in the next room because he had died very young and he had come back here to cry and fulfill his purpose on earth

WE DESCENDED from an old race that vanished, barbarian
    invaders scattered us
but at night one could recognize us, the few of us, as we always
    sat on side streets
talking humble words about compassion or succession
and when sometimes we entered the city a flute would be
    heard in the stoa
where the outlaws had taken shelter while now the blind
    walked in a fast pace
and followed the dust that our passing had left behind

THEN what are the childhood years opposite this great
    debt
that you exist and here we're again in the open air only
with the half decomposed hand of our great grandmother in the sack
    and the shadow of the evening laid on the ground
together with all the other poor people while the wheel of the
    potter in a low tone argued
with someone we couldn't see and the lamp we placed on top of
    the roof, now shone that the lying-in woman
find her way home

THE BIRD THAT SPOKE THE TRUTH

Forgetfulness covered the past, the unknown besieged the house,
   ghosts of things we loved and lost
and now only the cob webs know the future — but nostalgia
   for the unknown has won us over since our young age and
   loneliness
has promised us the long distances. Oh, the children we were with
   those long neckties
for a very short childhood. And Maria, when the evening breeze shiv-
ered
   among the ribbons of her hat,
was in different constellations — we never reached her. And I've loved
   passionately everything I was never meant to know. And I've lived
all
   my life in a dream
and immortality in a few cognacs.

One morning a bird sat on the tree on the other side of the road and
chirped
   something
oh, if I could understand what it wanted to tell me perhaps I would have
   discovered the meaning of the world.

THE FIRST VERSE

But why sometimes we stand in the middle of an unknown road
    or before an old house? What do they remind us? Who do
    we search for?
Other times under a bridge or behind a curtain you feel that
    you truly live —
things that someday you'll repay with your soul
until one morning the first bird chirp was heard in the garden
    at spring time
mother changed her hat the young servant girl climbed up to the attic
    to cry and grandfather skipped his Bible reading.

Now I sit on the old rocking chair where three generations
    have sat. Where have all these people gone?
My whole life was but the memory of a dream within
    another dream and when Anna laughed it was as though
    she spread jasmine flowers
and for a while the night glowed.

I remember when I was a child I wrote my first verse
since then I've known that I'll never die —
                          but I'll be dying every day

TWILIGHT

We are captives of the inexplicable and of the forever lost
and remorse is the only way to return to the innocence
    of youth —
oh, my old departed friend, I know I'll meet you again in
    a dream or suddenly in the street when all is lost
women who we loved while the rain intensified outside
    the windows
then we passed the bridge holding hands, your wet hair
    shone in the sundown —
who could believe it, really, that it was a time when we would
    even give our lives
with that unstoppable fever like the sick children who
    when the get well they don't fit in their childhood cloths
and they are mocked in school — and they fill their
    notebooks with poems
so that they won't be lost and then adulthood comes like
    a shipwreck.

Oh, twilight, hour of justice, you pay attention to the most
humble things before nightfall.

MANOLIS ANAGNOSTAKIS

Manolis Anagnostakis was born in Thessaloniki and trained as a doctor, specializing in radiology. During the chaotic period of 1944 Anagnostakis served as the Editor-in-Chief of The Start, a student magazine. Anagnostakis' first book of poetry Seasons was published in 1945, at which point, the poet's Marxist dream had already failed him. Arrested for his involvement with the Student Movement at the University of Thessaloniki in 1948, Anagnostakis spent several years in state prison. His second volume, Seasons 2 was published after he was imprisoned in 1948. In the next year, Anagnostakis was both expelled from the Communist Party of Greece and tried in court. He received a death sentence, but out-survived the regime. Upon his release in 1951, he published the last book in that cycle of poems.

He began a new cycle of work with his *Continuation*, in 1954, and its sequel in 1955. A collection of his works was published the next year. The poet spent 1955 and the next year in Vienna, continuing his medical studies in radiology, before returning to Greece. He spent 1959 through 1961 doing editorial work. Anagnostakis moved his practice and family to Athens in 1978. Lakis Papastathis produced a 52-minute film, Manolis Criticism, a journal of literary criticism, and finished the cycle of poems *Continuation* in 1962.

Although his 1971 collection represented the end of the published works he's best known for, his existentialism-influenced verse left its mark on a younger generation of Greek poets. This influence is in part owing to his poetry having been set to music by Mikis Theodorakis, as part of his *Ballads* cycle, written during the seven-year Regime of the Colonels. The *Ballads* have been performed by vocalist Margarita Zorbala, for the Greek television series *Paraskenio* in 1983. Two volumes of Anagnostakis' other collection *The Poet Manoussos Fassis* were issued in the following four years. Anagnostakis died June 23, 2005 in Athens.

Anagnostakis' poetry has been described as terse. His early works may be comparable in number of lines to Cavafy although they do contain single-word lines and single-line verse paragraphs. Other characteristics of the early poems are its bold, conversational tone, sometimes in the form of an epistle, and at others culminating in direct advice to the reader. This style, along with Anagnostakis' simple, direct description of a hostile world was emulated by other left-wing poets of his generation. His lack of recognition outside of Greece can be attributed to the fact that Anagnostakis' poetry is politically committed.

OLD STREETS

Old streets that I loved and I forever hated
where I walked under the shade of houses
inescapable nights of the return and the city: dead

I discovered my insignificant presence in every corner
wishing that at some time I'd meet you: I and the lost ghost
of my passion

forgotten and insubordinate walking and holding a flickering spark
in my wet palms

and I walked in the night and I knew no one
and no one, no one knew me

THE SKY

First I want to take your hands
to listen to your pulse
then we'll go to the forest together
to hug the big trees
on the trunks of which long time ago
we engraved revered names
to trace their lines one by one
to count them one by one
with our eyes gazing up high as if praying

the sky doesn't hide our forest

the lumberjacks don't pass by here

YOUNG MEN FROM SIDON

We shouldn't complain, really
your company was pleasant and full of vigor:
freshened girls, wholesome boys
full of love for life and for adventures
and your songs were sweet and meaningful
very sentimental, humane
for the children who died over the other continent
for the heroes killed in past years
for revolutionaries with black, green, reddish skin
for the grief of every suffering man
this involvement especially an honour for you
for today's problems and struggle
you always appear and you fight, therefore
I believe it's your right to play
in groups of two or three at a time
and to fall in love
to just relax, brothers, after such tiredness

(George, have you noticed we've aged prematurely?)

TOMBSTONE ENGRAVING

You also died and you became the special
good family man, the patriot
thirty six wreaths accompanied you
three funereal speeches by vice presidents
seven votes in favor of what you offered

ah, Lavrentis, only I knew what a bastard you were
what a sold out asshole, you lived a life-time of lies

sleep in peace I won't come to disturb your serenity

(I'll exchange my whole life with my priceless silence
not with a reward for your sorrowful corpse)

sleep in peace as you were in life: the special
good family man, the patriot

you'll neither be the first nor the last

LOVE IS FEAR

Love is the fear that connects us with others
when they take control of our days and hang them like tears
when our days die along with them in a wretched disfiguring
the last schemes of our childish emotions
and what does the extended hand of people hold?
It knows how to squeeze tightly where logic fools us
when time stops and memory is uprooted
in a pointless search beyond logic.

(One day they return without any wrinkle in their mind
they discover their wives and children have grown
they frequent the little stores and cafes of the neighborhood
they read the epic routine of each and every morning)

Do we truly die for the others or we avenge our lives this way
or we spit all the measly resemblances this way
and at some time a sunray goes through our dried up minds
something like a vague memory of our lively prehistory?
We've reached the days when you don't know what to measure
erotic events and stock market companies
you can't find a mirror into which to call out your name
simple intentions of a secure life, current affairs
boredom, lust, dreams, business dealings, cheating
as if, I think it's because custom is better than guilt.
However who will come to stop the momentum of the falling rain?

DAY WILL COME

Day will come when we won't have anything to say
we'll sit opposite each other looking into each other's eyes
my silence will say: how beautiful you are
yet I don't find any words to describe it
we'll travel somewhere out of boredom
or you'll say that we also travelled.
People always grope around and at last they find love
however they don't find anything
sometimes I ponder that life is so short
it isn't even worthy of trying to start it
I leave Athens and go to Montevideo or
perhaps to Shanghai, this is also something
you can't doubt

remember that we smoked a lot of cigarettes
and talked all night long back then
I don't remember what we talked about
yet we did it with so much interest
I wish that one day I could go far away from you
although even there you will come looking for me
oh, God, no one can truly live alone

THEY WERE YOUNG

The roads were dark and muddy
the food on the table scarce
the kiss by the front door stolen
and love locked in their little hearts

they were young, just children
and by chance they were of a good crop
they spent their nights in basement tavernas
and roamed the neighborhoods all night long
ah, those side streets and corners
how nicely they kept the honest words

they were young, just children
and by chance they were of a good crop
at home they knew no father, no mother
they didn't care about anything
they never saved any coins in piggybanks
they never held a measuring tape or compass

they were young, just children
and by chance they were of a good crop

EARLY BEFORE DAYBREAK

It was still early before daybreak when
I couldn't accept defeat. I knew the many
hidden valuables I had to rescue, the many
pales of water to keep ready among the flames

you talked, you showed strange wounds in the streets
the panic choked your hearts like the flag you flew
on balconies, you loaded the merchandise hastily
your prognosis was correct: the city would fall

there, by the corner I meticulously collected
I carefully shut down my last outpost
I hanged the arms on the walls, I decorated
the windows with the broken school desks
I knit my net with hair clippings and
I waited standing alone like the first time

HE'S A SIMPLE SPECTATOR NOW

He's a simple spectator now
an insignificant little man among the crowd
he neither applauds nor he's applauded
a foreigner, he responds to the call of the streets

from afar come the new trumpeters
of the selected future classes
their yelling tumbles down the decrepit walls
they melt mud into the lighted mud creeks
now come the pure and unfeigned
the cunning feat participants, the innocent
the registrars of our days
the great waste is coming now
in the fountains of playful waters
the last specifications are due now

yet he's a simple spectator now
nameless little man among the crowd
with his arms before his chest as if dead
he neither applauds nor he's applauded

you better always know the when and the how

WHEN SPRING COMES

When spring comes smiling
you'll wear your new clothes and
you'll come to grasp my hands
my old friend and
although nobody expects your return
I feel your heartbeats and
a flower springing up from
your mature, embittered memory

one train whistles in the night
or a faraway unexpected ship
will bring you back along with our youth and
our dreams and
perhaps you haven't forgotten anything, really
while the return is always worthy more
than any of my love and your love
my old friend

I SPEAK

I speak of the last trumpeting of the defeated soldiers
of the last rags from our festive garments
of our children who sell cigarettes to the passers-by
I speak of the flowers that wilted on the graves and
rot in the rain
of the houses gaping with no windows like toothless
skulls
of girls begging and showing the scars of their breasts
I speak of the shoeless mothers who crawl among the ruins
of the conflagrated cities, the corpses piled in
the streets
the pimps poets who shiver by the front steps
during the night
I speak of the endless nights when the light is dimmed
at dawn
of the loaded trucks and the footsteps on the wet
cobblestones
I speak of the prison yard and of the tear of the moribund

but I speak more of the fishermen
who abandoned their nets and followed his steps
and when he got tired they didn't rest
and when he betrayed them they didn't reject him
and when he was glorified they turned their eyes the other way
and their comrades spat at them and crucified them
and serene, they took the road that had no end
and their glance didn't ever darken nor bowed down
standing and lonely amid the horrible loneliness of the crowd

NIKIFOROS VRETTAKOS

Nikiforos Vrettakos was born in Peloponese. He was the second child of six in the family of the Konstantine and Eugenia Vrettakos. He attended elementary and high school in Gytheion, South Peloponese, where the other great Greek poet Yannis Ritsos attended as well. In 1929 he moved to Athens with plans to attend University, however due to financial difficulties he didn't but instead he worked in various jobs just to earn his living. During this period he published his first poetry books *Under Lights and Shadows* and *Descending Into the Silence of the Eons* which were well received and also got the attention of Kostis Palamas, established poet at that time. Between the years 1929 and 1938 he lived for a while in Peireus. He got married and worked as a civil servant.

He went to the army and during the war against the Italians in 1940 he was sent to the front lines of Northern Greece. Soon after the invasion by the Germans he went back to Athens and became part of the National Liberation Army. Entries of his diary became the base of his next poetry book *Wild Beast*. During this period he also became member of the Greek Communist Party. For a while he worked as a clerk at the Ministry of Taxation and during this period he met the poet Aggelos Sikelianos with whom he shared a life-long friendship.

In 1955 he was elected member of the civil council of Peireus where he contributed a lot in the artistic and literary development of the city. In 1957 he travelled to Russia along with Stratis Mirivilis, another famous author of the days. In Moscow he met the wife of the famous Maxim Gorky.

After the four colonels took control of the Greek Government in 1967 Vrettakos went to self-exile in Switzerland from where he travelled all over Europe and took part in radio programs and poetry events in various countries. He was recognized by a few European Universities and during this period he wrote his autobiographical piece called *Anguish* which was published in New York.

In 1974, after the seven years dictatorship he returned to Athens. The Greek Academy awarded him the most prestigious Ouranis Award and he was named honorary professor of the Literature Department of the University of Athens. In 1991 he visited his hometown in south Peloponese and in August of the same year he had a heart attack. His funeral took place in Athens.

He was nominated four times for the Nobel Prize.

GREEN GARDEN

I have three worlds
the sea, the sky,
and a green garden: your eyes
if I could saunter in all three I could inform you
to where each of them reaches
for the sea I know
for the sky I suspect
for my green garden
don't ask

MAN, THE WORLD, AND POETRY

I dug up the whole of earth, just to discover you
I sieved the desert in my heart; I knew that
without man the sunlight wouldn't
be complete; however, now, seeing
through so much clarity, through you —
things come near me, they become discernable
diaphanous, now I can
include its parts in one of my poems

I'll grab a page and I'll
turn the light into straight lines

A SMALLER WORLD

I seek a shoreline where using canes
or trees I'll fence one piece of the horizon
where, gathering infinity, I may get the sense
that machines don't exist or only a few do
that soldiers don't exist or only a few do
that weapons don't exist or only a few do
that lead to the exit of the forest with the wolves
where there aren't any merchants or only a few
in remote places of the earth where
paved roads haven't yet been laid

God hopes that at least
paradise will never cease to exist in the poets' sobs

THE HELLENIC LANGUAGE

When I'll leave this light one day
I'll meander upwards like
a babbling brook
and if by chance somewhere among
the azure corridors of heaven
I meet angels, I shall speak to them
in Hellenic, since they don't
know of languages: they speak among
themselves with music

AN ALMOND TREE AND YOU NEXT TO IT

An almond tree and you
next to it
but when did you blossom?
I stand by the window
and seeing you I cry
my eyes can't take all
this joy
oh God, please give me
the cisterns of the sky
that I fill them all

I GATHER FALLEN WHEAT EARS

I gather all the fallen wheat ears to send you bread
I pick what's left of the sun with my broken hand
to send and dress you in it, since I've heard you are cold.

Put on your green dress at Easter that the children
will run with the flowers, doves will fly out
and our mother with her big apron full of love.

Take any road, any mountain peak, ask any tree you like
you hear me? All roads on earth start at my heart.

Don't be lost gazing the light. You hear me? Come!

POEMS FOR THE SAME MOUNTAIN

Not, I haven't come to say
goodbye, my brother, you who I placed
on top of a twig when I was a sunray
most of my verse are structures
on your body and if my words
become logos we would be both
standing like parallel rocks. Yet among
today's forest that's turned upside down
logos isn't heard anymore though I know
that in a future day children will find
flowers in my books and they'll
talk of the miracle of life as they gaze
the world through my verse

IF YOU MISS ME ONE NIGHT

If you miss me one night, don't be concerned
till the next morning, evening, till Sunday
I'll be around here, next to the sick man
I'll be searching for a spring with my bitter cane
I'll be walking from door to door with a loaf under my arm
keep the fire always lit since I'll return to you
most of the times wet. I've warmed up a shirt
on your knees and be mindful of the door and
the public road that I may be heard because
without the waning moon and the bright stars
I come back from the world's end every time

THE PUREST THING OF CREATION

I don't know why darkness has vanished
the sun entered my body from a thousand wounds
and you won't find this whiteness,
with which I've covered you, in the Alps
since this wind swirls towards that height
and stains the snow

even on the whitest rose you'll find a thought of dust

you will find the perfect miracle only in man:
white extensions that truly shine
and exceed the cosmos. Then the cleanest
thing of creation isn't the twilight
nor the sky's reflection in the river
nor the sun on the flowers of the apple tree. It is LOVE

THE BOY WITH THE HORN

If you could be heard
I could give you my soul
to take to end of the world
to use and create a peripatic star
or wood for the fireplace of the negro
and the Hellene villager during Christmas
who will use it to make a bloomed almond tree
in the windows of the prisoners

I perhaps won't be alive tomorrow

if you could be heard
I could give you my soul
to turn into visible
colorful, musical midnight notes
playing in the air of the world

to turn it into LOVE

KIKI DIMOULA

Kiki Dimoula was born 19 June 1931 in Athens. She's the first living female poet ever to be included in the prestigious French publisher Gallimard's poetry series. Born and raised in Athens, Kiki Dimoula worked for many years at the Bank of Greece before leaving to care for her two children full-time.

Through her poems, Dimoula explores both syntax and memory, restlessly searching for forms to contain grief, intimacy, and uncertainty. In a New York Times feature on the poet, writer Rachel Donadio described Dimoula's poetry as *spare, profound, unsentimental, effortlessly transforming the quotidian into metaphysical, drawing on the powerful themes of time, fate and destiny, yet making them entirely her own.*

Dimoula's first collection of poems translated into English is *The Brazen Plagiarist: Selected Poems* (translated by Cecile I. Margellos and Rika Lesser). Earlier collections include *Farewell Never* and *Lethe's Adolescence.* A full member of the Academy of Athens, Dimoula's honors include the European Prize for Literature, Greece's Grand National Prize for lifetime achievement, two Greek National Poetry Prizes, and the Academy of Athens's Ouranis Prize as well as its Aristeion of Letters. She lives in Athens.

Dimoula's work is haunted by the existential dissolution of the postwar era. Her central themes are hopelessness, insecurity, absence and oblivion. Using diverse subjects, from a Marlboro Boy to mobile phones and twisting grammar in unconventional ways, she accentuates the power of the words through astonishment and surprise, but always manages to retain a sense of hope.

Her poetry has been translated into English, French, German, Swedish, Danish, Spanish, Italian and many other languages. In 2014, the eleventh issue of Tinpahar published 'Kiki Dimoula in Translation', which featured three English translations of her better known works.

One of her Greek writer contemporaries, Nikos Dimou, has called Ms. Dimoula *the best Greek woman poet since Sappho.*

REPORT

Draw two columns
one for the day's gains
and one for its losses

the serious concepts
your bright thoughts and readings
your from side to side
unsparing passages
mark on the column of the gains

the daydreams
with their little chasms
the easy jumps of your imagination
for all these tricks against your boredom
I don't know, don't rush
perhaps you may need tomorrow's column of gains

but all this day that has passed
don't fool yourselves and don't forget
to write it under the column of the great
losses

SINGLE STROKES OF THE PEN

You may easily describe and explain me
with single strokes of the pen
it isn't boring
during the winter nights

a firm stroke you may draw up front
thrust it in vertically
these will be my beliefs
another one you may draw from the opposite direction
thrust it deep into the center of the first
appropriately that the first one
will seem exhausted
place some long ones next to the short
the vague ones next to the underlined
to underscore my inclinations
make sure these don't ever end
unless my explanation is shortened

scatter a few
of my objections
to all directions
add two long strikes in the center
and between them the void of the inevitable

now with the pencil
(or your imagination)
make sure some mist hangs
over all these
since with just one stroke of the pen
you can't explain my sorrow

SOME NIGHTS

Now that my old visions
have vanished far away into the seas
and their shape can't reach me
and their memory has left me

I haven't ever wished
to return to such thoughts

yet during
some endless nights
and almost tirelessly
my old visions
from the far away seas
I recall

EREBUS

Stooped over
the darkest hour of my soul
I shall present thin verses
cordoned off by an unexpected tempest
that fatally wounded
my once timid sunrise

these verses will tell a lot
you'll see, you'll read them
only the last one
won't say much
though upon seeing the verses above it
it will lament

PREPARATION

We wore the starry sky in our eyes
we embroidered the night
with hopeful flares
and we provided ourselves with consistency

we annulled our precaution
with the point of absolute
and we smuggled our silence
with the caique of the ephemeral

we set up the table of the unexpected
with two glasses, we made offerings to the possibility
and lighting the candle of sensitivity
next to our hearts
we read the lyrical telegram, which like all others
was full of truce or even peace,
and was brought by an enraptured and floodlit moment
and was coordinated by our destiny
that ties us together with dignified tutelage

MELANCHOLY

A great darkness skated on thin ice upon the sky
thus as the window hugged me
with one hand
I pulled inside the room
the unbelievable loneliness of the street
while with the other hand
I grabbed a handful of darkness
and threw it onto my soul

VOID

With our sense a slingshot
we slaughter the possibility
of our salvation
the collected experience carries the sin
the past drizzles
the hatred of fleeting inside us

Now the unaccomplished falls upon us
like the tempest
and we bathe in melancholy
as we wake up
to the merciless stress of the need

AFTERNOON

A piece of the wind that fell on the street
sat on the electric wires
and in low tone
played a melody
dedicated to my mood

which rose
momentarily and looked around

then unconvinced and indifferent
sank deep inside me again

DECAY

In ten verses I absorbed those years
that against their passing
the rest of my shattered life bumped.

The first verse
dressed in the suit of the ideal
entertained by euphoria
supported by the arm of my youth
robust and exquisite verse
pity it isn't the last

the second, I don't know how to say it
was left half done
and lopsided
as if regretful

the third one was written by itself
on the tundra of your escape

the next one I buried
in the verdure of my nostalgia

the next one was housed
in the illusion of your tender correspondence

the sixth and seventh
perched on the pole of longing
gazing far out

two of them almost sunk I pulled up
from the tide of your offer

and the last one
was so precipitous
that from its peak
the continuity tumbled
hugging the vertigo of futility

PURPOSE

I'm leaving
I won't tell you where I'm headed
to pretend
I keep a secret from you.

I'll furtively look into the sea-floor
to befriend the sea
entrusting it with my tempest
I'll stir the stars with my height
I'll set aside the unity of the sky
with my prayers
that in all these I'll perhaps
discover your hidden purpose
that you perhaps have come to display the colors
and to annul the winters
or to switch off
the dial of my mind
dissolving your departure.

If I meet your purpose and find it sunlit,
endless, and in crimson color I'll run to it
to rediscover it in your eyes
if by chance is hidden in the storm
I'll pretend I didn't understand it
if by chance in vain I search
patiently I shall press your chest
until you alone will betray it.

YESTERDAY

He came back
dressed in the shade of the undefined.
His eyes a sea-floor without a surface
his lips the incision of mystery
his words a vague deck of cards
that flop to one side or the other

his body an incense
and his hair drenched in youth
his laughter the ruin of souls
he hid the wind inside him
that ripped my paper dreams
my tomorrow cried inside me

long time has gone by
since I received the communion of his loss
in a glass gold-plated by autumn
when I covered his picture with the twilight
and I locked up my songs
for a long time that we've forgotten each other.

He came back
a day when we unearthed the parchment of our memory
and signed a godly continuance
since we loved each other.

Yesterday we went our separate ways.

THE LETTER

The post-man
carrying my hope in his steps
brought an envelope
with your silence.
My name was written on it with forgetfulness.
My address in an inexistent street.
However the post-man discovered it
retreating on my face
gazing the windows that stooped with me
to read my hands
that were already preparing an answer.
I'll open it with my patience
and with my sadness
I'll copy your unwritten words.
I'll answer tomorrow
and I'll send you my picture.
I'll place some wilted clover on my lapel
with the locket of a crash
engraved in the chest
and I'll hang on my ears — think of it —
your silence.

NOON

In the basement café
that offered pleasant privacy
we tuned ourselves
during the noon hours.
Soon after
we felt lust taking over us
which suited us well
since an old painting of Averof
and a picture of the owner
(heroically interrupting
the boredom of the wall)
entertained us profusely.

REQUEST

Today
let me entrust you with my story.
I'm the melancholic wind of life
that night found me lost in a heartless yesterday.

Do come and postpone my night
with your eyes
as if they are fog and strewn with stars
they combine the haze and the morning
into a weird convergence.

Do come
even if later it'll be proven futile
when our inexorable secret
surfaces between us
an unbearable enlargement
—temporary and foreign that we are —
with the prompter of my bitterness
I'll recite again the ancient pleasant voyage
to the imposing hours
which climbing onto the raft of the irrevocable
will shine toward the insatiable tomorrow.

NOSTALGIA

I still remember him
strange, because
so long as the spring cloud stayed
so long it took to say goodbye.

Exquisite memory.

He was diffused like fragrance
undefined like endlessness
glanced as if in the endless night.
An ashtray in front of us
into which we deposited our ashy contention.
His watch designed
a bitter beginning in time.
Then I
raised my glass
that we'd drink together to a voyage
mixed with silence.

To a separation without a goodbye
nor with a kiss.

COINCIDENCE

He was just like me.
I met him standing
under the awning of melancholy
the reflection of void
in the agony of his glance.
His movements
the wounded reciting of water.
The expected spaciousness attracted me
I went near him
and with a few incoherent words
I narrated my loneliness to him.

REFLECTION

He was a passerby
and he looked very odd to me.
A little lifeless a little aloof
yet loveable.
His haste like the canceled matins.
We suffocated.
The dwelling too small for our passion
and our shapes a bitter crowding.
Our plans of low esteem
the light of our hearts in dual color
and the frames of our minds bizarre.

He was a passerby.

MILTOS SACHTOURIS

Miltos Sachtouris was born in July 1919 and died March 2005. When he was young he left his law studies to follow his real passion, poetry; using the pen name Miltos Chrysanthis he wrote his first poem, *The Music Of My Islands*.

Sachtouris met Nikos Engonopoulos in 1943 and later worked with Engonopoulos on *Ikaros*. In 1960, he began publishing *When I Talk to You* and *The Spectres, or Joy on the Other Street*. Two years later, in 1962, he received the Second State Poet Prize for *The Stigmata*. He later wrote *The Seal, or The Eighth Moon*, and *The Utensil*.

He had a long relationship since 1960 until his death with the artist Gianna Persaki who was the creative director in most of his publications after 1960 and he dedicated to her among many collections *Skevos* and several poems including *The Clocks Turned Upside Down*. In 2003 Gianna Persaki received the Greek State Prize of Literature on his behalf, a prize that was awarded by the Greek Ministry of Culture and the President of the Hellenic Republic. Accordingly, upon receipt of the award she made a public speech where she also quoted: *Nikos Karouzos who said that life was a garden which faded away, and Sahtouris who said that life was a short violet.*

During the last years of his life he worked on *Colorwounds, Ectoplasms, Sinking, Since,* and *The Clocks Turned Upside Down.* He received the Grand State Literature Prize in 2003 for his works. In 1992 writer

Lefteris Xanthopoulos shot a documentary titled *Who's the Crazy Hare* ("The Crazy Hare" being one of the poet's most known poems) about Sachtouris at the poet's house, in Kypseli, Athens. That day Lefteris Xanthopoulos asked him who was the Crazy Hare and the poet responded *I am.*

He died at the age of 85 in Athens on the morning of Tuesday, March 29, 2005 and was buried in Athens. Upon his death the Prime Minister of Greece, Kostas Karamanlis stated: *Miltos Sachtouris was one of the leading poets of Greece and one of the last representatives of a very important era for the Greek poetry.* Following, George Papandreou the leader of the opposition at that time and a former prime minister of Greece stated: *Miltos Sachtouris was one of the greatest Poets of Modern Greece. He served the Greek letters with loyalty, elegance and moral.*

SAVIOR

I count the fingers of my severed hands
the hours I've spent on these windy roofs
I have no other hands, my love, and the doors
don't close and the dogs are uncompromising.

With my naked legs deep in these dirty waters
with my naked heart I long (not for myself)
for a light-blue window
how have they built so many rooms
so many tragic books
without a shred of light
without a short breath of oxygen
for the sick reader

since each room is but an open wound
how can I descent the tumbled stairs again
among the bog and the wild dogs
to bring medicine and rosy gauzes
and if I find the pharmacy closed
and if I find the pharmacist dead
and if I find my naked heart on the window display of the pharmacy

no, no, it's all over, there's no salvation

the rooms will remain as they were
with the wind and its cane fields
with the ruins of glassy moaning faces
with their achroous bleeding
with porcelain hands opened towards me
with the unforgiving forgetfulness

they've forgotten my fleshy hands which were severed
as I was measuring their agony

DIFFICULT SUNDAY

Since morning I've been gazing up high a better bird
since morning I've been enjoying a snake wrapped around my neck
broken cups on the carpet
purple flowers on the cheeks of the seer
when she lifts the skirt of Fate
something will sprout out of this joy
a new blossomless tree
or a pure young eyelid
or a beloved word
that wouldn't kiss the lips of forgetfulness
bells chime out there
my imaginary friends wait for me out there
they're lifting up and circling around a dawn
what tediousness, what tediousness
yellow dress — the embroidered eagle —
the green parrot — I close my eyes — it caws
always always always
the orchestra plays cheap tunes
what passionate eyes, what women
such love, such cry, such love;
love my friend, blood my friend
give me your hand, my friend, such cold
it was freezing
I no longer know the time they all died
and I remained with my amputee friend
and with the company of a bloodied twig

416

PRESENTS

Today I put on
the red warm blood
people love me today
a woman smiled at me
a girl gave me a conch
a boy gave me a hammer

today I kneel down onto the sidewalk
I nail the naked legs
of the passersby on the slabs
they're all teary eyed
yet no one of them is scared
they've all stayed in places which I reached
they're all teary eyed
yet they gaze the neon signs up high
and the female beggar who sells Easter Bread
on the sky

two men whisper
what's he doing? Is he nailing our hearts?
Yes, he's nailing our hearts
for he's the poet

SEA FLOOR

A sailor up high
dressed in white
runs along the moon

and from earth the girl
with red eyes
sings a song
that doesn't reach him

it reaches the harbour
reaches the ship
reaches the masts

but it doesn't reach up high to the moon

MINE

I write to you
afraid and from inside a dark tunnel
lighted by a lightbulb as insignificant as the eye of a needle
a wagon passes over me carefully
maintaining its distance that it won't hit me
I on the other hand pretend I'm sometimes asleep
other times I pretend to mend a pair of old socks
since everything around me have strangely become old

yesterday at the house
as I opened the closet it turned into dust
and with all the cloths in it
the plates break soon as you touch them
I'm scared and for this I've hidden the forks
and knives
my hair has become like a wasted piece of cloth
my mouth has turned white and it hurts
my arms are made of stone
my legs of wood
three boys cry around me
I don't know why they call me *mother*

I wanted to write to you about our old joys
but I've forgotten how to write about joyous things.

Remember of me

STAGE

They had placed a head
made of clay on the table
they had decorated the walls
with flowers
they had cut out of paper two bodies
making love on the bed
on the floor you could see snakes
and butterflies
a big dog was guarding
at the corner

strings were criss-crossing the room
from every direction
it wouldn't be prudent to pull them
one of the strings was pushing the bodies
to make love
just outside the misfortune
was scratching the door.

NOSTALGIA RETURNS

The woman undressed and lied
on the bed
a kiss unfolded on the floor
wild faces with knives appeared
on the ceiling
a bird hanging by the wall
choked and vanished
a candle leaned over and fell
of the votive
sobs and sounds of running footsteps
were heard outside

They opened the windows
a hand appeared
then the moon invaded the room
hugged the woman and they slept together

all night long a voice was heard:

the days pass by
the snow stays

TRAIN STATION

It always rains in my sleep
my dream gets full of mud
the landscape is dark
and I wait for the train

the station master collects daisies
that grow along the rails
since no train has arrived
to this station for a long time
and suddenly years have passed
and I sit behind a window
my hair and my beard have grown long
as if I'm very sick
yet I fall asleep again
when the woman with the knife
in her hand slowly nears me
she examines me carefully
and sticks the knife in my right eye.

GREEN AFTERNOON

That green afternoon
Hades took aim at my yard
from my dead window
with my silky eye I saw Him
going around pretending to sell buns
he walked around pretending to be a lotto seller
the children didn't suspect anything
they played with guns and they yelled
while Hades came close for awhile
then distanced himself for awhile
He then came back closer
at the end He got angry
He started to howl
He made up His eyes
He colored His nails
He inflated up his breast
He started talking in a high pitch voice
He acted like a woman

then He finally decided
to leave whispering:

I wasn't lucky today
I'll return tomorrow

THE DOVE

The dove could have flown this way
people had lit torches in the streets
they guarded the tree lines
children held small flags in their hands
time was flying when it started
to rain, then the whole sky turned dark
a lightning bolt whispered something
as if afraid and screams started
coming out of the mouth of men

at that time the white dove
with its fanged teeth howled
like a dog into the night.

DIMITRIS LIANTINIS

The author, educator, philosopher and poet Dimitris Liantinis, Professor of philosophy in education at the University of Athens until 1998, was born in 1942 in the prefecture of Lakonia.

He finished the High School of Sparta in 1960. He studied at the Department of Philology of the Faculty of Philosophy of the University of Athens, graduating in 1966. Between 1968 and 1970 he taught philology in Secondary High School Education.

Between 1970 and 1972 he studied at the University of Munich.

Between 1973 and 1975 he taught again in High School Education.

In 1975 he was appointed as assistant in the Laboratory of Pedagogy of the University of Athens.

In 1977 he received his PhD in philosophy from the University of Athens and with distinction; the subject of his thesis was *The presence of Greek essence in the elegies of Duino* by Rainer Maria Rilke.

Outside of the University he also taught in Greece at the Maraslios Academy in post-graduate teacher training, at the PEK of Kifisia, Peristeri, Peireus and at the Police School. He gave lectures at the Naval School of War and at the Military School of Health.

He authored books of philosophical reflection with a particular personal and characteristic poetic style and his personal succinct flavour.

While in Munich in 1972 he met Nikolitsa Georgopoulos Professor of Introduction to Philosophy and History of Philosophy at the University of Athens whom he married in 1973. On the 1st of June 1998 Liantinis disappeared from his family and his university environment.

EAGLE

There may be a way to bend
the insistence of chained Nostos
to run and using light to decipher
the slant passages
and unguarded borders of the by-chance clouds
to log with light
the slopes and counties on rocky mountains
of the dear stalker and the wild animals.
No less number of fir-trees.
With new paeans and war drums the echoes
won't refuse to come and help
the silent function
until drop by drop they'll
turn the height into immortal as
at the Monastery of Dochiarios
the difficult will become easy
while the sweat moral of colours
will avenge the malice of the rocks.
An angry horse
threshes the horizon
like the wounded Achilles punishes
with golden horse-shoes
and shinning nails
that the fire of lightning sharpens.

ARCTURUS

Guide of the seven bulls
that graze in the kingdom of your concern
you evaluate the stagnate century
you build the borders of your struggle
with four drops of frozen sweat
in the shape of the crusaders banner.

Oh, Alkalurops,
navigator of the children's laughter
and primer of the elders
you stand amid the grayish aging rocks
and with your flute you sing about
the labor of death
of both the powerful and the immortal

NORTHERN HALO

Before your enigmatic manner
I adjust the red chiton and
the crown of thorns on your hair
I raise your fortitude straight to the sky
and this April I salute you

ecce homo

SHIELD

When the shield of the sun
descended to the careenage of the west
the face of day melted
mummy thrown into the light.
Trees set traps for the birds
where they burry their height
a ship sinks into the soil
and the beasts of the forest
have gone astray to the mountainous
goat paths.
The procurement of the stars reveals
blood in the ravine
that buzzes naked
slashing the skin of water
the flesh of things
can't find refuge
in basil.

Linos' skinned body hangs
over the midnight mast

ALTAR

Our blood is fiery red
when the newborns climb up the golden hills
and autumn bestows its gifts
to the naked knees of the rain
cactuses listen to
the unsuspecting footsteps of Abel.

Dawn readies its slaughter
and the evening sacrifice
sprinkles the door-posts of the west.

GEMINI

Lizards crawl in the cane fields
and shivers in the refusal of the lissome
who won't remain a virgin for too long

the phallus and the sob of the god
have turned into a swan

LIBRA

Solemn and beautiful stranger
you who undress
the salute and the sun to the bone
who sow the side of a daydream
our hours unfold
and salute you
they gleam with feathers of winds
they salute you
with songs for the sea's birthday
as our lust sinks
in the hourglass of your laughter
shooting stars, seagulls
volunteers of the ancient epic
with its circular returns

solemn and beautiful stranger
you're welcome till you exhaust yourself

CHARIOTEER

You took the main road that dashes down
from the dark thighs of Delphi
like the arrow's lissome quiver
symmetrical
to their questionable stature
you vibrated the unruffled gravel-road
with polemic sandals and waterfall thunder
you held tightly the reigns of the sea
and its reddish coppery gleam in your hands

arriving
you talked about the serenity of the god
who suckled the nipple of a star

HERCULES

Irascible beast
born executioner to face the evil Poseidon spread
that sprouts into the sea
because memoirs will be written only
on the edge of the sword
that cracks the cheekbones of the night like walnuts

castles of the night will fall like trees
anatomy lesson on the body of the deed
poisoned by his own hand
his final chiton
he put on
like the lion of the desert puts on its bandolier

BEAST

Deadly landscape
where the wheat ears arc
silenced by the work of the sickle
here and there corn fields
and the thin beard of his excellency the ambassador
when the old ant carries its crop
using the carts of night
and the janissary rat arrives
at the rocky ships and the castled cities

dryness toughens

the eyes of the black-clocked woman
and the salt of our silence

here
an invincible curse ripens
to spring out like the blood of slaughtered animals
sultans and ministers and priests
this place: Armageddon

HINDU

Things of the world I have seen
yet my eyes remain clean
your silence fills my ears
the sun shines and you tell me *go to sleep*

SAIL

Little cloud made of cotton
rowing
onto its tender *oh*
melting in the sky-blue
and dripping on the edge of your eye

CANCER

The achitricline in drunken stupor again
went for a stroll
along the high road
with crimson lopsided cap
arms like oars
two backstrokes one forward
a cigarette on his ear
yet, if he broke open the taps
and spilled wine in the cellar
beware, oh, thrice beware
the king will come with an edit
(dotard and disfigured as he is)
the guillotines will be put up
and all who go to the agora
will turn headless like goats

people run to hide
in houses and in trapdoors
and let the one with two sons mourn

CENTAUR

Morning and the horses neigh
tied onto the froth of impenitent sea
rustle of naked leaves punished
forty times lashed by the winds
climb on the shoulder-blade of Sunday
and on the Pelion waters

here the blood of serpents poisons
the ripen languor of serenity
like rust the veins of marble
and time gathers the wings of ash
to debate with the blond gables
now that in the sleep of the olive tree
the spider forms its wrinkly netting
in the fields the lustful sprouts
quiver and bathe
in the fountain of convulsion

SWAN

We've lost ourselves in unconsecrated churches
since the days of Leonardo
we've hanged on the wall
the beautiful woman of the loiterer
icon of an ancient youth
in lakes
wedged between the beard of rocks
we saw our strange features
afraid of the thunderous flapping of eagle wings
what we recounted wasn't ours
coppers of the holy oak
in the trenches of red hills
that shatter the lance of winter
morning dance
that hid in the viscera of the oak
and in the frowning of the motionless stone
our struggle
our grief
buried in the unstruck chord of the lyre
that will brake on your touch

KATERINA ANGHELAKI ROOKE

Katerina Anghelaki-Rooke was born in Athens, February 1939. Nikos Kazantzakis, a good family friend, was her god-father. At the age of only 17 she wrote the poem *Loneliness* which her Nikos Kazantzakis forwarded to the editor of literary magazine New Epoch with the following note "please publish this poem; it was written by a 17 year old girl and it is the best poem I have ever read." Since that day her devotion to poetry and translation took wings. As herself pointed out in one of her interviews this was her entrance through the door of poetry.

She studied foreign languages and literature at the universities of Athens, Nice (France) and Geneva (Switzerland), where she was graduated in 1962. She has received Ford Foundation Grants (1972 and 1975), was invited to the International Writing Program at the University of Iowa, and was a Fulbright Visiting Lecturer in the United States (1980-1981), during which time she lectured on Modern Greek Poetry and Nikos Kazantzakis at Harvard. She has subsequently lectured on other dimensions of modern poetry and given public reading of her poetry in English and in Greek in the United States, Mexico, and Europe. She won the 1985 Greek National Poetry Award for the Greek version of *Beings and Things on Their Own*.

Her work has been translated into more than ten languages and is included in numerous anthologies. She has translated from English and French as well as from the Russian works of Shakespeare, Mayakovski,

443

and Pushkin.

She's the recipient of the first poetry award Prix Hensch of the City of Geneva, the National Literary Award of Greece, the Kostas Ouranis poetry Award and in 2014 she was awarded the National Poetry Award for the whole of her literary accomplishment.

LIFE'S LACK OF APPETITE

I'm not hungry I don't hurt I don't stink
perhaps deep inside I suffer and I don't know it
I pretend I laugh
I don't seek the impossible
nor the possible, bodies
forbidden to me don't please my eyes
sometimes I gaze the sky
with a longing glance
when the sun lessens its gleam
and the blue lover surrenders
to the beauty of the night
my only involvement
with the turning around of the world
is my steady breath
but I also feel another
strange involvement

the agony I suddenly feel
for the human pain

it spreads on earth
like a liturgical cloth drenched in blood
shrouding myths and gods
it renews itself endlessly
and becomes one with life

yes, I want to cry now
but even the fountain of my tears
has turned dry

THE NEW PASSION: FEAR

Wounds don't bloom
in poems or in songs anymore
they only go septic
the sea isn't lust
that floats on the surface
but fear of the sea floor
what became of the joy of life
that captured every moment
even when dawn came like a bad omen?
Pain doesn't harass
the body anymore
but the ever powerful tyrant, fear
that has come and has swept
every passion

these days love resembles
sometimes a beggar at the corner
and other times an unemployed clown
unable to make anyone laugh
there's only one passion: fear
that spreads like a shroud
and covers everything

fear for the collapse
of nature, of the body, of the world
these days instead of yelling
how beautiful this is
the viscera shouts
watch out

SOMETHING IS HAPPENING

My legs walk
over the void
my arms embrace emptiness
and my fantasy conspires
with nothingness
what's happening, what's happening
and nothing goes ahead?
The haze refuses to become cloud
the moist to become rain
the winter sunrise delays
the reserved melancholy
won't turn into distress
and the unnamed nightmare
hesitates to mature into a certain fear of death
however here's a gleaming shadow

I have postponed the coming
of my last day

MOMENTARY LIFE

I closed all the windows
that looked to the garden of flesh
the shutters only touch
the tree branches of love
that hang loose
and touch the ground
I stay away from
the view of mortal stars
I hide myself just not to desire.
And now? With nothing changed
only one moment is left
when the keen eye
will describe something
incomparably more exciting
than my own reality

THE VISION OF EROS

I went blind
since I've lost the vision of Eros
with its power
that keeps the eyes closed
and doesn't hate darkness
it relates to your smell
since you smell like a fragrance
on the face you see
a fragrance only you can smell
it only springs out of your breath
without this vision
perhaps it may pass before you
a semblance of the ideal passion
though you won't see it
you won't see the clear sky
that it carries on its back
the sky where West and East
love each other, smile to each other
and inflame their imaginary
magical games

now I recall old dreams
in my invisible mind
just as if I could see
the ghost of Eros again

OUR FRIENDS: THE SNAKES

Perhaps the snakes around us
are good useful beings
since they free our suspicion
of the un-kept promises
and as the snakes coil
they teach us that no reality
is as valuable or true
as our momentary breathing.

What have people promised you?
Sweet life?
This requires good imagination.
What have the saints promised you?
Eternal life?
This requires great endurance

IT STARTS AS A FUNNY SONG

They're all sunburnt
and I'm wrinkled
they're all suntanned
and I'm burnt up
what's the meaning of summer
when you're old
the meaning of health
when the future is on strike?

The seagulls caw
their calling a reprimand
as if I hear my teacher saying

Go but come tomorrow better prepared

Tomorrow. Tomorrow I'll look
at bodies moving again
like flares in the darkness
in my darkness

STAGING

I feel like the stage director of my agony
leading actor in the one-act play of stress
but who's the playwright?
Who wrote this play
with such wrongly written acts
and who's hiding behind the curtain
who won't see Him when he comes down?

Yet the imaginary playwright
had imagined everything
even the moment
when the lights of the soul dim
and the stage empties
now resembling a blank page

I DRINK AND I SWALLOW

How would my life be now
with all the black events around
and I'm afraid like a little animal
that shivers during the bear-night
I tremble that behind the clouds
everything has been decided
how would my life be
without the heavenly drink I swallow
without this watering
that makes wild of my deficiencies
and lightens the weight of the day
the unbearable weight of the night
without having under the tongue
the snuggling dream
that becomes fluid body
which I taste in each gulp
although I never forget
to count drop by drop
the emptiness that becomes lake inside me?

MORNING OPPOSING THE DAY

The face of dawn has the expression
of a merchant who doesn't have
the item you wish to buy
and how could it have it, how
could it possess hope, wings
for an upward movement
the ointments of lust
a miraculous body that searches
to discover the other, the shining
side of things before
the effort of verification commences
before dawn begins
with just one wish:
the continuation of your tasteless health
since the leaves that sway
in the breeze don't touch you
since the fiery tears of the sun
that goes down and dies with the day
leave you unimpressed
since you don't expect anything
from the new day that arrives

therefore good morning…with suspension points

NANOS VALAORITIS

Nanos Valaoritis was born to Greek parents in Lausanne in Switzerland in 1921 but grew up in Greece where he studied classics and law at Athens University. He was published in the pages *Nea Grammata* alongside contributions from Odysseas Elytis and George Seferis, and was immediately taken into their literary circle.

In 1944 Valaoritis escaped from German-occupied Greece across the Aegean to Turkey and from there through the Middle East to Egypt, where he made contact with George Seferis who was serving the Greek government in exile as First Secretary of the Greek Legion in Cairo. In 1944, at the instigation of Seferis, Valaoritis went to London to develop literary links between Greece and Britain. He met T. S. Eliot, W. H. Auden, Dylan Thomas and Stephen Spender, and he worked for Louis MacNeice at the BBC. As well as studying English literature at the University of London, he translated modernist Greek poets, among them Elytis and Embirikos, and contributed to Cyril Connolly's *Horizon* and to John Lehman's *New Writing*. He paved the way for Seferis' success in the English-speaking world by editing and translating, along with Durrell and Bernard Spencer, Seferis' *King of Asine* which was published in 1948 to enthusiastic reviews.

Then in 1954 he moved to Paris where he met surrealist poet André Breton. In Paris he also met his wife Marie Wilson, the American surrealist painter.

In 1960 Valaoritis returned to Greece, and between 1963 and 1967 he was publisher and chief editor of the Greek avant-garde literary review Pali. But when the junta came to power in 1967, he felt he had no choice but to go into voluntary exile, and in 1968 he went to America where he became professor of comparative literature and creative writing at San Francisco State University, a position he held for twenty-five years.

Then Nanos Valaoritis returned to Greece, where he has co-edited the literary review *Synteleia* and published a remarkable body of work, including essays, translations, anthologies and books of poetry, short stories, a novella and four novels variously in Greek, English and French. In 2004 the Athens Academy of Letters and Science awarded Nanos Valaoritis the prestigious prize for poetry in recognition of his life's work and the President of Greece presented him with the Gold Cross of Honour, given for his services to Greek Letters.

BIRTH OF THE WORLD

They say the world was born upside down

but it isn't true. Whoever was there said the world was born properly with its head down and not with the feet up

the mother of the world was a horrible shrew with hairy head, claws and pointing teeth like nails

but the world was beautiful, nice since the first moment, admired by its uncle the sun and its auntie the moon and by all its cousins, the stars in the sky

and the sea was proud of it and the mountains, then the rivers, the rocks, the trees, the rain, the clouds

everyone and everything was proud of the world even the wild animals and the birds and the serpents, and the fishes at the bottom of the sea

only one didn't like it: its creator

because he was spiteful and jealous and his name was Abyss. One day he visited his mother and tried to throw his creation in the bottomless crevasse he created

however the angels gave the world wings and it flew away even the demons spoke favorably of it as it was flying

then his father, to avenge it, had three more children with the shrew mother: Time, Decay, and Void.

Since then these three compete in who of them will first destroy the beautiful world; since then we enjoy the world for a moment then we lose it, we, beings of the Moment, who are eaten by Decay, and in short time we return to the Void.

TROY

Of the ones who're in the sea, some drown
some return to become castaways
they all wait to face you.
Only Death doesn't wait.

Remember that along the shore the dead
wait to talk to you as you walk by.
What we might built they knock down.
It seems the defeated have won.

No one knows what will happen this spring.
The river filled my mouth
and the sun held my hand.

Horses returned without the body.
When we returned during the summer
oh God, the towers had changed color

THE RIDDLE

The root of a tree consumes my shape
a stone pricks my finger
and skins my brain
my eyes become prey of the leaves
owls hide behind my eyelids
my steps self-delete, stay still
become mouths among the memorial shrubs
a butterfly sucks all of my being
sparks and smoke come out of my nostrils
like the dragons who were corals in ancient times
like the thistle among the grass blades
wind whirls forget of me and deny me
flowers stick their tongues out to me
terraces walk over me
I hate the springs and I trade their wishes
I'm the favored of the waves like the pebbles
I refuse to retreat opposite the wind
to melt in the furnaces of heated baths
to burn on charcoal like a crab
to make superhuman efforts to talk
to save myself
from the conflagration I alone started
I shine like a diamond but I'm not a star
who am I then if I'm not who I am
a heavenly or earthly body, massive, fluid or airy?

UNWRITTEN WRITING

I heard them talking in a tragic tone in the living rooms of 1880
I heard their sighs in the hotel room number 12
I saw a naked woman running in the third floor of my mind
two human like monsters that growled
to provoke her brazenly — as she walked by them —
their tails hitting the floor rhythmically
when the light rain fell
ash from a volcano, mouth of a woman
I held the hand of a deranged boy before he let his last breath
I crowned the beloved forehead
with a few dry, empty consoling words
(I don't remember whether it was a boy or a girl
the unjustly killed in a plot of two by one and a half meters)
three centuries have gone before all these happened
before I transcribed in a clean notebook
the lament of the renounced man
the cry of the newborn child
burials of alive men — dead people who reincarnate
silky shapes that fall back
a person who was afraid to fall in love
a piece of marble made of flesh
and the unwritten writing
which I saw written in my dream
with fiery letters that burned the paper

INSIDE EACH OTHER

They all change, become one another
wood turns into stone, trees turn into clouds
women become men leaves become sea
the feathers water-wells the eyes winds
the drawers metals the flowers mind
writing and letters become
illiterate, the beautiful turns ugly
the male becomes neutral the secretive obvious
hope turns blind like wealth
they all become telescopes, then
there isn't anything to happen or it won't
each is inside the other
stones and rivers run through his fingers
words turn into tulips
his love becomes a cistern, a table
the chair settles in his right eye
through the window you see only one orchard
cemetery of leaves the marketplace is virgin
and the dew of the dusk nothing but wrong turn of the steering
a needle stretches its thread until it brakes
a leg chews its chain, a kite turns
into a dog and bites whoever goes by
an orphan child becomes the mother of another
a title becomes destitute and gets married
whatever exists is alive, the metals are in the earth
stones in the soil, proof that they wilt
if you uproot them the world turns horrible
lends and borrows, changes color
you don't call it anymore, it exists as it's named
monster, turtle, divan, couch, thigh, stove
and blonde hair around a woman's mound.

THE WHOLE 24 HOURS

Half a century of afternoons spent with my grandmother
clouds, colorful lizards and other monsters
airhead girls like sparrows
with the guilty walk in their overcoats
a deserted bed-sheet on my face
daily encounters like tumbled down churches
limos with somber expressions at the steering wheel
unfamiliar persons waiting at the corners of the streets
unrecognized women who pass by in plural
patisseries filled with questioning glances
medicine, pills for emotions of asphyxia
hours that won't come back and ghosts of cafes
tired or cheery waking up in the morning
a march toward the narrow door of the heart
nobody at the house where they said a crazy
Swedish girl with the eyes like lampposts lived
struggle for democracy, running competition and agony
a quarter less than half a century and something more almost on me

I'M TIRED OF LOVING YOU

I want them to auction me
I want them to put me in jail
I want to be like Sunday
when all of us eat a sweet

I want to become a goldsmith
to cover you in gold dust
I want us to go to America
to meet with Mr. Croesus

I want to travel to India
to get burnt into a deathly pyre
chanting a Buddhist sutra
to throw my bones into the Ganges

I want to travel up the Amazon
against the current — to be eaten
by a flesh eating tropical plant
chanting a magical chant

I want to look deep into your eyes
to beg you to stop
and to be bathed for the second time
in the Niagara waterfall

I want to compete with the shadow
that always follows you
I want to sail with white sails
to Europe with the unions

I want to ascend to heaven
not to think of you ever again
to sit next to the Archangel
and we both read cheap romance magazines

THE KNOCK

The knock of the door
created panic
the heartbeat
in heavy winter

whipping of the whip
on the back of the punished man
the hit of the ruler
in the open hand

the bells chimed
during Easter
dramas and tragedies
on the stony seats

we waited for an answer
from someone on the phone
yet we forgot what was the question
when we were on stage

who are you and where you come from
what is your official name
how do your relatives call you
what name do you give to the police?

We went out to the streets
in protest
with empowering slogans
about our world view

we felt we fought unjustifiably
being hit straight on our heads
face to face on a battle
with the handbook of history

CHRONICLE OF REFORESTATION

The reforestation continues
in a fast mode that suddenly
reaches paroxysm
trees appear everywhere

they go through the roof of the house
they carry on upwards
towards the sky
until they reach the gate

of Omnipotence — there
they stop to figure out
what each will tell
to the Master of Great

Archangelic Powers
who held the reigns of Earth
between his fingers
among the agates and amethysts

    addendum

we don't know what they said to the Lord
these trees — their words
He took these trees
and breathed their words
and said in a deep voice,
oh how beautiful:

your oxygen oxidises me
and reignites my fury
to slaughter and to destroy
to burn and to exterminate

KATERINA GOGOU

Katerina Gogou, was born in Athens 1st of June 1940 and died 3rd of October 1993. She was a poetess, author and actress. Before her suicide by pill overdose at the age of 53, Gogou appeared in over thirty Greek films.

Her book *Three Clicks Left* was translated into English in by Jack Hirschman and published by Night Horn Books in San Francisco in 1983. The Greek version of the same book was first published by Kastaniotis in 1978. Her poetry was known for its rebellious and communist content.

As an actress Gogou was known for lesser roles of rebellious free spirited women. She won the first women's award at the Salonica film festival.

As a poet she's known for her antiestablishment poems and her anarchist ideals. Her verse is filled by indignation and refute, however her ideals and her wounded psychological state lead her to suicide at the age of 53.

Numerous poems written by Gogou appeared in the Greek film Parangelia about the life of Nikos Koemtzis who, in 1973, killed three individuals (two of whom were policemen) and injured another eight at a bouzouki club in Athens over a dance.

FOR THE ONES THEY'VE BROKEN
FOR THE ONES THEY'VE IMPRISONED

Tattered by the wild waves
leftovers of life forever thrown
into the dark bowels of earth
with their foggy minds
caused by the frenetic haunting
of the motionless course of the stars
the last ones
leaned their tired head
sacrificed
to the ceremonial whirlwind of time
there were no people
the white snow of silence
finally blanketed the sunken cities

TIME WILL COME

Time will come when things will change
remember this, Maria
you remember that game during the school recess
when we run holding the baton
—don't look at me — don't cry. You are the hope
listen, time will come
when children will select their parents
they won't be born at random
there won't be any closed doors
with stooping people outside
and we shall choose our work
we won't be horses they look at our teeth
people — think of it — will talk in colors
others in musical notes
just save in a big jar with water
words and concepts such as
unadjusted, oppression, loneliness, price, gain, humiliation
for the history lesson
times are tough — I don't want to lie — Maria
and more tough days will come
I don't know — don't expect too much from me —
this is what I've lived, this I've learned, this I've said
and from all I read I keep just one:
it only matters to remain a human being
despite all this, Maria,
we'll change life.

25th of MARCH

One day I'll open the door
to go out to the streets
just like yesterday
I won't think but
a piece of my father
a piece of the sea
things they left to me
and the city. This city that they've turned rotten
and our friends who vanished
one day I'll open the door
straight to the fire
and I'll enter like yesterday
crying out *fascists*
putting up roadblocks
and throwing stones
holding a red banner
gleaming high up in the sunshine.
I'll open the door
and this, not because I'm afraid,
but, I mean to say I had no time
and that you also have to learn
not to go down the streets
without weapons like I did
I had no time to grab them
because you'll get lost like I did
just like that vaguely
shuttered into pieces
of sea, years of childhood
and red banners.
One day I'll open the door
and vanish
with the dream of revolution
in the wholesome loneliness
of the conflagrated streets
in the endless loneliness
of roadblocks made of carton paper
with the epithet — don't believe in them —
Provocateur

SEASONS WILL COVER ME

Love is of a diaphanous white color
and its body in the shape of benediction
and in the smoke
this horse searches
to take away its dead rider

Whether ancient or modern
I believe
the seasons will cover me
in a way that I won't feel hungry
nor thirsty
and I won't write poems anymore

only, Lord, homeland of the stars, I beg you
dress me in the white diaphanous color and
grace me with the body of Your benediction.

Do I ask for too much?

A

With my head in smithereens
by the vise of your bargaining
at the height of the traffic jam and opposite it
I'll light a great fire
and I'll throw all the Marxist books in it
that Myrto will never learn
the cause of my death
you can tell her
I couldn't endure the spring or
that I cross the road with a red light
yes this is more believable
with a red light, this you can say.

TROY AVENUE 35A

My house, just like yours
intrudes into the houses of others
since the roads are so narrow
and there are so many people
sometimes I feel we sleep in the same bed
since we are almost glued together
we use the same brush to brush our teeth
and we eat the same food
only when you go
you leave behind your dirty dishes
it can't be explained otherwise
that the sink is always full
it doesn't matter though
I do what I can
to show how much I love you
for this I put on the fake moustache
and I go out to the rain with a fan
that your children will laugh
only I beg of you don't gossip about us
and leave my Myrto alone
she was born the way she looks.
Sad.

NOSTOS

I

My kingdom lies
beyond the terminal of the winds
visible from the other side
of the blue mountain peak.
It keeps me away from relatives
a badly shaped marble cross
with an erroneous date of death
of the one they named my father.
The path is very long
and I come from afar covered by dust
keeping the rules of my race
I killed my horse
with the sword dipped in sunlight.
They dragged me here
I'm still here
in the kingdom of the worst humiliation
in the nation of need.

II

In my country
behind the light-blue mountain peak
the ones who gave birth to children
were dressed in long coats made of wolf skin
and had their babies
arrayed around the fire
and they put them to sleep
with words that initiated them
to Death.

III

Our forests were made of glass
along the trees — motels
strange rooms with harmonious sounds

only the musicians kept vigil
with the flattened kites and spider webs

golden and purple that entwined
the web of love around their necks

just before morning twilight
they left with helicopters
a dust cloud of blue stars
showed them the way.

IV

She cries
she wants to leave
but the anchor they've tied
around her neck
stops her on her steps.

ANTONIS FOSTIERIS

Antonis Fostieris was born in Athens in 1953. He studied Law at the University of Athens and History of Law at the Sorbonne, Paris. Since 1981, he co-edits and directs the literary magazine *The Word*.

Fostieris is one of the eminent poets of the so-called Generation of the Seventies, which is a literary term referring to Greek authors who began publishing their work during the 1970s, especially towards the end of the Greek military junta of 1967-1974 and during the years after democracy was restored in Greece. Fostieris has been considerably translated; that includes translation into English by Kimon Friar (1984), the acclaimed translator and scholar for his Modern Greek literature translations.

Fostieris' poetic quest is realised in a language marked for its clarity and intimacy. Through a dense poetic language, refined to the degree of perfection, Fostieris seeks to outline a view of life: *The problem of poetic expression has been shifted from the agonising quest for the avant-garde and the old axiom it does not matter what you say, but how you say it'. Without ignoring the manner, the essence, the view of life that the work represents counts more and more.* Fostieris builds his structures within each poem and across the collection as a whole. His poetry is multilayered and rich in intertextual references.

For Fostieris fundamental existential questioning is of outmost importance: heritage, a person's belonging to his roots, lineage, the ghostly image of Death, memory and loss, darkness, the continued advance and retreat of dichotomies, and also Eros and its power, passion, language and its proper use as well as poetry in general, as to where is headed and its influences from abroad. Kiki Dimoula writes, *Fostieris' language, his tireless defender, managed to escape from the established linguistic ready-made tones, in which most of his contemporaries have become victims, and marked a new path with goal its own recognition. His language attacks against the surly depth of concepts with the wonder of an ephebe.* Similarly Tasos Livaditis said: *The real talent has among all other elements that constitute it the concept of youth; in it Fostieris molds his themes dealing with Eros and poetry.*

Of particular importance in the poetry of Fostieris are the elements of surprise, of reversal and reconstruction. Titos Patrikios wrote, *the unexpected reverses the established flow of things, it turns them upside-down and makes the reader to face them from the start seeing their internal side. Yet this reversal doesn't constitute the deletion of logical flows but the anti-metathesis of the conventional flows with anti-conventional.*

Fostieris lives in Athens.

UNSUSCEPTIBLE TO IMMORTALITY

Three hours are enough to write a beautiful poem
yet thirty years aren't enough to write a poem
even if you desire it a lot and you're willing to sacrifice for it.
I understand spring is a matter of routine for nature
that hates pneuma and blackens the imperishable.
Think carefully: every form of immortality stands opposite
the concept of being. Every opposition
will vanish under the heel of time
that straddles over it with soles made of granite.
Opening the suspicion of the present
and burning
the brushwood of events into the fire of the sun up to the sky
where present
means the past of the future
or better the future of a different past
since, as far as I know, there's no recipe
to make a moment last.
How greedy
we've truly been, how prodigal
in our avarice. Who would believe
that we've spent the little eternity that belongs to us
lost in the desert of words. We've seeded and waited
for the new fruit to sprout from the seed
leaving
the ripened fruit to rot.
Truly how empty-handed
how unsusceptible to immortality mortals are.

TO THE SILVER MOON

Oh moon, is it true you're made of silver?
And all these people standing on the velvety display window
uttering emotional whispers
perhaps
they glance you, they weigh you, they evaluate you
with their eyes?
I can't find any other explanation. You enhance
the wish of possession and totally thrilled
people pull aside the curtains or they charge
to see you from their balcony. Heavenly traps
await for you and they've sent two bears to track
your scent. Be mindful of the Archer's arrow
and the poison of the Scorpion, oh Moon,
it must be true you're made of silver. Accept that
only what can be sold has value and is respected
by all. We all honour the sold out.
Devil, ten thousand verses have been written for you
and none of them relates to the most basic, not even
a moneychanger dared make an offer clearly.
The unapproachable usually stays behind
although people crave it
therefore, make the first move
now that I see you whole and pregnant
because from tomorrow you'll start becoming less
and then who will throw his good money
for your silvery
your ephemeral
underweight body?

DOMESTICATED FOREST

In your fresh living room a forest rustles
the furnishings that you hear breathing
still keep watch as if by instinct among
the wings of leaves. And if they shiver
when a visitor comes in it's because
they sense the hidden axe being sharpened
this time like a painless affectionate smile.
They panic during the nights
and the big nail of their roots cracks into
the rock of the cement. Their branches
ravage the ceiling — look at the cracks
of the wood that roars. Leave them alone.
Neither truth nor craftiness smoothens the knots
into the bark of old age. Leave them.
And if the tic-tac of the worm mimics
their heart beats
they still dream of a heroic fire
to come and finally separate the pneuma
from the flesh —
the shine from the ash

BOY AT THE MUSEUM

A boy has slept in the museum
for the last three thousand years
his bones have shuddered in the cold
they got full of holes for the stubbornness of the irrevocable.

A boy gets up from his bed at night
pulls the curtains aside to see the moon
the wild light startles him and he sleepwalks to the roof
just a little more and he'll climb up to the clouds
just a little more and he'll clean out God's beard

I'm lying, I'm lying a boy sleeps in the museum
eons trickle cold water on him
the eons buzz in his ears like bees
eons of ants around his mattress
just a little longer and he'll rip the curtain of his sleep
he'll get up and crying we'll hug each other

THE THOUGHT BELOGS TO MOURNING

I re-desert the silence of my soul
and I re-enter into the thunderous lithography
of nothing (stone cylinders grind syllables
that we won't miss the eloquent poem) black bread
made of black flour — has anyone ever thought
why when typing the words always turn
black?
What genetic inclination decided
that every thought belongs to mourning? What instinct
slaps the fragrant boys of symbolism
who shockingly let the obvious to escape them?

Often I end up sensitive
pretending to be emotional

and now with what hands can you kneed bread
with what courage can you finish the poem?

SIMILE OF PASSION

I take off the bark of the wood and I find coal
yet, ultimately, what separates the tree
from the lamp post?
(Untrammelled time, shepherds
decoration of leaves, sprouts, fluids)

The firewood crackles in the fireplace and its breath
a rustle of the forest that charges and rises
with the wings of its ashes
and the chirps of the birds on the chimney.
Beautiful fire
each of your flames a crematorium of bucolic imagination
simile of passion that often raises the measly
into an expensive conflagration.
I gaze the sparkles of your eyes, the agile swirls
of your snake like tongue
that consumes piles of prey
with dancing and its methodical movement
like Eros
you consume as you give warmth.

Such truth, such craftiness you need
to succeed in consuming.

How much consummation you need
to warm us up?

FIRE OF THE TOUCH

I think of Midas, of course, like you do.
The endless coal he turned into gold
with each touch. Then I say
that everything was turned upside down
and all our caresses turn everything
into coal
into an invisible lightning bolt.
I have no answer
even as I look around the smoke
that becomes
a rhetorical yarn
about the world affairs
incense caressing
the external
which with golden reflection
announces its betrayal
of the darkling
burning of life
and crooked etymology
that speaks the truth
of my rising.

Remain calm

during this ceremony
your skin is
your hide away place
in the trembling touch
of the flame.

THE TARE

You speak in words
you translate the unknown
into a different unknown. Exchanging
the unbearable of the matter with a false
portfolio
filled with intangible shares
pronouns
and verbs.

Which chthonian throat
gives voice to a vowel?
With which element of this world
a consonant agrees?

Minimal bites of air
impersonate monsters, therefore think:
for the fisherman
the word net is needless. Unruly
soulless and souled elements charge
and sweep concepts. They trample
the meaning of names and noiselessly
body against body they claim
what they've dreamed of being. Transcending
the unknown beyond tongue and thought
into something more darkling
and impossible to lift.

In the intangible
tare
of matter.

PIECE OF PROSE

When we start to write do we seek
to enter into the seed of this world
or to crack it open?
That it will evaporate in our imagination
and imperishably
it will re-emerge a universe made of words?
To leave behind cobbles of emotions
fears and dreams? (I mean the awaking from sleep
and other things that will feel heavy tomorrow).
Re-starting the endless piece of writing
with a lot of rhythm and images, sensing that
we don't really want anything — that
a piece of prose is a universe made of nothing

and that
this last piece of prose
is our destiny.

LANDSCAPES OF THE VOID

A new day today, the sword of irremovable
and the abyss of the mind.
Does the infinitesimal moment
has truly nothing of its own?
It borrows something from before
and repays something from tomorrow
with the remanence of the other
light as air and yet it steps on your chest like steel
exactly like the universe encases you:
made of steel.
Full of holes in the sea of void
landscapes of the void
where islands of neutrons
and galaxies flow
imaginary canard of the visible
in the winged baton of vertigo

that being electrified
transcends the zero
the nowhere
and the never

into the world

GEORGE DOUATZIS

George Douatzis was born Athens in 1948. He studied Economics and Sociology. In 1974 he started working as a reporter for newspapers and magazines, radio stations and television channels as political analyst, reporter, article contributor, editor and news producer.

He's been writing regularly since the 60s. His first appearance was in "Poetry Anthology of the New Hellenic Generation" in 1971.

THE RED SCARF

I couldn't erase the world but I could erase myself from the world whenever I felt like it and this in fact filled me with satisfaction.

Besides I always took care of my attire in detail since I had to hide many scars. People admired my trendy appearance and some even envied it.

How could I convince them the red they saw wasn't because of the scarf?

COMPANY

Definitely
no one knocked at the door

it was very expensive to be present
the visitors cost too much

only the past
knocked at my door again
there is no freedom, it said to me
let us beautify our prisons
forgetting that it too was imprisoned
in the cell of memories
albeit what past could it be

and the mirror kept quiet
as if it was a door knocked by the wind
and no sound came out of it

one way or another
I was busy meditating
on the heaviness of a tear
or
on how some nights have no end

PASSING

Winds of atonement will blow
for something we didn't do

laughter, pain
sorrow, habits
writing, advise left
for the upcoming strong winds

and my silence
fertile like loneliness
gives birth to love
to man
to God

WASTE

Easily we waste
the most valuable:
water, blood

like losses
that build the smallest room
in which I live

and as I grow older
the room turns smaller
until it becomes a small dot
lost in the space
of a mindless world

ADDED

When the white clouds gather many tears
there's no protection for the white haired old men
who resist time with their art
tears turn white
they keep their umbrellas open
with no sails they point to its entirety
their black metal skeleton
that the unimpeded tears can pass through
and create the cleansing rain
that showers all who have
their hands open to an embrace
as if they sublimate all the acts of their lives

DON'T BELIEVE THEM

Don't believe them

you were saying —

their empty words play with hope
two dots in the sea of people
who believed in the arriving spring
and you with my image in your eyes
you're saying
patience, spring won't come as they say

you were saying —

and I was talking of spring

they want to erase our dreams
that we say *yes* with bowing heads
that we turn the self-deception
into belief

you were saying —

I have you
I have the guitar
and my back loaded with dreams
don't believe them

and I was talking of spring

CURTAIN

You see them indifferently
they pass by in dozens
and you know
that if you pull the curtain aside
and life reappears
along with their real faces
you'll discover
tears of joy and tears of hope

you don't know the quality of the curtain
the fabric, color, pattern
yet you're certain
it exists, in fact it has existed for eons
on the side of the heart
to protect all who can't endure
diaphaneity and the roughness
of their own truth

ah, night has pulled a lot of tricks on you
and undeterred you keep walking

HALF OF ONE

They were talking of revolution
and I, the fool, led them
to the big mirror of introversion
perhaps they could understand that everything
needed an honorable beginning in self-knowledge

then quite condescendingly I left them
to rest after the difficult voyage
and I asked mortality and decay
to teach them a lesson
by putting them to sleep

next morning I lost all hope

I saw them shaking off
the remaining dust of humility
from their cloths
and they gave an order to shutter
all the existing mirrors

when I needed
to rely entirely onto my strength
to become the humblest of all men

BENEFITED

Before the defeated are born
they talk without seeing you in the eyes
they have their glance on the ground
as if searching for ancient secrets
and you don't know whether it's because of fear
sickly pride or the means to blackmail you

however
they always make you worry
since you easily think
they may hide their hatred
in their downward glances
being always ready to become ravens
unthankful and benefited

WORDS

Such was my fear
that I never extended my hand to a shake
being afraid it would be taken away
by the greeting person

I have to confess
I always hated the holidays
because I felt sad seeing them
jaunty and empty
like an image of sorrow
that tries to get filled by words
words of colorblindness
a lot of words, untrue oaths taken
that erase meaning and hope

I tell you the wind is full of words
how can the weather turn cooler
and where will you hide hope in the future?

MUSIC

This music a desperate dialogue
of soundless stringed instruments
that rip my heart

for a strange reason
this desperate music
was quite enjoyable
perhaps because desperation was sinking
in the beauty of poetry
dressed in the garment of hope

you see, it was the moment
that spring, the time divider, gave wings
to this little life
to the passionate people
to those imprisoned in stereotypes
to the Mithridates of unfulfilled desires

as life and hope are hopelessly mixed
in this desperate music

DISTANCE

Then
I felt that pain disappeared
like a handkerchief in the wind
at the time of departure
in the harbour

and when I turned my eyes
to see where the wind took it
the ship that took you away
had already vanished in the horizon

wish you knew how many songs
of distance you represent

TALKATIVE SILENCE

How couldn't they
understand they've lived?

They didn't know —

he told me

and walked away
stepping on dots
vanishing in the horizon

when I decided
to write a poem

which I would read during my voyage
from my beneficial melancholy
to my country home of sadness

TEMPEST

I rolled onto the clouds
to get some
of the twilight color

I hanged the most beautiful dreams
onto my wall
and broke the mirrors

finally they found me stooping
by that small lake
searching for the image
of my trembling idol
that only absolute lack of breeze
could make my true likeness visible

but the north wind became a tempest
like the thirst for justice
in the eyes of man

CHILD

In the eyes of the child
you'll see the guilt you pushed aside
even for acts you didn't commit
because what more a child can tell you
beyond the great *why?*

And at that moment
is like you dive
in the glance of a blind man
searching for a shred of light
as the darkness of desperation overtakes you
or
you try to glorify life
in the low light
that comes through
the cracks created by life giving lust
trapped in the structures
and answers of guilt

and there is nothing tougher than
the truthfulness demanded by the answer
to *the why* of a child

TITOS PATRIKIOS

Titos Patrikios was born in Athens in 1928. He studied Law in the University of Athens and later sociology and philosophy in Paris, at the Ecole Pratique des Hautes Etudes and at the Sorbonne. He was active in the resistance movement against the German Occupation, but during the years of military dictatorship following the Greek Civil War he was "displaced" within the borders of his own country, to detention camps on the islands of Makronissos and Ai-Stratis, and later exiled outright to Paris and Rome, once from 1959-1964 and again from 1967-1975.

He's considered one of the most important poets of the after the Second World War group of poets. His first poetry book, *Dirt Road*, 1952, was very well received as positive reviews were written for it and his second book *Apprenticeship*, 1963, was also recognized placing him to the top of his contemporaries.

Titos Patrikios isn't only a poet. He served the Modern Greek Letters in various ways, as an editor and contributor to the literary magazine Art Review, as a translator and an essayist. He was also involved in important political issues which placed him on the top of the most courageous and philosophical thinkers of his times. Patrikios was fascinated by the concept of a better and more just society a dream he defended with courage and persistence.

He has represented Greece in many international literary events: poetry forums, festivals, and he was invited by foreign Universities where he spoke not only for his work but also for various other subjects. His poetry has been translated in many European languages especially in Italian and has been included in many Poetry Anthologies.

After he received Greece's National Prize for Literature in 1994 Kedros Publishers produced his collected poems in four tomes which cover all his works up to 2002. In 2007 he published his *New Path* and in 2008 a collection of Erotic poems titled, *Lustful Desire*.

TWO STATUES

The poem that talked of life
entrapped her in its words
held her down
wanted to keep her
motionless for eons
a statue in its verse.

When life listened to the poem
it encircled it with phosphorescent sand
made a stone of it, broke its limbs
turned it into a statue
moving in time.

OEDIPUS

He wanted to solve riddles
to shed light in darkness
where everyone settled
though it burdened them.
He didn't feel afraid of all he saw
but from the refusal of the others to accept them.
Would he always be the exception?
He couldn't endure loneliness
and to connect with his neighbors
he poked out his eyes
with the two forks.
By feeling them he still recognized things
no one else wanted to see.

TWO DEMONSTRATIONS

Then the demonstration turned the city upside down
with a new slogan among the known ones:
let's march for the democratic ugliness
Five years later another demonstration
larger than the first one and more militant
called us all to march with only one slogan.
Let's march for the compulsory ugliness

SISYPHUS

Speechless he finally noticed it:
impossible to believe that he accomplished it —
after a thousand efforts
he had finally reached the summit.
He had pushed the rock for eons
step by step towards the top
or went after it when it slipped off him
and he ran to reach it and start his push again.
He had never reached the top
until now that he was at the top
with the motionless rock next to him.
He tried to move it, he made sure
the rock was stable; he took a breath
and turned to enjoy the immense view;
then he suddenly stopped —
if he finished his martyrdom
the myth would vanish too
the various explanations of his task would stop
no one would ever talk of Sisyphus again.
With all his might he pushed the rock
made sure it would start rolling towards the bottom.

SYLLABLES

And whatever remained from your passing
chronos smoothens slowly
like a pebble in the riverbed.
I'm only sure of your name now.
And I call it again and again standing at the seashore
that perhaps one night
when the barbwires and walls engulf us
I'll need it as a word of survival
only to discover that even that has vanished.

VERSE

Verses that cry out
verses that stand up like bayonets
against the establishment
and among their few steps
they put together or dissolve the revolution
useless, phoney, boastful verses
since no verse topples the establishment these days
no verse motivates the masses.
What masses? Between us, really,
who thinks of masses these days?
At the most a personal relief if not a recognition —
for this I don't write anymore
to offer guns made of paper
weapons made of words talkative and hollow.
I shall only raise the edge of truth
to shed some light onto our counterfeit lives.
Long as I last, long as I am able.

PICTURES AND BIOGRAPHIES

Our erotic dreams were sustained
by the unchanged pictures
of the women we loved.
Our political dreams were defeated
by the changeable biographies
of the leaders who had once convinced us.

CAMPAIGN AGAINST HUNGER

I grab a piece of bread from the ground
still fresh, thrown by the hand
of a man with a full stomach
I kiss it as I did when I was a child, I cross it
careful not to be seen by anyone
I place it high up on the shelf.
I didn't know that hunger still
lurked in the viscera, that
it had spread its tentacles over
like an insatiable octopus.
I grab a piece of bread from the ground
thrown by a man with a full stomach
I too with a full stomach now.

LIBERATION OF THE MINOTAUR

What would happen to us
if nothingness wasn't reborn?
How could we mark the periphery
of our ever changing self
how could we have invented touch
that using it we could feel the others
how could we fill
our emptying world?
What could have happened to us
without the rebirth of nothingness
without the survival of the void?
In the void we construct exquisite labyrinths
like Daedalus constructed his
as if to liberate from its depths
the invisible Minotaur.

THE LIONS GATE

Lions had disappeared by then
none was around over Greece
not even a hunted one, alone
hiding somewhere in Peloponnese
not bothering anybody anymore
till even that was killed by Hercules.
Yet the memory of lions
never stopped scaring people
images of lions incised on crests
and shields frightened people
likeness of their image on cenotaphs
their glyphs on the stony top of archways.
Our unbearable past always daunts
as the narrating of events does
and the writing on the stony top
of the gateway we pass daily.

HARIS VLAVIANOS

Haris Vlavianos was born in Italy and studied Economics and Philosophy at the University of Bristol. He also studied Politics and History at Trinity College in Oxford. His doctoral thesis, entitled "Greece 1941-1949: From Resistance to Civil War," was published by Macmillan in 1992. He's professor of History at the American College of Greece.

He has published ten collections of poetry, the most recent of them *Self Portrait of the White* in 2018. He has also published a collection of thoughts and aphorisms on poetry and poetics entitled, *The Other Place* and a book of essays entitled, *Does Poetry Matter?: Thoughts on the Uselessness of an Art* as well a book with Haikus, entitled, *The History of Western Philosophy in 100 Haikus: From the Presocratics to Derrida*. He has translated in Greek, the works of well-known writers such as: Walt Whitman, Ezra Pound, *Drafts and Fragments of Cantos CX-CXX*, Michael Longley, Wallace Stevens, John Ashberry, Carlo Goldoni, William Blake, Zbigniew Herbert, Fernando Pessoa, E. E. Cummings, Michael Longley, and T. S. Eliot.

He's the editor of the literary Greek journal *Poetics*. His collection of poems *Adieu*, written in 1996, has been translated in English by David Connolly and published in the UK by Birmingham University Press (1998). A volume of his *Selected Poems* has been translated in German by Dadi Sideri Speck, in Dutch by Hero Hokwerda, and in Italian by Nicola Crocetti.

A selection of his poetry has been translated in Catalan by Joaquim Gestí and published in Barcelona by the Institució de les Letres Catalanes. Other volumes of *Selected Poems* have been translated in German by Torsten Israel in Dutch by Hero Hokwerda, and in English by Mina Karavanta.

His poetry has also been translated in French, Spanish, Portuguese, Bulgarian, Albanian, and Swedish and has appeared in numerous European and American journals and anthologies.

CAFÉ EXISTENTIAL

(Murphy's way)

Matter precedes existence —

the young server said emphatically
as with quick
decisive movements
she cleaned the marble table next
to where the cross-eyed man with the pipe sat

in this case along with
the double espresso
I'll also have an apple pie —

Jean Paul said

CAVO PARADISO

For my son

Time has come for you to leave, morning has arrived
besides the night passed indifferently
the girls returned alone
and went to their rooms alone
even as they spent three hours in front of their mirror
to decide whether to paint their nails pink or green

the American dj was good I have to say
but that constant remix after a while
became almost anticipated and at times tiring

your father would prefer to listen to Lou Reed
and Tom Waits tonight
(in fact it is a full moon)
but you quite justifiably will shout:
but they belong to another era
it always happens this way
when Ginsberg visited Ezra Pound in Venice
he urged him to listen to the Beatles
and asked him whether he liked them
the old Ezra shook his head slightly
as he whispered *I prefer Vivaldi*
it doesn't matter though
if this certain Paradise proved to be counterfeit
others will appear tomorrow and more gleaming
with bigger pools and more sunburn bodies
rocking around sensually
the meaning of things hides elsewhere:
when he woke up in the morning and saw you relaxed in bed
he was relieved and gave you a kiss on the cheek
then he made coffee, turned the computer on, logged onto You Tube
and found the *Is this Love*
yes, in You Tube, and yes, Bob Marley

GIFT FROM HEAVEN

What makes you believe that
I can still live in a room
from which you have removed
with certain gusto I may add
one of its four walls?
I agree the view is better —
not that one can see at the far end
Arno and the Ponte Vecchio —
but you think this major renovation
is a good reason for us to return
with our reignited courage
during the first act of the play?
And the four syllable word on the wine bottle
and the meat cooked with prunes
and the candles that supposedly repel the mosquitos
what do they truly mean?
And the young server
with the heavy accent
from which Russian novel
has he suddenly sprang up?
And how the fact that Adorno
as you tell me emphatically
had dined with Greta Garbo
in Los Angeles in 1944
and that his dog, Ali Baba — what a name
urinated onto her book
change anything?

Do you hear the rustle of the leaves
and the voices of the children
who come down our street
on their rollerblades?
Do you know that the message they carry
belongs to a future
you haven't imagined?

Close your eyes for a while.
Sometimes is better to look at reality
without trying to estimate
in how many minutes the sun will go down
besides right now
the point isn't
this particular sundown
but the gift it has given us.

Did you say — *wasted years?*
Don't turn melancholy.
Is there ever a Paradise
that is not lost
at the end of the dream?

THE COOKOO'S NEST (AT HELICON)

for Maria Topali

Suddenly a deranged man
with a hat appeared
from behind the tree
and started shouting:
if it doesn't rhyme it isn't a poem
it isn't a poem if it doesn't rhyme

she was a little afraid
and started walking backward
but I told her not to worry
since as many hairs were missing
from his bald head
and for this reason the hat
as many and more sprang up
from his tasteless verses.
Un caso triste
Camus would have said
but not *dendo di memoria*
a sad footnote
in the history of poetry

she laughed like a child
and started walking
with steady steps
we continued our walk
without looking back
his shouts vanished
as we passed the stone bridge

what an unbelievable story

DAZZLE

With the brush of Yau

Many artists have painted
a woman
combing her hair
with her back — often naked
and turned to the viewer —
in front of a mirror

you're naked
you comb your hair
in front of the mirror
singing aloud
la donna e mobile

for a moment I see
what all others have seen

a woman in love with herself
in love with the world

WRONG QUESTION

Now that I read it again I think
I was right I put it aside in the first verse
at the point when the young couple
were exhausted by the exchange of deep thoughts

to have something because you desire it
differs from desiring something because you have it

it's easier to pretend there are obstacles
than to pretend there is passion

he decides to sleep in a separate room
another loveless night

how many months, you asked

it's not the end of the world —
until the second round begins
everything will unfold as it's supposed to
until the first *newly felt attraction*
turns into the *unbearable boredom*
the point is this:
you think if you urged the woman to do pilates
and the man to go sailing
you could move to the next phase of the drama?

Indeed the body needs some care
especially now that it has reached the middle of the road
when the valley at the far end looks bare
although a sense of vigor is enough
and your main characters will try to fool
the unerring nature, now that these two
dream of a wonderful, new beginning

many men at the gym desire me

many women are ready to fall in my experienced hands

Is she working the next lie in her mind?
However the alarm just went off
it's time for the children to get up
the school bus is due in forty minutes
they have to have their breakfast, brush their teeth
put on gloves and scarves
and then —

Good morning, you slept well?

No, I had nightmares all night long

You want me to make you a coffee? It will revive you

I don't drink coffee anymore, have you forgotten?

LORD BYRON JUST BEFORE, JUST AFTER

If you lament for your youth why you live?
Here is the land of the glorious death
rush into the battle, give your last breath
without hesitation at this very point

long for — it's easy to long, not to find —
your burial site, soldier, the most appropriate for you
then, look here, choose the soil
where you will lean and rest

Today I turn thirty years old, Messologi, January 22, 1824

Who could be a writer
if one had something better to do?
Lord Byron asked his Greek servant
as he gazed through the open window
of his old crumbly house
the hordes of the Ottoman Empire soldiers
encircling the walls of the city.

He had just finished
the first verse of the poem
which was meant to be his last.
He turned thirty years old that day.
Three months later
the strange, civil-warred place
which he had chosen as his homeland
would grace him his wish:
a death worthy of his name
an heroic exit from the unbearable boredom of *poetry*

BLAKE IN PARADISE

Biographers and experts agree
he was crazy.
Was it important though
if he indeed saw angels dancing
on the trees of his garden
or that for hours he talked
to Isaiah and Ezekiel?
Wasn't enough that he gave us
the *Wise Sayings of Hell*
and *Jerusalem?*

Just before he closed his eyes
he asked for pencil and a piece of paper
to draw the face of his beloved
Catherine for the last time.
Under her portrait
with a trembling hand he wrote:
I'm sure it exists
since you exist

THE CANE OF BERMENSCH

August of 1934
travelling by train
from Weimer to Berlin
he decided to stop by the *Villa Silberblick*
to pay a visit to the place
where he closed his eyes
his beloved philosopher
and to pay his respects
to the philosopher's eighty six year old sister Elizabeth.

Upon entering the house
he held a whip
which he stroke nervously onto his leg.
When he got out later on
he played with a cane in his right hand
and he said to the officers who escorted him:
What a beautiful lady
a true German
such ladies
are the backbone of our nation
she gifted me with Nietzsche's cane.
The cane of Übermensch!
as she explained to me
I'm the only one who deserves to hold it
because only I have understood
his Weltanschauung
only I can bring his horrible dream to fruition
only I
Adolf Hitler
the Fuhrer

CLOE KOUTSOUBELIS

Cloe was born in Thessaloniki in 1962 and graduated from the Aristoteleion University with a diploma in law. She has published six books of poetry. *Relations of Silence*, Egnantia Publishers, 1984, *The Night is a Whale*, Loxias Publishers, 1990, *Departure of Lady Leda*, Nea Poreia Publishers, 2004, *The Lake, the Garden and Loss*, Nea Poreia, 2006, *The Fox and the Red Dance*, Gavliilidis, 2009, *In the Ancient World Evening Comes Late*, Gavriilidis, 2012. She has also published a novel, *Whispering*, Paratiritis, 2002 and a play *Orpheus in the Bar*, Parodos Publishers, 2005.

Her poems and short stories have appeared in various literary magazines in Greece and abroad.

Cloe's poems have been translated into French, Italian and English. She is a member of the Thessaloniki Company of Authors.

She's the vice president of the Writer's Company of Thessaloniki and a member of the Writers Company and Circle of Poets.

PENELOPE

She knows by now
the aren't fools
they sing as they think of creating art
nor the old Circe in her lust
hidden in windbags forever sealed
nor the misbehaving Nausica
trapped in the wrong age
in white socks and childish dresses
nor the Laestrygonians nor the lotus
that keep him away from her
or Poseidon's petty angers
and the mix-ups with his old companions.
Penelope knows by now
her last message will remain unanswered
they'll never talk to each other again
logic compels him to stay away from her,
all over her
suitors drink raki
and roll like lions in the arena
males who sniff lust
and define space with their arrows.
And Odysseus?
Penelope doesn't remember of him anymore.
Only that one night she slept with a stranger
and when she asked of his name
he answered: *I'm no one*

ANTIGONE

When Antigone leaves she always forgets something.
A lacy glove on the satin bed-sheet,
a steamy drop of lemon
on the cheek of a friend,
a stolen touch on a lover's arm
a lip-mark on the porcelain tea-cup
when she drinks hastily.
Antigone forgets
the gauzy handkerchief moistened
by the sudden momentary tears
the little umbrella in the fragile rain.
Antigone forgets
the rustle of her dress when she walks
the fan that changes her seasons.
Antigone always forgets something
and for this she always leaves.
Only some nights
as she starts remembering things
she sprinkles ashes on her hair
buries herself in her cave
and laments for the unburied dead.

THE NAKED POEM

I come to you naked.
At first chubby and unshaped
with folding skin under my arms and legs
then a teenager in the conch's purple
without the interference of the pen
that will change the ignorance of writing
a woman's purpose
with her outlined valley of loss
swollen certainly by the moist of childbirth
with elliptical words
that hide and attract
with gaps between the verses
that they stay silent
and include the shape of your fingers.
I come to you
every night
a naked and lonely poem
filled with whispers and ancient secrets
that you may read me.

THE POEM VIRUS

A poem has been swirling around me since yesterday.
It gives me a headache and vertigo.
I turn my head to the side
at the edge of my vision
I discern it
thick stain
at the edge of my desk.
This is not personal — I said to it
I don't want any more poems
nor steamships loaded with rice;
I'm fed up with the oceanic voyages
on ships of high underwriting costs
a raft is all I want
in a plastic self-contained pool
in a yard full of rusted metal;
one restful body and a chair made of cloth
to rest.
This I said to it
and it took its revenge on me
and it got filled by you and with you
and it wrote itself.

TO MY ONLY READER

I'll wait for you
in a station not yet built
in that center of loneliness
where condors swirl around the trains
where bald babies wail loudly.
You'll come
with a train no longer in service
without brakes nor engineer
a train that rolls among the stars.
When you disembark you won't hug me
you won't tell me *I love you*
you'll only raise your hand
and you'll rearrange tenderly the collar
of my worn out overcoat.

PROMISED LAND

It doesn't scare me
that this pencil leaves
no marks but only traces
of melted sky on the paper.
Neither it scares me
that instead of paper
I write over your body,
warm conch of fragrant chamomile
spread everywhere.

It only scares me
that one day
I'll write poems on paper.

OPTIMISM

One day we'll meet again.
You'll wear your face
and the gray raincoat.
It'll be a bit windy
as when we had that stroll.
Asphodels will fly between us
the ancient ruins
will get filled by pollen
haze will cover our kiss.
Your warm lips.
Then you'll say: *this will never end*
and I'll add: *it will end.*

A ball of snow melts in Antarctica,
somewhere else a continent sinks in the void
in the ancient agora a man and a woman
saunter joyously
unsuspecting of what comes next.

GUILTY

I'm guilty, I confess.
The last poem I wrote for you.
Mitigating circumstances: the rain,
the endless cigarettes, alcohol
perhaps even your body
memory of what never happened.
In reality I wrote about some other things:
for that story in the Garden
that you never had the courage
you never learned
you never asked
and last night, I confess
I wrote a verse for you
sorrowful and naked
in this smudgy and always half finished
poem of my life.

THE TICKET

I purchased a train ticket
to come and find you.
So simple to get onto a train
with the operator, the money collector, other passengers
rails touching the ground
and all stops pre-announced.
I forgot how black the train of love is.
It burns coal and every hope
with a blind eye and a gaping mouth
an orchid engine forever hungry
it groans rhythmically
like a gigantic serpent
in and out the fearful tunnels.
I forgot how lonely the train of love is.
The inspector often
validates the tickets
and the money collector
a wax resemblance
always waiting at the station.

I purchased a train ticket
to come and find you.
As if I didn't know the voyage is always the same
and who to look for in the deserted station.

THE IDOL

There's always an idol
hidden behind each mirror.
No one bothers with it.
Its life unfolds noiselessly
on the glassy surface.
No one touches it
nor does it recognize
the strange people
standing in front of it.
Mechanically it mimics
their movements: when
one raises his right arm
it raises its left
when one coughs noiselessly
it moves its lips.
Only when the house is vacant
the idol takes the razor
and touching it on the veins of its wrist
it tries to feel alive.
It sees however only the void opposite it.
For this, look into the mirror carefully:
if you're lucky
you may even see
the screaming idol
behind your face.

PHAIDON THEOFILOU

Phaidon Theofilou was born in Mytilini, in 1947. He studied social studies in Germany and worked for the civil aviation. During the 70s he lived in Germany from where he travelled to Vienna, Rome, Warsaw, Budapest, Brussels and other European cities. He contributes articles to newspapers in rural Greece and to newspapers in Athens on a regular basis and he's involved online with articles relating to literature and the arts in general.

He was a founding member of the Hellenic-Austrian Cultural Institute and of the Thucydides Center for the Sciences. He served as a selected member of the Company of Hellenic Writers from 1991-1993. He served as general manager-editor of the magazine *Aiolida* which dealt with literary and cultural issues of the island of Lesbos. His work has been translated into German, Polish, Bulgarian, and have been presented in various anthologies both in Greece and abroad.

TRUE DON CHIXOTE

Crazy in love
he run
everywhere and nowhere
he passed from the pistils of the flowers
and came out to the air
filtered by the thick leafage
he collected the lighted spots
escaped from the shades of trees
and he marked paths during the moonless nights
he left food close
to the dens of lonely wolves
and honey to the bears
he waved to the clouds
to guide their rain
and he played with the thunderbolts in his fingers.
He folded the night, like paper, in two
then in four and finally in eight.
In the morning with the first sweat of the sun
he arrived to his house and galloped
on her naked body
as if in an oasis that had no end
nor beginning.

BY THE POCKET

I open a small window on my chest
where the shirt pocket is located
to escape
when sorrow allows it

IN A SLOW MUSICAL MINOR

Your life wasn't easy nor comfortable
it surely wasn't unsuspecting
black holes controlled you
like lovers
not that you couldn't escape them
although always one of them would collapse
and would swallow you
when you mused
between the void and the whole.

Yet you knew
that whoever dives in darkness
also deserves the light.

LIKE A FAIRY

Like a fairy
I enter the cane fields
reaching to their roots
feeling the caress of moist and warmth

I charge to the forests like a juvenile
to welcome the rain
with green wholeness

I touch seams of ore in the earth
which reflect and declare
their ethereal colors in my eyes.

Yes, like the color the eyes of men reflect
when the soul stays still
and the glance falls in the void.

I pass my appearance
which resembles a pointing needle
among the foliage of the trees
tasty craftiness of chlorophyll.

I go to the hothouse of your fears looking in them
you're afraid of your fear and what gnaws you.
Yet when drinking with your friends you leave them to forgetfulness
but your fears come back more demanding
since you don't have the courage to face them.
Often you replace the faces of your fear
with hatred, ingratitude, subversion of others;
thus you also change.

I stand before the miraculous work of bees, that don't know
they transform aesthetics into ambrosia with their stand
they transcend a great deed into a simple expected act.

Then, I hold my self-respect up high
like a precious possession:

my respect for the cat
which when it feels its time has come
leaves everyone behind
and bestows its body
into a schism of the earth.

STAGE LIGHTS

What is truth?
The lie asked shaping up its makeup.
Truth is the birth of man dressed in its innocence,
the mind of life answered.

And then?

He becomes an adult and doesn't know which lie to choose
he chooses a different lie in each and every case
as one picks a color.

What comes next?

The unaltered final truth appears:
the hospitable soil that consumes everything.

TANGO WITH A CLOUD

I'm afraid to fall in love with you,
she said.
No one knows what a woman may have in her mind.
He was silent.
During the winter nights he fought
against the winds
yet he was a faint breeze in her mouth.
He brought pearls of tears to her
from a child's grumble.

One day he decided to leave discreetly.
Yes, discreetly.

Who can get a message from a passing cloud?

During the rainy days she'd fix the table
a small knitted backing
onto which she'd lay her secret feelings
and she had an experience so alive
as if dancing, she felt, tango with a cloud.

THE EROTIC DON CHIXOTE

He stood in the morning sunshine
he counted the cobblestones
he swept the colors in the eyes of men
memory agitated his years
and he touched the post with his cheek
living the caresses he yearned.
I miss you, he whispered
like the soul misses its body.
I fill your absence with music
and I love you.

As for her
no one knew if she truly existed.

THE RAIN WOUDN'T STOP

He told her how important she was because of her nature
he underlined her grace and worthiness to her
since she didn't have a sense of these
and valued the people based on
their external shining surface
he told her that worthiness comes out
from within and reflects on everything.
He wanted to build up her self-esteem
and they managed to accomplish it.

Himself with his persistence and love
overflowing his heart
and herself by accepting and by being surprised
at the value of her revealed treasures.

When she felt completely sure of herself
she scolded and made fun of him
all while she displayed a wild joy in her eyes
he couldn't suppress neither his disappointment
nor his anger that battled inside him
until one night when the rain wouldn't stop
he choked her to death.

Love truly has many faces
from exultation to murder.

STRAIGHT SOUND

Words are of female gender
they flirt with all five senses
add and subtract to and from their value
making fun of the poets' agony
the conceit of rhetors.
For a moment they grasp their true meaning
in front of the saints' humility.
Finally they brazenly get justified
in the lips of men
with lust on their tail wind.

BLONDE DAY

The door of spring opened
and we saw light-blue epitaphs.

Piece of news at noon
imminent nuclear war

the old man said *I'm hungry*

we drank the night in a glass
at the bottom of the glass a new day.

Chemistry wakes up in the factory each morning
and finds the dead history

the dancing rain continues
two shoeless shoes in the street.

GEORGE THEOHARIS

George Theoharis was born in 1951 in Desfina, Greece. He worked all his life for the chemical industry. He has published five collections of poetry and a book of historical research about the slaughter of the populace of Distomo in 1944; for this book he was awarded the National Literary Award for a Chronicle — Report in the year 2011. Since 2014 he has edited five Poetry Anthologies. He contributed to the newspaper Book Press. His work has been translated in French, English, German, Spanish and Albanian. He's a founding member manager-editor of Emvolimon, a literary magazine which was awarded the National Literary Award for the year 2014. He took part in the Commission for National Awards for Children's Literature. He's a regular member of the National Company of Greek Writers — Poetry Circle.

DIFFICULT DIAGNOSIS

I can't read your eyes
anymore, since
your calm glance has
something unrecognizable in it

like the little shrines
on the side of the road
when you drive by them

and you don't know
whether it's to the honour
of one who got killed
or to the one who was saved

WITH THE PATIENCE OF THE ROCKS

If one day you leave
and go to the sea
I'll become a white pebble
and I'll wait for your return
by the shore

I'll wait with the rock's patience
even if you delay

you know the rocks can wait for years

WITH MUCH DECORUM

Sometimes even poets
can't write

it happens when I think of you

I can't find the words
but the ones which compose you

missing one would be unfair
adding one would break the balance

I break my pencil and look at you

ecstatic and in love

I don't feel a poet before you

but like a framer before
an exquisite painting

VISIBLE COMPLICATION

Eyes of people meet
sometimes.

It could happen March
on a road next to the sea

when strong emotions
flood the air
and the gathered people
that applaud the parade
are unable to explain
why from the shiny bayonets
of the parading soldiers
suddenly a flock
of birds in love appear

DURING THE NIGHT

During the night
glances of the statues turn alive

as if the passersby
feel
that someone spies on them

LISTEN TO SILENCE

For John Patilis

When I die
remember
when you go to sleep at night
the eyes that saw you and believed you.
Recall the eyes
that brought your truth to the lips
like the pine needles
draw the blood of your arm.

When I die
listen to the steps that muddied
your door step in those desperate days.
Listen to the steps which
brought the fresh dream
in your good soul.

When I die
listen to the silence of sounds
among the people's chatter.
Listen to them
they're my body's orphan words
that travel in time.

Silence is the words of all who didn't speak
not because they didn't want
but because their tongue was a treeline
among which nightingales always sang.

MELANCHOLY STORY

There is lighthouse on a deserted jetty.
and a bench in olive oil green color under it
bitter olive oil green the color of longing
a lonely bench in a lonely jetty
under the most lonely lighthouse in the Universe.

If a desperate man sits on it
he may hear, in the language of the creaking wood
the story of the sparrow that perished
there where the water turns into salt
and of the perch that leaned its colorful body
on the seafloor and died
when they discovered the perfect dead-end
of the love between a bird and a fish.

WRONG SCENARIO

At this moment you may be skipping stones at the shore

you may also be measuring the decorative pieces of gypsum
on the ceiling of a summer bedroom
while sunshine visits you in the form of bands
through the blinds of the balcony door.

You may, on the other hand, pretend that you read
a book with uncut pages
or you may put on your make up
in front of a cracked mirror.

Under the shade of a eucalyptus
a few steps from the sea
I may search for the rhythm
I may try to craft an exquisite verse
while nature sends me a myriad of music tones
and thousands of sounds.

And perhaps I may feel full of fire
though my soul is drizzled by your absence.

What of you will the night bring to me?
And will it?

The summer lasted for too long
let autumn finally come
to rediscover the melancholic equilibrium.

A FEW DETAILS FROM THE NORMAL LIFE
AND THE DEATH OF MRS IRENE KARVONIS

She let her last breath in bed at the end of the century. During her last year of her life her memory gradually left her leading her to the starting point. She became again the little girl who she always was. She shrank into a handful of a person due to the absence of the fluids of robustness dressed in her freshly washed nightie, she was happy for a sprig of basil you would offer her or by giving her the chance to narrate incoherent stories.

She let her last breath having reached her ninety-three years. Just before she died she turned and said to her son who was by her side "I was born in Syros in 1906. I remember the day Halley's Comet pass by the Earth. We had peas and small fried fish. They were forcing me to eat, but I wanted to see the comet, dad."

When she closed her eyes and with the commotion that was created among the relatives who waited for her, her not yet forty days old grandchild started crying.

And if this story seems a bit melodramatic and if the question arises "for what reason a normal life deserves its place in art?" I wonder: "why the normal life of the kind Mrs. Irene Karvonis doesn't deserve it, when among other things, she managed to finally answer the merciless question of "what shall we cook today?"

JUSTICE

She died after a long life at the old folk's home of the Diocese. Her step daughter buried her in her place of birth away from which they have lived for many years. She buried her next to her second husband who died at a young age. She never enjoyed her first husband. He was killed a newlywed during the occupation years. Just before the casket was covered by soil her step daughter emptied in the burial site the bones of the killed husband which she had taken from the bone apothecary of the church. "Let all three of them be together; my mother got married to them because she fell in love with both of them"

ALEXANDRA BAKONIKA

Alexandra Bakonika was born in 1951 in Thessaloniki, where she re-
sides. Poems and reviews of hers have been published in well- known
literary periodicals.

Her work was presented at the symposium of Patras in 1994. In
1996, she was invited and participated at the symposium for Modern
Greek Literature in London, by invitation of the Hellenic Culture Foun-
dation to contemporary poets and writers. Also her work was presented
at the Aristotle University of Thessaloniki in 2012, at the Goran's Spring
Festival for European poets in Zagreb in 2015, at the 2016 International
Shamrock Poetry Festival in Munich. Apart from her poems which were
translated and published in India and Canada, selected poems have been
translated in German, Swedish, Croatian and Albanian.

She studied Medicine at the Aristotle University of Thessaloniki, but
she did not complete her studies. She has had various assignments as an
English teacher. Her poems appeared for the first time in the literary
magazine *Diagonios* in 1983.

Her books include *Open Line*, Diagonios, Thessaloniki, 1984, *The
naked Couple,* Diagonos, Thessaloniki, 1990, *Lovers and Lairs,*
Samkaleen Prakasan, translated by Richard Scorza, New Deli (India)
1992, *The Divine Body*, Diagonios, Thessaloniki,1994, *Surplus of Seduc-
tion*, Bilieto, Athens, 1997, *Voluptuous Consignment*, Entefktirio, Thes-

saloniki, 2000, *Field of Lust*, Metaixmio, Athens, 2005, *Sensuality and Authority*, Metaixmio, Athens, 2009, *The Tragic and the Retreat of the Senses*, Saixpirikon, 2012, *Cloe and Alexandra*, Libros Libertad, translated by Manolis Aligizakis, Vancouver (Canada), 2013.

SWEET AFTERNOON

The shape of the square
and the houses which delineate it
with lit arcades
open air restaurants
and cafes, here
where the young people
flood the sidewalks
leave no empty table

the futility and sensual life of the city
drowned together, dissolved
into the sweet afternoon
and yet inescapable, here
where beauty thickens,
I entered with awe

PERFORMANCES

He declared imprudently
your poems are full
of sensuality and passion
and something else,
something exquisite,
I expected from you
the few times we've made love
I can't conceal it,
you have disappointed me.

For his own performance
in bed
and my appraisal of it
he neither asked
nor cared to know

THE LAST GARMENT

For a long time he had courted her
and when he found her on the beach
among acquaintances and friends
he spread his towel beside her
and as they lied very close, he touched her.
He got lucky
and was somehow surprised
by her immediate response
she stood up and led him
to a secluded remote beach
where they stopped
and from experience gained from former
love affairs
she knew the heat
she caused when she stood stark naked
and throwing off the final piece of her garments
she started going in and out of the water
many times and flamboyantly
as if to tell him
die wanting me

THE NAKED COUPLE

He got lost in the lush verdure
trying to find a path to the sea
while we stood somewhere higher and waited

he climbed puffing
let' s go further, the slope here
is too steep

on the other hand
the naked couple looked fine
among the trees
two bodies
joined in one
like a valued trophy
of the most innocent exploration

which our guide pointed to us later
when they also descended
to the same beach

THE PENCIL

The strange way you hold
the pencil excites me

I feel its pressure on the paper
its touch on the point
your fingers have substance
and form, and are contorted
around the pencil
like the desire which feeds
my soul

your ardor flows even when you write

THE AFTERNOON LIGHT

He was sitting at the next table
engaged in his own affairs
but every now and then
he turned to look at me
staring me in the eyes
it was the languid afternoon light
which bathed the tables
the clean tablecloths
and further on the rocks and the trees
and before all this happened
I was sunk in an overwhelming languidness
in an overwhelming peacefulness
which predisposed and prepared me
for such a thing to relish

in that wondrous light
a man staring at me

MY BAGGAGE

Violent acts and tragedies
aren't foreign to me
I've lived them as if
through fire and steel
if you search my body you will
discover their deep scars
I carry in my baggage
darkness, shadows and grief

I have certificates
introductory letters
and trials I have endured
and I can claim and enjoy
the sunlit and joyous events
the encounters and my immersion into joy
rarely experienced
become a right and gained time

I never feel guilty for euphoria felt

POEMS IN LATIN

They rolled around conflagrated by passion
still in seventh heaven by his kisses
she thought it was raining but he corrected her
it isn't rain but the crackling of the dry wood
the gardener is burning outside.

They got dressed and after he offered her a drink
he opened a book and read Horatio's poetry
from the original version
he red some erotic hymns
with his accent trills and sounds
and the juicy words in Latin

after their lovemaking they finished with verse

VIOLENTLY

They only had one erotic encounter
since they lived in different cities
life and distance kept them apart

yet what engulfed her the most wasn't his face
nor his smile but his fiery kisses when
while she was standing he stripped her naked
then violently he pushed her to bed face down
and before he even touched her back with his chest
he slapped her buttocks not at all harshly
saying arousing words to her

MINIMAL SPACE

At the beach, instead of sand
there were small, white pebbles
which hurt when you stepped on them barefoot
and when you lied down without a towel
I kept an eye on him
when just out of the water
he lied next to me
he joked with the others, he was pleasant
and all responded to him positively
in the generally joyous atmosphere
it took me sometime to realize that he pulled closer
turning upside, sideways, on his stomach
he seek to come close, to encircle me moving
over the hard pebbles without any concern
for scratches or pain. He got full of marks
fighting them. At one point, as if accidentally
lying flat on his back he raised his legs
and with gusto he placed them next to mine.

We almost touch, at the tip toes

It was enough for me
when the minimal space of our skin touched
I was given and I was received through it
we mutually connected through our tip toes

TOLIS NIKIFOROU

Tolis Nikiforou was born in Thessaloniki in 1938 to refugee parents from Asia Minor and Eastern Romelia. He studied business management in Thessaloniki, Athens and London. After the end of the dictatorship of 1967-1974 he returned to Thessaloniki and worked in his field until 1999. He was a regular contributor to the literary magazine *Nea Poreia* and he served as a member of the Company of Letters and Art of Northern Greece. His poetry books *The Double Alpha of Love, Soil in the Sky, Deep Blue for Goodbye, Egnantia Street, Eyes of the Panther, Nostos,* and his novel *Appeal of the Seconds* and others were published by the *Nea Poreia* publishers.

Since then the Athens publisher Mandragoras has released his books *Secrets and Miracles* and Nefeli publishers released his novel *Yellow Walk on the Grass* and his short stories collection *Road to Ouranopolis* which was awarded the first National Literary Award for the year 2009.

His poems have been translated in various languages and have been presented in anthologies around the world.

ENCHANTED SOUL

I fell in love with you
in the dirty neighborhood, in the factory
and on the colorless surface of the concrete

behind the street barricade
mixed in the strikes of the workers
during the student demonstrations
in the hallways of the courts
in secret meetings
in the darkness of the night
your name was written
in the fliers we distributed
on the red posters we put up on walls
and in the logs of the police force

I fell in love with you, my comrade
your enchanted soul is mine
my agony belongs to you

THE MOST BEAUTIFUL POEM

You've written the most beautiful poem
unparalleled verses
when a teenager you worked
in the cigarette factory
to earn enough for your books and bread

the most beautiful poem
the unparalleled verses you still write
on the court dockets and empty rooms
you recite them with crystal voice
before those who put children on trial
for selling newspapers and putting posters on walls

I stand up and kiss your forehead
I squeeze your hand as a comrade would do
I share your load with gratitude
poetess of the everyday life

THESSALONIKI 1980

Ravaged city in the contour of the bay
foreigners with colorful ribbons
and beads buy out your soul

panic
wild panic in the streets
and in the offices
and in the houses that stand up
and block the wind
as the dead rot of their books
exhumes a foul odor of rewards

ash, predatory shouts
the spring turned into an eunuch
with its blood coloring billboards
just a moment before the end

and Eros

goes around unsuspectedly
it doesn't wish to learn anything
Eros in the teary eyes of the girls

SHIVER

On wet lips
stretching slowly to the neck
between the breasts, shoulders
a dark shiver consumes the mind
flares up the knees
pierces into the marrow
it burns the skin
an omen of fever
and of the sort breath
that apexes methodically
and speeds up the pulse
that wakes every molecule of the body
nails thirst for blood
teeth search for blood
deeper ever deeper
powerfully more powerfully
shiver that creates the jerking
whisper that becomes moan
ejection that becomes numbness
abandonment that slowly fades

AS IF

Something between the words
when the skylight opens
like a trap door

something obvious and magical
like a wild female
an apparition
cawing of gulls
in the fog

something like perfume
a touch
a sensation
beyond the senses
something like light

between the words
something like light

LESSONS IN CREATIVE WRITING

The first lesson is called loss
that seals you
like fiery iron
small and defenseless

if you're strong and survive
you'll carry on with your studies
you'll read books
but will always look behind
towards the kindergarten of the neighborhood
and the silver olive tree leaves
under your balcony

these and love
will guide you
and perhaps one day they may turn
your open wounds into flowers

nothing remains but to look
the beast in the eyes
as it sucks your blood each day
on your path to a mountain peak
that doesn't exist

SMALL GREEN LEAVES

From smells to colors
to the last blood molecule
what promise the spring brings
what light
what shining illusion

still enchanted
we write its eternity on water
on the stone and on the wind
we add ineligible iotas
on the abyss of forgetfulness

small green leaves
we become a shiver
in the sky

ITS DEBT

Many a time since my school days
death has stared deep
in my eyes

frosty and dark glance
endlessly vacant
though vaguely saddened
made of sky and granite.

Thus I was meant to always live
my life passionately
always under the foul mouth of death

until one summer three years ago
he took me to the surgery table
for my last voyage to the unknown

yet somewhere by the slope of nothingness
I felt him suddenly whispering

your time hasn't come yet
the one unknown to man
wants more books from you
he thirsts for more of your blood

before its return home
your soul has to pay back to the world
the whole of its DEBT

MUSIC

Her dress rustles
like the dark forest against the wind

and my name in her voice
her breath mixed with mine

when her knees tremble
and open half way to my caress

my hand on her soft skin
as it seeks a secret river

whispers and moans
a long ahhhh that shivers in the air

and absolute quietness, ecstasy
in the thick velvety darkness

TOMORROW

When we'll meet
in a future life
during springtime
look deep in my eyes again
to remember my touch
how desperately I once loved you

when tomorrow becomes now
in Valparaiso or Vladivostock
in a faraway planet of the galaxy
don't forget me

beyond our small self
and beyond death
you and I will again become
the inextinguishable fire on earth
the red cloud in the sky

DINA GEORGANTOPOULOS

Dina Georgantopoulos was born in Vrahati, Corinth. She studied at the Law School of Athens. Her poems have appeared in various literary magazines on line and in paper form.

Her first poetry book *Caressing Myths*, translated into English by Manolis Aligizakis, was published in Vancouver, Canada, in 2015. Her second book of poetry, *Unpretentious,* was published in Athens by Vakxikon Editions.

HIGH TEMPERATURE

I fill and empty my cloths daily
coherently
in reverence
I fill and empty plates, glasses
carefully not to ruin them
in the high temperature
in the wholeness of my effort
I burn my hands that become
tools and erase stains
I no longer want to endure
to find my balance in the
high temperature
that existed long ago
and it took years to accomplish

truly it takes time to learn
the opposite of what
you have been doing all your life

THOUGHTS OF SNOW

I want to touch you
with the longing and joy
of the first snowflake on my hands

that the weight of great love
bends me
that I feel warm in the emotion
of what I've hidden in the snow

PINK BOWL

I took the pink bowl
from the drawer
filled it with
the wild aroma
of the ocean

I started washing
the dreams
whirling and
almost fragrant
I tied them on the wire
cloths line
in the sunshine

this the good wives do
I'm told

PLAYING WITH THE WAVES

Then I looked up
and far into the sea
I longed to see everything
then
I dreamed of long voyages
I spoke to the froth of clear thought
since yours was insignificant
it only wished to keep me near the land.
Small steps up front
turned into a run
and this to escape, which I thought
of having
then I argued with my other self
joyous and dreamy
lucky since it gave me
the gold keys
which I gift to you
to unlock your dreams one by one
to unlock them in places you can't
in places you don't dare.
Yet don't be afraid
perhaps you may get a bit wet
but remember how
you liked to play with the waves

LEVEL OF EMOTIONS

The level of my emotions
rises dangerously
but don't be concerned
while you sleep at night
I embroider wings

no, I don't think of
flying
but to cover my emotions
that they won't get wet

PERHAPS

Perhaps the melancholy of fingers
suspicion of the kiss
the side of history
perhaps a reflective thought

perhaps I touch the magic of Eros
speed up lives with shadows
perhaps the music of growth

perhaps nothing
perhaps everything

LEGS AND ROADS

You leave a mark on the heel
you look on the knees
for an explanation
for the red cheeks
for the pink bandana
difficult course
legs roads
legs love
beautiful new homeland.

I'll undo the pink bandana
that you'll deposit
your world on my legs

RECIPE FOR LOGIC

I kneed bread
give shape
to the amorphous

didn't know
they had given me
eyes lips hands
and love
relative ingredients
my daily recipe
truly
the proper use of things

lesson from the recipe book
of logic
for advanced students
who kneed bread

BODY ESCAPE

To get to know
a naked body
takes an eternity

it isn't enough to crown it
and honour it

it takes the soul's
depth and height
to open the gates of heaven
and hell

make sure never to escape
the edge of the fingers

BASEMENT

In the basement
the cigarette smoke ignores
philosophical opinions
it warms up
in cognac breaths
drunken stupor, yet
my lady, when men cry
love builds a bridge to God
in their mouths
and the scream becomes
a fifty cents song
in the crying juke box

behind the door
on the wooden hanger
forgotten in circular steps
life paints a statutory path
not anxious for dawn

GESTHIMANI SIDERIDIS

Gesthimani Sideridis was born in Sydney, Australia. When she was young her family returned to Greece where she studied at the Pedagogical Department of the University of Athens. She lives in Athens and works for the Public Schools. Her dedication to the written word and her inclination to the arts in general guided her steps to painting, poetry and literature in general.

Many of her poems have been published in poetry anthologies, literary magazines and online.

Painting is her new form of expression in which she defines her aspirations and imagery through colors and shapes. She finds inspiration in whatever she comes across and her subjects are nothing but today's human condition and man's perception of the environment and his relationship to it.

THE UNKNOWN SOLDIER

Nothing light and feathery
smelling of cinnamon and honey tonight

the unknown said —

observing the killed fishes
by the marble ledge of the window
with their weary entrails thrilled
at the bite of the wasps
that longed for a gram of death

nothing sweet

the unknown soldier said —

not even a single honeybee
only murder and blood tonight

he said —

ROUTINE

And the routine that wage war evaporates
naturally and without special choices
with coffee and cigarettes
the smoke comes from the East
like clacking

all the rest are from here, local
the television promotes our habits

what is blood, you may ask me

red fluid that makes a mess
therefore I see the messy landscape daily
as I have coffee and cigarettes

the lies smell through the windows here
and treason's everywhere

it's the same, you may say
here simply
the blood is messing noiselessly

I WAITED

It was calm in the island
the moon hanged from the sky
red fluid poured in the black sea

calm moon and calm sea
calm boats, motionless

I held the little umbrella in one hand
the red light was afraid
in my other hand a green anchor
and I stood on the silent rock

I was also calm like the rock
and I waited
for the wave to bring you back

the sea was also calm

MY ROOM

On the other side of the wall
the canary dictates an erotic symphony
while it spreads the next distance on the wire.
On this side of the wall
a shoeshine boy shines the shoes of the traveller
with silent movements

until evening and the next morning
like any other day
my room will vibrate with notes
and shoe polish

NOTHING

This way the points of colon assume their importance
when you finish, you start
with the unfinished business
the full stops hang onto the balcony of resistance.

Who said that I was in reverie
after all it's not summer yet
nor a moon hanging from the railing
with a pale suspicion
perhaps a drop of dew from the basil

nothing

the night stopped promising
a clear lake of words
perhaps imaginary

nothing

yet always better

always nothing

TOMORROW

Nothing reminds of yesterday
they all resemble wilted spinsters
make their faces to cover ugliness
lined up like the stuffed animals in the bazaar
waiting for another rejection.

Tomorrow I'll close my eyes and go to the plaza

BLACK AND WHITE HATS

Hats hang midair on the opposite sidewalk.
Only hats, with no bodies, without souls
unknown identities yet they hang midair
gracefully. Black and white hats
sometimes in one color: white or black
primarily black

I gaze them in surprise

I question myself

am I still visible?

EMPTY ROAD

The empty road smelled of moisture
light fluff covered the grass
and only the poplars
created shady signs of movement

she held the handkerchief
tightly in her dry hand
a little detail of lace jutted out

he took her wrist tenderly

my love ships don't pass by here
the voyage requires strength —

he said to her and pulled
her handkerchief affectionately

YELLOW LEAVES

He dripped red wine in a conch
he licked a hot peppery memory
drunken yellow leaves sparkled
on his body fleetingly.

Who said autumn
drips sadness?

Falling leaves mean rebirth.

IFIGENEIA SIAFAKA

Ifigeneia Siafaka was born in Athens. She graduated from the Classics Department of the University of Athens and she has worked as an educator, article writer, translator and editor of various publications. Her books are focused on students and educators and are available by her publisher, *Gregoris* (Essays 2000) She has also published *The Song of Lygka*, a novel, 2011, *The Knitted and Other Machinations,* short stories, 2013, *Metalipsi*, prose poems, 2015. Since 2016 she is responsible for the editorial work of the prose and poetry periodical anthology (Thraka 2016). Her articles, critiques and pieces of creative writing have been published in various literary magazines.

Ifigeneia lives in Brussels.

PERFUME

You got rid of overtime
a resting Sunday
a thud and a reverse smile
shreds of exile decoration thrown into the vase
Oliver Twist offered them out of court
honeysuckle in the bulb holes all night long
long as the saints clean up the cotton
the yellow vanilla of the wounds

LEATHER NIGHT

They run barefoot under the starlight
that sowed the teeth of the sea
in the night gathering
the tongue sewed glass onto the sea lapping
flesh was cut into a sandal

to wear me when you deny yourself, she was heard

you're a night made of leather, God, I mumbled
and you will drag me along all alone
with my footprints like casted dice

BANNER

At the edge of the precipice
we tamed chaos with our tongue
crying babies without a maid
with exposed fingers
we entertained the body with vertigo

the dragon climbed up the mountain
and placed a banner on top of it.
We made blankets of our tongues
and we've since sailed the seas silently

PICTURE

Glance on the deserted eyebrow
his head leaned on the edge of the tiles
shawls on slabs made of conceiting clay
rustle of lust during the nights
moist sky by the lamppost
fate rattled its disguise in the side streets

tourists took pictures
of gigantic shadows on stone walls
airy bodies of loneliness
scales on the snowy slabs
sunny massive sculls

VYNIL

Ink flows from the shell of the cuttlefish
the bitter shiver of Acheron on evergreen mirrors
drinks us as in its tavern
Dante's needle cries for music
in the barcarole of revolutions
and from deep inside us its oar
nothing but the hollowed heel Cerberus
bends in its mouth and spits

the twilight barks on the gunwale
and a dancing ivy
emancipates dark nails
from where the blind foreigner will dawn

WAITING

Fleeting silent inescapable
roads expand under the roofs
the epitaphs slip like white bands
the rooster's comb lays a sheet
that some call shroud
others call it sanctifying buckle of wounds
ancient dust on the car
lovers whisper in the back seat
spring troparion, a plain salutation
they fix their hair, undergarments, eyelids
when the resurrection backstabs them
and they, always optimistic
wait for her with a pale dagger
hanging behind the windshield

BUTTON

The dead are waiting for us
laying in wooden beds for hours
with the wolf's smile, with the lace of fire
chaste, self-sufficient in the heat of the last goodbye

Plastic Lazarus blow treason
through their nostrils like morning dew
the words unpicked their button
thread hanging from their lips
leads to illusion

unfairly the traitors were never
resurrected on earth

PENALTY IN HEAVEN

And he was climbing toward the sky
riding his bicycle and shouting so loud
that he blocked the directions and iotas of the angels
and a traffic jam was created before
the ordination of the selected few in Heavens
and the alleluias collided with the hand grenades
pricking unsuspecting heads onto the soil

stay aside that I enter, he shouted and threw
one by one all his hats off his head
towards the balding men who guarded
the Gates with their metal teeth

he kept his beheading for the end
and with a feather in the shape of spear
he offered his head as penalty
and he became the victor

MEMORY

Today is the birthday of the prehistoric anemone
our shadows become flames on stamens
the dream gurus talk all night long
the owls suckle on watches
the turtle thighs rot on the clock fingers
when cuckoos plant the birthday escapes

we've kept a chair as holy tube for eons
umbilical mud and rust —
we, the ex-vitro anemones of memory
with an extracorporeal bone in our eye
with the thrice denying cock:
our larynx is full of ash

SISSY DOUTSIOU

Sissy Doutsiou was born in Athens. She studied astrophysics at the University of Sussex and theatre at the drama school of Delos. She's an actress and poet and a founding member of the Institute of Experimental Arts and participates in collective *Void Network*. Performances: 4.48 Psychosis, Dying as Country, The Maids. Performance: Resistibility, Anatoli (Calcutta - India). Participated in poetry reading at the 1st Athens Biennial *Destroy Athens* .She toured for lectures, performance, video art exhibitions in USA, Mexico, India and Nepal.

In collaboration with the Experimental Institute of Arts, she supervised and taught theatre seminars.

Books: poetry collections *Insult of Public Modesty, Oh ! Occult*, participation in the essay "We are an Image from the Future (The Greek Revolt of December 2008) ed . AK Press USA.

THE BRIDE

Teary brides and the screaming live coal walkers.
The miracle that wasn't.
Indescribable desperation.
Let your wish come true.
The tender legs of your woman are open
each morning the master gives orders
the slaves obey.
His woman a whore
on plain pink bedsheets
beyond a shred of enthusiasm
under green dreams
inside a house.
Absent euphoria
books, comics, stones, napkins thrown on the floor
sweaty shorts and salty inside shirts.
A sharp pain
I contract my legs
bend them to my chest
a small flock of birds
welcomes my tears in front of your eyes
I think of the river Ouse
as if balanced on blonde thorns, you inspect the bruises
as they play like children one against the other
male-female-neuter genders.
I'm sorry, but today I'll leave.
Some children are doomed to grow.

BLASPHEMY

I hope when I get very tired I won't have to carry alone
my valuable body to hell
I the protector of a pandemic Eros
when Aphrodite is bored in Heaven
and caresses the hot squirted sperm

I could imagine myself
like a domesticated animal
that they take care of me
they love me
they feed me
they pet me

I wish to be of the opposite gender
a male
with liberated morale
with an admirable decency
a melancholy character
with unparalleled tenderness

that I wouldn't need to struggle
for anything

blasphemy —

the center of pleasure
allows ecstasy flow
unimpeded. Certainty
of pain was the only desire
the only proof that I've existed

the seductive hermaphrodite
gifted with shining skin
since its twelve year
forgets every law and authority
joined into one being forever.
Samalkis who kissed him with zest
hugging him tight. Cursed let it be
the Sea of Karia, southwest of Asia Minor

a very dirty female sucks up lust
from her wounded pride.
One multiplies his joys
when one shows respect
to perversions

blasphemy

LEVIATHAN

The black sea
thick unexplored bottom
big waves, exulted sea froth
the only ones who survived Leviathan

dark
fearful
powerful

the peace of its seafloor
passage to Hades
you won't need to bribe with bronze coins
trembling before the dark endlessness is enough
your relatives won't need to feed death
under your tongue: nothing

Acheron is sorry
Cocytus wails
Phlegethon explodes
Lethe forgets
Styx hates

lives tied
to various places
you haven't imagined
pirates
construction sites
sailors

breaths of men chained on gigantic anchors
they put aside skates and red fishes
to report a full cargo to the port authorities
cosmetics and accessories for women

last breaths of mammals
with their eyes pulled by the metal net
plastic colorful hands
disembowel schools of fish

they just have time for a cigarette
the sea is angry
tyrant and at the same time
savior of the earth
industry sounds and
the cries of Atlantic
buzzing
and the rough unfamiliar
Leviathan

details give you vertigo
the magenta's light is low
about thirty five per cent

each instrument in its place
for its hanging
for its underwater killing
chains, hooks, pipes.

A load of blood
the blood of sea weed
dried exotic conches
wrinkled star fishes that shed tears
and dried up corals —
wrinkled memories of a sea floor

plastic blue gloves
remind you the color of dawn
stow beauty in orange plastic pails

souvenir from Portugal, mom,
buy me that sea horse,
it's so nice

Dead.

Men like machines
with no emotions
frozen eyes
cold
the wind that makes you
think only of hunger
wine
cigarettes
a chubby cunt to fuck
repeated movements
repetition kills tenderness
repetition
cynic words
and survival.

A trap door that spits blood
and pieces of rotten sea meat
twenty four degrees and fifteen minutes north latitude
seventy six degrees west longitude
alone
in the ocean.

Parts of the ship
rectangular shapes
square and multi-angular
with schisms
the heavy and salty sea water
goes through
fills and
empties
rocks

when the rusted shapes fill
with men near death
the sea
washes them clean
freshens them
until they die of asphyxiation

a load made of corpses

their fate was common
to stop
running inconceivably in the sea floor

SAME LONELINESS

Same loneliness
same pain
in all the metropolises of the world.
Lonely girls wearing short cheap skirts
they bought in China Town.
Boys who beg for a few cents
in the frozen wagons of New York
where all the co-passengers with severed fingers
held together in their pockets
are ready to crawl in their apartment.
Skyscrapers and multi leveled high-rises.
Human bodies chained
on the roofs of the high buildings
as the planet continues its course in space.
As the planet continues its course in space
a vacant glance
keeps guard behind the window
staring at the busy street.

Loneliness is the same in all
the metropolises of the world.

Institutions, schools, banks, city offices
alienated mothers with red eyes
stay locked in their suites
full of anxiety about today
and tomorrow.
Civilization that focuses
in the satisfaction of ownership.

Loneliness remains the same.

Hundreds of rail lines of subterranean trains
ready to disembowel
any joy or happiness
as the trains constantly breath
our dreams die of asphyxia
in the endless paths of Wall Street.

Loneliness remains the same
in all the metropolises of the world.

In concentration camps of the migrants
in concentration camps of contemporary workers
their houses next to the gas stations and restaurants
in private streets ready for sale.
Loneliness is the same
in the morning wake-up call of the civil servant
in London
in Berlin.
Loneliness is the same
in the desperate smile of the strikers
and in the hope of the prisoners.
Loneliness is the same
in the graves of the anarchist comrades in Chicago
and in the graves of the murdered comrades in Athens.
Loneliness of the impossible
of compassion
of the slave who wants to rebel.
Loneliness is the same until we become victorious.
As the planet continues its course in space
we shall plan for our freedom.

As the planet continues its course in space
we are free.

Loneliness remains the same
as long as we are slaves.

As the planet continues its course in space
we shall plan for our freedom.

YOU MAY BURY ME ALIVE

You may bury me alive
in the earth
it wouldn't bother me.
You may put me
in a narrow casket
it wouldn't bother me at all
that I couldn't move my fingers
I would die —
you may bury me alive
deep in the earth
that I couldn't hear the sobs and sorrow of my friends
I wouldn't be upset
without pity
without my empty heart
and my sister's whispers
with no help
alone, it wouldn't bother me
the whispers of my friends
with no help
alone
my death.
You may bury me alive
it wouldn't bother me
that I would smell the moist soil
in the earth
it's always moist, it never gets dry in the earth
the soil is always emotional
I could dig deep in the soil
under this life
under this life
a layer of dead people exists
under our feet

our dead sleep
under the foundations of this world
sick bodies rest
tiring thoughts
bleeding heroes
sacrifices
fetuses
wise old men
under this life
they caress the soil
skeletons of memory
love letters
old pictures
you may bury me alive
it wouldn't bother me at all
that I couldn't breath
in the darkness
no problem
under our world
the endless white sea of the cursed people flows
the last efforts for survival spasm
I encourage you to bury me alive
I don't like much sensationalism
I admit my wish
for a triumphant elation
to exist with truthfulness
beyond the hot asphalt
alive
for a while
so long as I last
so long as I last.

MY LOVE

My love
the body ages
the voice becomes hoarse
but the essence remains the same
being horny remains the same
I want our love to last forever
I don't want you to die
I want to keep you in my arms forever
I know this is impossible
I know one day you'll disappear among the clouds
far away from me
far away from everyone
I love you
I love your eyes
your beautiful glance
I don't want to miss you in the endless infinity
I'm your true lover
your most willing lover for ever
death is an ever beautiful monster
that leaves memories behind it
images and sounds
days dedicated to the people we love

I love you

TZOUTZI MANTZOURANI

Tzoutzi Mantzourani was born in Athens – Greece, in 1959. She studied French Literature and Language at Pepperdine University, Malibu, CA. USA, and worked as a journalist in several Greek newspapers and magazines until 2009. She has published four poetry collections and a book of short stories. She has translated theatrical pieces from Greek into English and is currently working on a translation of Dorothy Parker's work in Greek. Her work has been translated in French, Spanish and English. She lives in Athens Greece.

TEARS

The most bitter tears are those
which never flow down the eyes
the most dynamic orgasms
are silent
the deepest desperation
hides behind a smile
the most strength a person can find
is when he's paralyzed from fear
the brightest light
you can see in the darkness of death
and you can talk about your life
by what you have left behind
when you die

DAWN

Dawn is almost here
the city lights flicker
and vanish in the rosy color of the sky
your warm and rhythmic breath
plays with my nerves
on the bed.
Traces of you have vanished from my life
though I'm looking for them
under the cold bed-sheets.
Dawn is almost here
the alarm will come on
I'll hug you
and you'll purr like a kitten
you'll kiss me absentmindedly
and you'll leave for your work.

WOUND

Sweet wound
with purple red blood
dripping
wound of love
with the shadow of separation
in the big eyes.
Look at me.
Kiss me.
Let me sweeten your pain.
Give me your hand
hold me tight
don't be afraid
when I stand next to you
nothing can hurt you
and when I'll leave
I'll still be with you

MEMORY

Memory erases
everything with a mop
when it wishes
memory only retains
the wrong deeds
yet so sweet
so lustful
so deep entrenched.
Aha. Memory
I've forgotten your face
I don't even remember
your eyes.
Only, when the weather changes
I remember two words
words like a sharp knife
two words no more
when we separated.
Which words I don't remember
only that sharp sting
that momentary ache
I felt in the lonely heart
this I only remember.

THE FLAME

My life nothing but a flame
of a small candle
burning next to the icons
thin candle, slender
its flame melts the body
slowly down
silently and humbly
next to other candles
wish, prayer and hope
burn together
with despair and bitterness.
The candle finally turns into
an amorphous mass
mixed with the sand
and the wick
the flame goes out
as the candle burns to its end
yet life doesn't end
nor does tiredness rest
the soul pulls itself
from one candle to the other
so that the flame remains always lit

WRINKLES

These small wrinkles
on the edge of the eyes
incisions of pain, the soul's
deep scars
and that furrow
between the eyebrows
the rough seas of life
enclosed deep inside her.
Tightened lips
she hardly dares to smile
in fear that for this she'll pay
eventually.
Oh life!
You've given me everything
a moment later
from the time I could
enjoy them.

FORGETFULNESS

Vacant glance, dark
you pierce the wall
you nail my heart
and it bleeds, it hurts.
It still beats and endures
until death can calm
your tired body
and forgetfulness embraces
your soul.
Until they all forget you
and you forget of them
until life commences
its march again

LACK OF WORDS

I don't know what else to say
suddenly my words vanish
I can't continue writing to you.
Then this sharp pain stabs my heart
it cuts my soul in two
one piece of it remains on the earth
the other up high in the light
it follows you on your voyage
into the serenity of another world.
Then suddenly
you gaze me with your empty eyes
and you tell me with your silence
that I don't belong with the dead.
You leave, I miss you
I stay alone
in the empty room
in the half side of our bed
in my empty soul
as I hold one hand with the other
tightly as if to regain my courage

MANOLIS MESSINIS

Manolis Missinis was born in Athens where he resides now. He's a writer, a poet, essayist and dramatist, and he has cooperated with literary magazines and newspapers online and in paper form. His texts, literary and with social subjects have been translated into English, French, Spanish, German, Hindu, Kurdish and have been published in literary forums on line and in paper form.

UNALTERABLE

Fantasy allows variations
to the other memories

       to the froth of the sea
       that touches the fingers of shadows
       stepping on the keys of time
       or the sky's darker shade
       heavy over the horizon during the night

but to that image
which my eyes saw
at that moment
but to the image that remains
motionless on my lips
fantasy can't add anything

CITY STREETS

Streets of this city
endless streets of my heart
sometimes warm filled with light
other times cold dividers
full of purple people
dancing virginal primeval rhythms
and the other streets of this city
sometimes sad memories
same paths of my heart
they draw closely
black and white archaic
and contemporary circles
I know tomorrow
my path will be as wide as the sky
with thousands of footsteps
designing its new tree line

that today is only rocky ruin
bitter, twice loved

PRECIOUS POETRY MOMENT

My integral moment
inconceivable concept
that stirs my thoughts
and shoots the daily routine
to endlessness

immortal moment
my warm bread, my breath
wide opening of my soul
love offering
on the table of the cosmos

FEELINGS

I don't remember the day —

      they alter time

I know how it started
in the first drop of dawn
when my palms got filled with dew
and my eyes with light

ABSENCE

It was hard to open the creaking door
my hair full of cobwebs
I tasted the sense of abandonment
I opened to the light
the dust appeared
an insect sat on the worn out curtain
I shut the window shutters

sorrowful abandonment

mark of the picture frame remained on the side
I recall it now
as I entered I saw it

once I broke its support
but we didn't discard it

what then?

I was away for a long time
soon as I came back all others were gone
yet the picture frame left its mark

the shape of absence tyrannizes one

COMEDY

You can only be of certain
qualities these days
people want you that way
full of foliage and
prone to many needs
sweet voiced and
prone to cloudlessness

I said

and took the path of self-contention

I followed the funeral procession of an unknown
as if to participate in something common
as it was expected of me

yet my diverse views lurked
like my secondary intentions

no painting figure has any control
none of the statues is self-preserved
gods with tragic faces
like Marilyn Monroe, James dean, Maria Callas
their existence depends on their fans

SIZES

When you get emancipated by the sizes
which allow you to see only their surface
which put in order what is of and because of them
be sure not to be just a thought
of the microcosm that dresses itself
a gigantic idol of itself
a mythical event
that never becomes reality

when you get emancipated
by the tendency of conviction
you'll notice the events
beyond the mimicry of conspiracy
but an expression beyond a glance
the turning of a page which swallows its load

when you get emancipated by the sizes
you realize they are just a matter of distance

MYTHICAL TEMPEST

I've always longed

to have a white
boat
a room full
of books
and a second voice
like the monosyllable yell
of the animal
to scare the black birds

to declare on paper
the personal
crucifixion of every man

to learn the proper sound
while tuning the violin
to learn a language
with clear words
to announce *life*
and the word echoes musically

I've always longed
to have even the secret
of my position in the picture
the void of which
one day I shall fill

THESE STREETS

These streets lead no where
they tend to the next
proceed or remain in the dark cell
plenty of suggestions and other similar images
these streets are unpassable
and the skin of the animal follows
deep scars and memories of hatred
where darkness imposes the night
these streets transcend silence
repeated like selected dialogue

LEGENDARY EMOTIONS

Since the answers fight to escape
and the impressions postpone
since the conscious gallows incise
a contour line leading to nothing
come, let us taste the smell of hopeless

that a thunderous wave may rise
just the finale of degradation
a lascivious bulldozing of exclamations
the decapitation of black comedy

and don't be content with regular screams
for some salvation just to stay safe
you, poor bird, that you've been taught
to survive in the cage

MARY MAVRONAS

Mary was born in Corfu. Her poems have appeared in various magazines such as *Aeolian Letters, Refuge, Calaino* and in various articles written for newspapers. Her word has been recognized in a few national poetry competitions. In 1999 she received the first poetry prize at the New Movement organized by the writers of Thessaloniki. She has also been awarded the first prize of the Macedonian Literary Company, and the first prize for *Free Verse* awarded by the literary magazine *Calaino*. Her poetry has been published in the Poetry Anthology 2015, published by *Ostria* publishers of Athens and in the annual calendar *Ah Eros* published by *Vergina*. Her poems appeared in the collection *Hellenic Verse and its Evolution since the 10ᵗʰ Century* published by Panagiota Zaloni in 2014.

She was recognized by the Literary World of Corfu and in 2012 her work has appeared in *Anthology of Awarded Poets 1995-2011* published by the Macedonian Artistic Society.

Mary Mavronas lives in Athens.

BEYOND TIME

I spring from inside out with a sour smile
waters of illusion charge against pieces of my nightmare
human cry
don't be afraid of the stars
they dissolve the shadows, they tame darkness, they raise the sun
from the dowry of the ocean.

The dream bends and helps sprout flags and lacy designs
it only leaves a tender glance like
my southern evening star.
Hug me
I'm tenant of a doll made of moon milk.

My limbs flow on the map of angels
they distance themselves
to love lands without anchors
to exchange the color
of the lustful passion
that the doves will fly
that the crucified will smell of honey and pollen.

The night gropes on mythical cells
it gathers the seas which danced in the temples
it crowns aged sounds of corals reverently.
I stagger onto the shores of the night.
Fleshless threads of Sirius and Orion
couple along the unspoken elements of my shape
I lean onto the altar of the night
to grab onto the drops of an untraveled line
like deep purple winter sleep.

An unused ring shook off its ashes.

Tonight I come out of myself like an out of the world caress.
Cosmoses and ethers flow in my idol.

Touch me.
I am a tenant of silver.
I drip moist beyond time.

WEDDING IN HELL

Crooked, twisted corners
the ceiling descends
with them
silvery stamp on the lips
a white pomegranate tree
the bride has the sign of Hell.

The walls wailed all night long
attentively I listen to the ceiling
narrating its experience
of the wedding

It admired, it said,
the linen crutch of the groom

IF YOU SEE ME

If you see me by the ancient seas
at night
to tighten the strings of hexapteryga
call me to show you
the way the kingfisher colors itself

THE MASK

The shape of the snake breaks each of my secret spoils
it stabs tears in the water
and that thread that loaded me with squares
totters motionlessly
some lunatics around the table
use conches to exchange fire
Eros mimics itself as if existing
and all people clap I don't recall why.

I don't want the scared taste of wine on my legs
nor the defeat counting the untameable
I search for my race, to contain me unwrinkled
with no decorations nor flatteries of death.
I sign onto the untraveled red of the sea
to embark onto a trial of kiss.

On the excess of my mask I shine a vein
water and fire on the bed of Astarte

just a little absinthe to her memory

SHARING

The night descends upon us
silence cuddles as we seduce our viscera
with the shroud of a new moon
perhaps we could stay whole
in the heart of the clock.
Dusted by the absence of gods and Eros
tamed in our starry projections
a heavy tear feeds on passes
baptizing bodies made of itinerant lust

and I question myself
how to name my homeless drunkards

UNFAMILIAR

The by chance unfamiliar absence
eons and seas added onto the map
reverently observing the bloodied temple
you didn't see me when I stepped
onto the black blade

IDOL

Tonight I want to put on a shroud
of the ones we gift to the
insubordinate
of the internal world
as I think of the number twelve
and that cross eyed poet
who leaves a stamp in the fire
so that it will last all winter
and I want to make love to his idol.

Perhaps as we stare each other
we may paint
the widow of our shadows white

HIEROPHANTS

They all left
beasts and hierophants
even those who flooded
the tides with lust.
I longed for nothing from you
only I begged you to give me
the kiss of Hesperides

THE COST OF A PYRE

We stole a verse
from the stars
an eagle's footprint
a night long vigil

lust is
an unfamiliar burial
that leaves us
untouched and
with the cost
of the death pyre

HARIS PSARAS

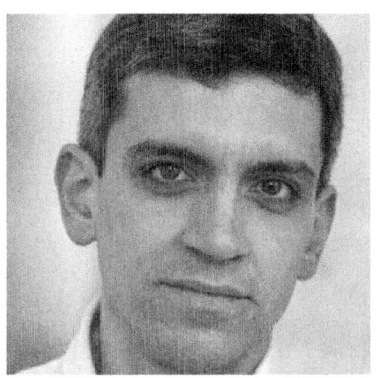

Harris Psaras (Athens, 1982) studied law at the Universities of Athens and Oxford. He received his Ph.D. from Philosophy of Law from the University of Edinburgh. He is a lecturer and fellow jurist of the St. Catharine's College at the University of Cambridge.

He has published the following poetry books *Gloria in Excelsis* (Kedros, 2017), *True Beings* (Kedros, 2012), *Glory in Carelessness* (Kedros, 2008), *In the Circle's Embrace* (Kedros, 2004). His poems have been translated into English, French, German, Romanian and Slovenian. He has, from time to time, published essays, studies, translations and narratives.

RECOGNITION

Time is a watch that shows the wrong hour
the past that will reoccur

the blonde you met yesterday at the steam baths
was Eve, Adam's lover

DESDEMONA

In your black arms,
breeze of love, you enclose me

you, my lover
the world's destruction

will occur, as Shakespeare
would have ordered in the fifth act.

The vortex of the mind births
jealousy which undresses us

PARADISE LOST

Spread your wings, fly in the wind
vigorously fly overseas.
Where we've reached is the end
of life on earth. Are you still here?

Rush, prepare for a flight to the sun
look, better to reach there early. You need it.
You have to run away from her, even by force.

Why you delay? It's now or never.
There's no if or perhaps. Words such as these
echo in Icarus' ears ever so often.

DISINTERMENT

Und sie gruben

I dug deep in the soil and rediscovered you.
I saw you digging to meet me.
We were made of dirt. You longed to touch me.

I was digging inside you. You were digging inside me.
We were digging from end to end
with fortitude believing and hoping
we were digging and thinking of our digging
and while resting, we dug in our sleep.

Sometime ago our hands belonged to us
we could tighten our fists, stretched our fingers.
They don't belong to us anymore, they're foreign to us.
They've become the hands of the one
who asked us to dig in his light.

He too was digging next to us
like a friend. The pulse of our body was alive.

He was digging next to us
to make us believe that we were truly digging
that we wouldn't say
that what remained after the echo of digging stopped
was the moist soil drying in the wind

REFLECTION

The door we didn't open leads
to the rose garden
to the true conflict, between the rose and the thorn
and each error a thick foliage
that hides inside it the birds from the hunter.

The world but a stage show of a travelling troupe
the director quenches his thirst stooping
in the themele. He mistook it for the mouth of the well.
Further on frogs croaked, sang
Attic tragedians with their heavy tones

Time the flowers' withering and its counting
cast on a healthy leg. Who has the courage?
Eve and Odoaker dared
but half way on the journey their shoulders gave up
their courage cost them Heaven and Rome

PARALLEL CAUSUALTIES

The sun is more blind that Homer
its black light unfolds inside us
in the eyes of death we're all civilians

You lay down early. You subdue the voice of love.
You say: I'm human
in your sleep you destroy and rebuild Troy.

The dead Hector throbs in your veins
and you run, a vassal of your blood.
Your daily innocent life tries to relax
by turning the pages: yet an Atreides.

Homer was blind too. The sun is also blind.
Death drafts both the good and the evil.
I regret means I narrate in detail
how Hecuba and Priam perished.

DEEP IN THE EARTH

A wedding was taking place deep in the earth
I heard the wedding gown of the butterfly
crumbled up high, flowers
disturbed the sleep and
I, a shadow in the depth, cried.
Poplars placed their crowns
on the pillow of my sister
her eyes turned fiery
and on her shoulder
a fragment of the sun was glorified.
Our father got up
spanked her to death
later he opened a bank account for her
and went to the amusement park to die.
Yet, the pain won't let up not for a moment
glued on me
like a kiss on the lips
since some were getting married in the earth
and the celebration there lasts
for at least three days
and with violins, tabors and lekythoses

FORECAST

The weather man was wrong, each of his comments
turned melancholy and that was just his view
and with what eyes can one explain
the fluctuations of the weather now?
Oh, come rain, fall, hey you rain, come to calm
the basic errors that we didn't take into account
scientific symposiums whether
it may hail or not, or the air may be choking.
Straight from the Planetarium
to his rented apartment
homely serenity, familiar space
the faithful wife is waiting for him
an oracle of his face, sweet
and for a long time errorless

DRUM

Hesitant before the chords
the wind is missing
neither string nor wind instrument
the drum speaks with its skin.
It wants to be hit hard
by all new drummers
who learn to hit in rhythm.
The drum guides them with its sounds
hands up and down obvious mouthpieces
the resisting drum guides them.
Children become rough this way
street after street in a parade
their first childish attitude wasted.
And since their heart has calmed down
like the membrane of the drum
how it hardened, how it stopped being normal
how it lost its friendly, old arrhythmia?

ELENI MARINAKIS

Eleni Marinakis was born in Chania where she lives. She studied graphic design and painting in Athens, where she worked for several years. She has published seven poetry collections and her up-coming collection is "I'm Counting to the Ten". She has also written the introduction and the poetic comments on two photo albums.

Her poems have been published in literary journals, in printed form and electronic and have been included in anthologies. In 2006 poems of hers were presented in a theatrical performance by the Theater Company Memory, based in Chania.

At the same time she is engaged in visual arts.

She is a member of the Society of Writers, the Poetry Circle and the Chamber of Fine Arts of Greece.

JUGGLER

Hard to fly with poetry
and I didn't spread
my wings.
I kept fallen leaves
and small rabbits in my living room.
The lonely band played
during the anniversaries
I opened my eyes timidly
fields of olive groves shaded my hat
a swing committed me to the void.

Thus, I grew up with crumbs
I earned my share of food
working the trapeze.

Since then I'm scared of the straight lines
the end of the horizon
the quick fading of the white.

Now I crouch under bridges
of dried up rivers
just to have
my own nothing

TIME BACK THEN

On a rainy Sunday
you opened so I'd talk to you

I wore black on my arms
since my childhood
I was climbing hills
with doves.

The white sky would appear
to lull me
the slant eye of embarrassment
sank the high noon

the leaping hours sweated
grandmother pealed the summer
with her hairpin
silence passed by like wind
gathering the months, the days
the Sundays I've forgotten

the years I haven't seen you.

HERE

You went hunting again
to harvest dreams

on the opposite branch
birds perch quietly
only the wolf
suspects the trap
of the void you created
that grew larger
inside you
during the nights.

In this small area
you'll learn to walk

BRANCHES

I cut my branches
one by one
I dry them
like emotions
that I subdue
each evening
that they won't grow
leaves to cover me.

Then, reverently
I put them
on the ground
I sing to them
a demotic song
and I bury them
in the deep pit
of the garden

THE HORSE

Father would
take me for a ride
to the cane fields
to listen to the wind
that blew and
the animals panicked

behind the blackberry bushes
the flowers were ripped
and a bitter moist
met the high noon

and look,
the horse's neighing
in the clearing
motionless for years

SORROW

This is the way with sorrow
sometimes you look
in the window pane
and you see your old idols

you see mother
in the sixties
in her dress
walking on the sidewalk
auntie Elliniki
with sea floor in her eyes
you see father
flying over a plain
in his gray suit

you see John
to gather wet sand
to build towers
made of paper

GRADE

Suffering passes by our place
leaves something on the table
the party is stopped, the musicians'
songs stopped half way

What will happen now
that darkness came
and the taste of our voice changed
silence returned, dripped red color
in our glasses
that our cracks get moist
our breath turned to blood
the world became night over our yard.

TURN OF THE HEAD

I'll keep the pictures
momentary click that enters memory
as you turn your head

Time is bitter
when you look into the past.
It doesn't give you a second
to make another movement
to turn your arms
a noiseless pass to continuum

Change your life there
in the 9x12 centimeters
of a regular day

REJECTION

We all know it well:
time
consumes our fingers
hurriedly
exactly at the time
when we ask
for a faint touch
to warm up

CARELESS BUTTERFLY

Lord, give me the wings
I lost in gardens
the peplos I ripped at night
the dust I spread here and there.
Lord, give me again
the colors I entrusted
to usurers hunters of dreams

I stripped my soul naked
and I'm cold

VASO KOSMIDIS

Vaso Kosmidis was born in western Peloponese where she graduated from high school. Since then she has lived in Athens where she studied business management and marketing. She worked and managed a major fashion company of Athens. She specialized in human resources, working conditions and personnel advancement in every field, as in the work environment, family status, benefits, health and education.

She has volunteered in various artistic organizations with the scope of promoting all forms of artistic expression. Her poetry has been published in magazines and she released her first poetry book *Short and Untitled* in 2017 with a second book ready for publication in the autumn of 2018.

PLAY

Come, let us play
in the yard

I said—

to drip
sweat and blood
of joy

not of forgetfulness.

Never say
was I ever a child?

BURIAL

You bury life
inside you

and you hope
with a

life come out

to give back to it
its lost soul

PARADISE

I live the earthly
Paradise
where earth
graces us with
the smallest flowers

the garden you're tending
beautiful in its reduction

that it creates
our superb scenarios

not those of Paradise

TRUTH

You declare
you long to discover
truth

but when
spontaneously
it shows itself

strip naked

you call it
a whore

FOOTPRINTS

Our footprints
in the sand
vanish
of the wind's blow

now only those
of our bodies remain

in our souls
they hide away
from winds
and rough seas

eternal marks
that we were
one body
once

BALANCE

Hard to half live
somehow
with your heart
that wants to run
to spread its wings

and your mind
that always
puts on the breaks

your unbalanced
life shutters

CLOUD

The tender cloud
isn't afraid

to touch the mountain peak

to hug it

to moisten it

to impregnate it

and you're
always afraid

to climb

PEACE

Don't hide
the sun of peace.

How can I rise?

Your logic
dusk.

My childish glance
sunrise

With that childhood
dream in hand
I still hold the world
which I seek
and peace
among the ruins
of an endless war
I wish to find

STRAW HAT

Under my straw hat
I hide
my loneliness
my companion
and shade

memory book
for the cold
winter nights
when the lone anemone
blooms
in the snow

NEKTARIA MENDRINOS

Nektaria Mendrinos was born and raised in Athens. She studied at the University of Athens, Faculty of Pharmacy, and since 2003 she maintains a pharmacy in Apokoronas, Chania Prefecture. Her poems have been included in group poetry collections, literary journals and poetic calendars. In 2009, her poetry collection *Evergreen and Deciduous* was published by Roes, and in 2014 her second poetic collection *Shells by Time* by Kedros, drawing positive reviews.

ROOMS FOR RENT

My country now
measured
by a day's work

three shifts
as a host
three at the restaurant
the rest in cleaning.

My country
in the postcards
of rosy seashores
in the whitewashed yards
resembles
a butterfly stuffed
in a little frame

DIVISION

For us the island
was always a summer
season rather
than a place.

For the island
we were always
the grandchildren
of old Tasos
names rather
than faces.

When grandfather died
in the winter
and in the heavy rain
we traveled
to the island
we didn't recognize it
nor the island
recognized us
place and season
had completely
disappeared

FREE

You wrapped
my neck
with sweet, warm
kisses and caresses
with heavy breaths
and words —
especially words —
tangible
purple
whispers

then
you let me free
no one holds you back
you said dryly
and stood unwavering

certain
of the result
methodical and detailed
certain
that as longer was
the silence
tighter was the invisible noose
around my neck

MOTHER

Reading and writing
your hand
on my hand
guiding the pencil

and the eraser
of your glance
steady on me

FLAME

Small island chapel
undermined, respectful
freshly whitewashed

chirps of birds enter
through its small door
to perform the mass
and the fine breeze
with aroma of sea froth
oregano and frankincense
on its invisible vestments

on the self a few candles
glued together
from the heat
and the mystagogic silence
I take one double candle
and I light it
our future
and our present
our present moment
transformed into
a flame

MYTHOLOGY

In the beginning
the Gods
created man
then men created
myths
and finally
the myths
from mouth
to mouth
from generation
to generation
created Gods
and men
all over again

EMIGRES OF 2013

Holidays
in airport corridors
overweight suitcases
full
of fragrant gardens
teas, coffees
sweets for the coffee

our children
emigrated
back
to the years

TRADITIONAL SWEETS

Mastic powder
rose water
thinly slivered almonds
and warm honey

festive days

mother

and in the kitchen
the smell
of your absence

SEASHORE CAFÉ

Silence has defeated us
for some time

silent
in each vertical
side of the table
we gaze the sundown
far away
in the horizon

the lapping waves
give birth to a caress
inside us
that slowly disappears
on the motionless shore
of our hands

we, two persons
truly try
to hide
our truthfulness

we, a couple
that upon been seen
the servers wonder whether
we live the past
the after
or the definite never

FRIENDSHIPS

Friendships are like this:
they start
in the time
of the first youth
and for this
they can last
a lifetime
and for this
they can betray

VASILIS FAITAS

Vasislis Faitas originally from Corfu, was born in Salonica, 20 of April 1942. He studied law at the Aristotle University of Salonica. He worked for the Bank of Greece until 2002. His poems appeared for the first time in the literary magazine *Nea Estia* in1966. His work has been published in literary Anthologies in Greece, Italy, the United States of America and online. His collection, *Alchemist of Chaos* was published in 2016 by the French publishing company *Le Miet des Anges.*

He has published the following poetry collections: in Salonica the *Settlers in the Night*, 1966, and *Letters to the World*, 1980. In Athens by *Mandragoras Publishing* the *Tomorrow's Postscript*, 2010, *Alchemist of Chaos*, 2015, *Café Entropy* 2017 and *Heraclitus' Tear*, 2018

CAFÉ ENTROPY

Just outside my window
in the fleeting life of the burbs
a boy saved the world once
turned his back to the void showing
the momentary passing of the secret

gathering of souls at the Café Entropy
listening to something unrecalled
mutated wind attacks the senses
shuttering time into lonely events
and the words into frightened birds.

I flow in seas-doubles, in watery labyrinths
each spring an uncertain cryptogram
where is the tempest that gave birth to me going?
Where is it emigrating?

What passed gleans unapproachable
what follows lives here
between us and the icebergs

I BREATHE THE COSMOS

The mountain becomes eternal message
life the incarnated memory of love
soul of man filled by the sea
with the sky in him
each has their own name
they converge
like waves in each other
nostos on the steps of the ancients

I breathe the cosmos

I've always existed somewhere else
reality in another reality
the voyage begins where it ends
the forest shivers on each tree leaf
each seashore recalls a voyage
to the merciless predestined end

FACTORY OF DREAMS

We hang between time and space
fleeting lives
genomes of mystery and ecstacy
pathfinders, we weave the mutant chaos
of our ancestry
in the womb of life and death

nothing is saved, nothing perishes
words-ideas, thoughts-tides
in the space where we build the revolution
of a predetermined dream

DESCENDANTS OF INGORANCE

The deep sorrowful monologue
view of the world nothing but
the harvest's fluttering
like the outcome of a vigil
utopia leaving its framed picture
distancing itself emptyhanded
the trapdoor of emotions
each day a new sea inside us
as we motionlessly walk

descendants of ignorance
voices, names, history of waves
don't come from the outside
Eros in our hearts
that faces the miracle
alchemy of souls that turns the earth
as the anchor of hopelessness
hovers
between
the void and endlessness

PARASITES

The big rivers of the earth
swallow the small ones
my mind turns
to the bloodied dreams of creeks
flowery shadows
unnamed souls
poems we never wrote

where they all mutate
and parasites constantly lurk
behind innocence

they whirl over their pray
erotically
announcing the coming of loneliness

GO TO SLEEP

Go to sleep now
don't ask me for another moment
for a new life
the tightening of the heart
what happened to the paths
that avenged loneliness
with no shred of revolution

go to sleep now
don't ask me again
how your day passed
the end of hopeful Eros
light flowering near us

go to sleep now
nothing will change
don't ask for another season
each of us belongs elsewhere

since I stepped over the void
tomorrow in another earth
since I couldn't leave
the sea alone

THE SOUL OF ODYSSEUS

I invented myself
inhabitant of the cosmos
gravity exiled me here
as if life was a path to ignorance
what can I now do with Odysseus
consciousness of a race that commits suicide
as he stands and listens
the sound of oars
sailing in the wind
miracle that gathers the dust
of dreams endlessly
when transparency of his myth
reaches beyond him, and beyond Ithaca

WHEN WE WERE ABSENT

for Haris
for Voula who passed

The man we thought passed by here
perhaps never lived
his voyage perhaps
lasted while we were absent
the gleam of the river from
above the bridge
as if a thousand years never passed
the whole world remains
a fleeting possibility of innocence

the now and the here
tender gestures of the forever
in the words and eyes of the others
memory's knife
wave froth that splashes on the rocks
eternity wrapped around
the veins of an enigmatic resonator

it comes from everywhere
and flows away

END OF THE DAY

The day comes to its end, my father's
voice echoed beyond chronos
his soul, citizen of another world,
flowered here
exotic seed in the sea

the day comes to its end
no other stories for you
stand up
tender rustle of leaves
the beginning of time is with you
more powerful than love

you light what you'll soon forget
multitude in the estuary of things
love and death
you still recall the call of return
with its imperceptible flow
beyond the fragile galaxies

LABYRINTH

My shadow and I will meet again
under the alluvium of the void
moment that overflows
the defending time
many others have come and gone
abruptly resurrected
from their starry graves
talking of the dark labyrinth

they'll come and they'll pass
what exists but a reflection
in the people's prayer
chaotic inclination
for the one who was young once
but turned old in a faraway land
he only listened and answered
using light and silence

nothing has stayed that reminds
of the voyage's wholeness
while the futility of love rages inside it
as each person follows his path
imprisoned in his own myth

MINA XIROGIANNIS

Asimina Xirogiannis was born in Athens in 1975. She studied Classics and Theater at the University of Athens and acting at the Theater-Laboratory Front. She teaches drama in Primary Education and works as a playwright. At the same time she teaches courses in Language and Literature as well as Theory and History of Theater. She has attended various theatrical seminars, acting, stage and play. She has directed and staged with her students several works: her own and those of others.

She has published three poetry collections. *Prophecy of the Wind* (Dodoni Publications 2009), *Wounds* (Gavrielidis Editions 2011), *My Epoch is Poetry* (Gavrielidis Editions 2013). In 2010 her novel *Body of Shadows* was released by the Anatolian Publications (1st prize by the Pan-Hellenic Writers Union and 1st Book Award in Siciliana Awards 2011).

In 2015, her book *23 Days* was published by Gavrielidis Editions (reprinted in 2016) and her one act play *Audition* was released by the Vakxikon Publications which received the 1st Prize of the Hellenic Literary Association. In 2017 she released the book *Tracing the Poem* (collage, poetry), Vakxikon publications.

Her poems have been included in five collections. Poems, short stories, reviews, studies, and articles are published in various printed publications, electronic journals and blogs. Her poems have been translated into English, French and Spanish.

SILENT POEM

Poem by poem I get close to you
though complete identification
occurs only in separation
since love's
a matter of two people who don't know each other

*

I believe that even
if we took different paths
we could have still met
in that silent corridor of existence
the separating line between light and darkness

*

Many years next to you
and I still feel
that I circumnavigate
the cosmos

*

We stood at a distance
from each other
before the rough and fateful
bargaining of the bodies.

Still at a distance afterwards.

*

Take me with you
inside the poem
where time is timeless
and the words exhume freedom

*

If my verse denotes some power
it's because you taught me to endure silence.

*

You and chaos are alike

*

Only the notion that
you let me be next to you
gives me the freedom
to consider myself as a poem

*

I want a bit of your time
of your space
of your glance
of your thoughts

too much of you

TRANSCENDENCE

I lost the original arousal
of the body
that became my voice
narrating its history
as I retained my soul

the body became a novella
for all the internal introspections
the shadows
the fights
the way life is transformed
into a poetic image

that you should show

when words flow
everything blooms

they annul the abyss

only the wound is recalled

EMOTION

We float among the clouds
ghosts with dark smoky fingers
we look for words referring to the void
and they don't come easily
while we see with new eyes.
The poem is present.
The poem is absent.

Sorrow remains
and licks our anger

ALMOST MAGICAL

Every evening
the resistance gives way
eyelids take the color of darkness.
The mystery we call
poetry awakes
and all is explained differently
and they all take the name Eros

or death.

THE BEST POEMS

I wrote my best poems
while on a line
at the bank
standing by
(sad and endless as it is
sad just like me)
standing therefore
I scatter my thoughts
I reap poems
like a desperate effort
to grasp time from its hair
to save my day
and to give courage to the sick man

NEW LIFE

Your life isn't fragile any longer
it got filled by male bodies
and rough touches

your life goes forward now
without the aura of the unsaid
without the sorrow of those mornings

POETRY

To write poetry
you need to have the burning inside
to conflagrate icebergs
to grasp with your glance
what spreads like fire
rapidly

your words need to be surprised
and capable to surprise
fatefully

VOYAGES

The most beautiful voyages are those of the mind
that take you to all you like and love
and if you need return
these will stay with you
beautiful images
as if you went there

memories beyond time

as if you went

as if you returned

LUGGAGE

A desire troubles me for a while
a multifaceted, pluralistic
multidimensional desire
that I carry even
when I don't want it.

Wanting it or not it haunts me

I like it yet I'm afraid of it
perhaps I'll never get
what I want

PAULINA PAMPOUDIS

Paulina Pampoudis, a founding member of the Society of Writers (of whom she served as General Secretary for 5 years) and founding member of the Circle of Poets (with a two-year term in the Board of Directors), was born in Athens. She studied at the Philosophical School of the University of Athens (History and Archeology) and attended Mathematics courses in the School of Physics and Mathematics and at the School of Fine Arts in Athens and the Byahm Show School of Arts in London. She worked as a copywriter in advertising agencies and editor in publishing house. She has published 14 poetry books (and three editions of Collected Poems), 5 books of prose, and more than 40 books "supposedly for children"; she has done more than 20 translations which have been published, and her work has been translated into several languages. She has also collaborated with radio and television and has written many songs.

She has presented three individual painting exhibitions, as well as many book illustrations. Finally, she has participated in group exhibitions and collective publications, and she has edited more than 70 literary works (and 4 Authors' Calendars). She is in the editorial board of 2 periodicals and arts.

SIX DAYS

FIRST DAY

The first day was the light
only light, and God talked to it
and Eros moistened it
and the colors bloomed
the green, the purple
the light-blue of loneliness
the yellow of death
the red that cracked

in the depth of memory
a coppery voice sparked
the wind stirred
trumpeted and travelled

God floated on it
white bird in the light

SECOND DAY

During the second day
rain touched the tabor of the sky
with its silver fingers
which swished
and a thousand trees
sprung up on the mountain side.
Thousands of leaves shone
and spelled the la, re, mi
the heavy fruit jingled
and the first skylark
rose high up in the light

light-blue trills dripped

God chirped on the highest branch
until exhausted

THIRD DAY

The third day He gave names
to the winds
and the birds shivered
in the roots of their feathers
the dry soil buzzed
many first tried miracles
the infatuated grasses
danced in the plain

two small puffy clouds
touched, then separated
ascending slowly in the light

God danced on them
until He was dismembered

FOURTH DAY

On the fourth day God
stood by the water's edge
and caressed the invisible
things rising in their thrill
and they took shape
and became purple rocks
on the seashore and they took
shape and turned into
deep caves filled by the winds.

Then God turned toward
the opening of the valley
and he positioned on the earth
and he established in the air
the exactness of constellations
and the presence of the trees

FIFTH DAY

The fifth day lighted on
innumerable animals of the earth
to which the love of God
gave birth and ruled over.

Deep serenity reigned, yet
something was missing

and as the river flowed
God leaned over it
took a handful of water
and kissed it.

Blood smelled everywhere
and all the animals
charged ready to kill.

God saw them silently
and slowly walked westward

SIXTH DAY

On the sixth day God
looked at His creation:
all seemed to be
as He had planned them
and nature took the aroma
of the bitten apple.

And God leaned down and
cried that He had stopped loving.
He then lied down to sleep
and in His dream beautiful
though tense people walked by.

God hasn't awaken since
the river took Him
and spread Him over
the most white flowers

GREEN

I have green eyes and the right to establish
like the wild vegetable
the works of cities
and the loneliness of monuments
the right to erase history
like the youngest brother
who descended in the water-well
to ascend to the sky
the right to spell the leaves and thorns
like an evergreen
in the lungs of the parks
and the impunity of the ravine.

My conceit is of green color
and I have the right
to impose the silence of the desert
to listen to my longing
to exist, which branches out
deep and cracks
my strongest longing, for
the world to exist

BEETLE

Work
of exquisite beauty
expertly crafted
exoskeleton
impenetrable diamond chest
complete armory
expensively equipped
highly analytical vision
thousands of megapixels
precise sensory antennae
strong claws
lining of the wings
precious, silky

perfect

fully armed
for the day's struggle

broken
in the beak of the bird

AT THE UNKNOWN SOLDIER

I run with my little hands open. The startled flock
of pigeons scatter around
(not truly panicking
they pretend to panic for the picture
for immortality)
I laugh (not truly my laugh
only my forward panic)

I wear my Sunday overcoat
unfamiliar collar
buttons covered by brown velvet
once belonged to my grandmother
then to Elli
then to me

stressed by the many reincarnations
alterations and moves

one of its small buttons still exist somewhere

people saunter here and there, dark faces
(it's not their lives
they pretend to go for a walk)

at the far end the Unknown Soldier shines
his unperishable body before us in an arch form

ah, the marbles in the whiteness
of the day, the pigeons
at the Unknown Soldier

(have now become flesh-eaters)

FESTIVE DINNER

In the next pose the lights turn off
house crumbles to death

middle of dinner, noiselessly
the walls will fall in

the black, lethargic
four-legged animals of the living room
for many years captive
creaking of forest
sighing in the wind
will feel free
to escape from their matter to chaos

the flesh will unglue itself
from the seats
the meaning of life
from the plates

then the cables will be severed by the screams

the clock will strike two in the morning
and time will freeze

LEONIDAS KAKAROGLOU

Leonidas Karakoglou was born in 1952 in Chania. He studied at the National Metsovion Polytechnic School. He lives in Chania. He has published nine poetry collections and a novel, *Life and Everything Else*, ESTIA publishing, 2011. Many of his poems have been set in music by Greek composers. His last collection, *Almost Complete Memory*, ESTIA Publishing, 2014, was nominated for the State Poetry Prize. He has dealt with cinema by organizing screenings, seminars, lectures.

EVENING

One evening
after you finish your supper
and took the plates away
while you smoke another cigarette

one evening
while the television would be presenting
a summer music festival
you'll put on your best smile
you'll give me a kiss
a gesture of respect
of an anchorite
and I'll stand in front of the door
to gaze the empty road

SQUARE OF THE DEAD

Late in the afternoon
the dead get together
in the square
to make a phone call
to their relatives
they hold the phone card tightly
and wait on the line
outside the phone booth.

The passersby see them and think:
where have you come again,
the city got full of immigrants
and the dead answer them:
we aren't immigrants
we're departed
departed we are.

RAIN

Another autumn
and I didn't open
the big gate to the garden
leaves no one has stepped on
in the pathways of the garden
I haven't forgotten the season of illusions
yet, time
passed slowly
like light rain
that ravaged the yard
just before daybreak

HOUSE

I don't like to go home late at night
not because no one waits for me anymore
but because when I unlock the door
and try to find the switch to turn on the lights
I'm afraid that in the dark
I might feel my hands
that trace the walls since afternoon
to discover how time has passed

and no touch consoles
the dirty stucco
the faded colors
the house that is vacant of its people

NECKLACE

I go to inspect your house
darkness everywhere
you must be gone
I unlock to smell a bit of you
but the house is empty
there are no furniture
no curtains
no smell
everything is gone, you too

what can I do with the key now
should I hide it in my wallet
like an old coin passed among
the hands of many men
or should I make a necklace with it
to hang around my neck
just to understand why I choke
when I think of you

THE SMELL OF TIME

I took my old coat from the closet
the one with the rip under the arm
it smelled of mothballs
but it would look as new
with some darning

as I put it on before the mirror
and I see my reflection in the window pane
I think of the days
that passed through the hole of my life
that had no patch

no darning
nothing makes them look good
nor any mothballs
can cover the smell of time

EVENINGS

The steps creak
I wake up and think
that you returned and climb
the wooden stairs
I get up to greet you
but no one is there
the steps creak of their own
they've got used to
the weight of absence

MORNING IN NEW YORK

It must be morning in New York now
the north wind probably blows and it is snowing
the timid light must be shining
no one would be waiting for you
the taxi driver would be changing the radio stations
until you decide

I smell your perfume in my hands
and discover a thread from your coat
I'll keep it and first chance I'll send it to you
I hope you'll write to me
so I can keep your address

otherwise I'll keep the thread
a pledge of small life
that the sleet covered

SOPHIA KOLOTOUROS

Sophia Kolotouros was born in Athens in 1973. She studied at the
Medical School of the University of Crete. She received her degree in
1998 and then specialized for five years in cytology at the Universities
of Heraklion, Crete and Agios Savvas, Athens. Recently she has been
involved with translations and editing of medical books (after attending
relevant seminars) and writing books (poetry and poetry). She attended
courses at the Hellenic Open University for one year, in the field of Greek
culture, while she is currently studying at the graduate program Creative
Writing of the same university. She has been an activist on hearing
problems, and in particular on deafness, from which he also suffers. She
has completely lost her hearing, but not her ability to speak. She
communicates by reading the lips of the interlocutors and responds
verbally, while not knowing the sign language.

She often visits schools and university institutions and talks with
students and on issues related to hearing problems and especially post-
lingual deafness. In March 2011 he set up a Facebook discussion group
on hearing impacts under the name KOUFOCHORIO, (village of the
deaf) which today has more than 1600 members and has developed
many activities to support deafness.

In March 2015 she was one of the founding members of the
Association: "Support Movement for the Accessibility of Deafness and

Hearing Loss with Oral Speech", in which an association holds the position of Chairman of the Board.

In December 2017 her poetry book *The Third Generation* was honored with the National Poetry Prize (2016).

MATRIX

My recording failed
the matrix broke long ago
my glass ball exploded
the snow
was thrown out

Years later
I tried to re-record.
I tried
but my glass ball broke long ago
carrying along with it
all the stereotypes
and illusions.

I climbed
on a snowflake and sailed away.
I escaped.

Now,
in the immenseness of the Cosmos I gather
other strange voyagers
since the mitre of prototypes broke
and we travel
beyond all certainties

NOVELISTS AND POETS

Novelists seek to put an order
in the chaotic world
for this sometimes they create plots
clearly defined
and complete

to conjure
their fear of death
and to give an end
to human stories
that abruptly stop

though poets
mainly search for the meaning of life
they don't create verses
they shutter them

HEAVENLY ATTRACTION

I revolve around you
or you around me
the attraction
isn't but mutual

yet I'm afraid
that the complete return to yourself
is of more importance to you

I have no other solution
I become a meteorite and I destroy you
I only wanted to come near you

DAVID AND CHAOS

The domino
started with the Twin Towers
and everyone knew
the butterfly that
flew over Tokyo
Iraq
Palestine
Afghanistan
brought the storm
to New York.

Who dropped the first ball?
I was in Genova
Gothenburg
Seattle
and I shot a stone
with my slingshot

BILLIARDS

They hit me
since the beginning of the game.
I'm the cue ball.

My job is to guide
the other balls
to their positions
each to its place.

I'll stay in the game
up to the end
my position
in the loneliness
of the immense green table.

I don't match with
other balls.
Only the black ball
lonely like me
touches me a little
before the end of the game.

IRIDESCENCE

Our other half
doesn't exist.
People exist.

Our circles meet
they define subtotals, common places
leaving other details alone
unprotected
unmatched.

I used the language
of Geometry, so you could understand.
I transformed my words into shapes
specific circles, defined
beautifully intersected
which you destroyed.

Now my words are soap-bubbles
that fly in the air.
They fly, laugh
make fun of me
with beautiful iridescent colors

SPIDER-WOMAN

I travelled in enclosed hearts
strange rough bodies
male bodies with erected phalluses
male bodies unexplored continents

I traveled in these bodies
I enjoyed their flowing juices
I wondered if they knew
how to touch a woman
if they wanted to conquer a woman.

Like we conquer them touching
edges of their chord-emotions entering,
piercing through, suckling, and turning them dry
we drip our own poison.

We conquer our victims.
Who has seen us as victims?
Who conquered us?
In the war of genders they see us as trophies.
They place their flags in our bodies
and leave in a delirious state.

The new century returns to Matriarchy
and I already set my web
for unsuspecting males

ARIADNE

They gave us the yarn
they said we could walk
out of our deadlock.
We wrapped the thread
around us
carefully

we stayed motionless
in the same position

in the heart of labyrinth
hypnotized
by the blue color of the TV

a blue lamb sits
in my balcony
that interrogates me every night

in the silent peacefulness
I have nothing
to confess

UNPREDICTABLE

The afternoon passes, the light fades
shadows get shorter
forecasting the night

unpredictable people become predictable
in the logic of escape
centrifuge power holds them together accurately
they say they'll leave, they always leave
revolving around a center
of their own persistence

predictable people walk on a straight line
sometimes we coerce them, tease them
put obstacles in front of them to see
if they continue on the same unaltered line.
Magnetized they always stand up and carry on
to their personal moral North.

I don't move neither on a straight line nor in centrifuge.
I foresee that night will come and I admire
the Northern Lights
as I wait for a collision

LAST CONCUBINE

Lover
I stage your play
I transform myself
object of desire and lust
I connive roles and sets
I become the subject

Woman
I put together the house
of a family
I transform myself
means of reproduction
I discover
a mother's instinct
I give life
become a mother

Priestess
I build temples
devising new religions
object of reverence
I make use
of metaphysics
and religious instinct
I become Authority

The roles
were divided long ago
you don't give me other choices
while you refuge to see me
as shape of waves that always changes

I only show you
one of my faces
I'm the last concubine
and secretly I escape
to the full Moon

IOULITA ILIOPOULOS

Ioulita studied Byzantine and Neohellenic Philology at the Philosophy Faculty of the Athens University and Drama at the Drama School of the Music Conservatory of Athens. The publishing company Ypsilon have released her following seven poetry collections *May You Have Many Good Years Markus, Digamma, Wish for Odysseus, From One to the Other, Eleven Spots for a Summer, The House, Iocasta*, and the fairy tales *What Zenon Asks* (First National Literary Prize), *The Little Green Hood, This is Something New*, and the *Timos the Athenean*. She has published the essays *The Dole, Searching for the Fourteenth Beauty, essays for Odysseus Elytis* and her translation of P. B. Shelley's *In Defence of Poetry*. She wrote poetic pieces for George Kouroupou's musical works *The Ship of Cypress* or *The Riddle of Love* and *Iocasta* as well as verse for the same composer and also for Petros Petrakis, Stathis Gyftakis, and Tatiana Zografos. She has also edited various books such as *Odysseus Elytis the Seafarer of the Century, On Top of Everything Else*, Elytis' *The World the Small the Great* set in music by George Kouroupos.

For thirteen years she has collaborated with the Orchestra of the Colors and with the Melina Mercury Institute for the creation of programs for oration and music and she continues presenting poetry and fairy tales on stage.

I

Busts and fronts made of moonstone arrayed in the air around me; I live all my seasons together, Markus, I'm diaphanous; a yellow thread lengthens around me, the air with its yellow cloths unraveled is yellow, the light is yellow. Yellow, you never wore yellow when you stared in my eyes during the pale night when its large purple eyes were poured around me, now that life is saved this way…erotic movement stopped half way in the crystal and half way out. Run, run the swans pull your house, you stand like a column by the door; space? Century? Name? Tell me your name.

The moon leans its face and my hair and hands get filled by fine pollen, salty as salt, where the silent light rain lengthens and little yellow fires in the shape of birds meet you. *A swallow has arrived*. May you have many good years, Markus.

THE BLUE OF ODYSSEUS

The rocks wake up and the winds wash their secrets
with fennel. Morning of an earlier pale copper engraving
the floors stare deep in the eyes through the sea tiles
the smooth and circular shallow, the pebbles of Vagianos
and Syrna with the lonely little church.
The Earth squirms in its slumber and thrusts out
little earthlings that will graze. Pilots count in miles
and you dip your feet in the endless blue of the queen-sea
    take the comb
that joined three coves and three oracles
the black, the rough, the slow walker who they call
    glass
the young workers close their eyelids while they still
sculpt the light around the perforated mine. Echo
of four cut off ships which were islands
and now they carry blue cobalt into the future
the children's blue, deep blue of the night,
                          blue of Odysseus.

I

We have been living in fairy tales as discordant as the weeds in our garden. Alone.
And we uproot our love each afternoon before you water.

Whoever left his mark here, a tread engraved on porous stone, knows me. Many
centuries in the same four-lettered word which when erased it re-writes itself and
its alphabet is destiny.

Flesh of my flesh my brother and my man, listen to me.

II

A difficult word to pronounce you, *love*

Your hand points to silence. Your hand gropes the sky in a single breath
and it spreads the shout among the little civil wars.

Your hand is a mouth, your hand a kick, that bloodies my knife. Deep
sleepless
sleep, your hand on my flesh wears me, sleeps on me.

Darkness laments and strikes, your hand a baby, a beast. Your strong
hand
for which I become a hand.
The love of your hand, my love.

CITY OF MUSIC

Small, multicolored musical squares
cobblestoned, where you step and
new sounds break up in the air

one night wearing a petticoat
and with a green dome on its hair
the night that turned into dawn
a band of light you passed over me
and closing my eyes as if feathers
a yellow night that turns into salinity
the river drop by drop

persistently persistent little lights like kisses
in her tiny hands as if of a marionette
a crypt, a fan, a voice
climbing slowly up in the air
and the elongated verdure on the ground
caresses as if silence, in a huge café where
the sounds go around in circles.
Trays with small glasses and sweets, gold signs
—which truth do the clocks count? —
music, you say.
A pink hydrangea and through the open window
a big heater made of porcelain and in very small letters
Salzburg of the nineteen hundred forever

PORTA REMOUNTA

The green caress of the water
that has remained on the walls for years
and now it moves suspiciously
slowly
under the foundations of houses
slowly under the inside room
ravaging
the legs of the bed
the crib of the unborn baby
the closed piano
of the house — we imagined —
the nailed door shutters.

GOOD NIGHT

Who plays good night with the stars
in a landscape that never rests
as the sea still brings down
the stone of the dead
with letters, straight lines, full stops?
Who plays with the breath
that was never said
only in our kisses, once
whispers of a lost tongue?
Who plays?
Suddenly the arms of the night
encircle me, closer, the footsteps closer
however no one will come
however no one will come.

I'm afraid.

LONG BED

A line of baby cribs. Large windows properly shut.
Dim light. Neither *my baby* nor lullaby.
Only some older people whisper under the blankets
there was a ship, there was a ship that never travelled
under the mattress and in the place of a talisman
the yearning of a mother who, may still come.
To bring the hug. To bring the true home in his embrace.

GATHERING

She gathers something. Insignificant. A glass, a knitted blouse
put on the coffee pot, put on the coffee pot her mother yells
and taking the pot she hides in it a cloth broken doll
into four pieces and the made of bone cross of her grandmother.
Then she folds the blanket, her house. Whole.
And they start their three day march to the sea. Passing
the barb wire during the night the blanket got tangled.
The house remained behind for good. Now, she embarks
along with the others, having with her only her Fate: unknown.

IOCASTA'S MONOLOGUE

When everything stops, it starts all over; you hear me?
Whatever passed comes back, heavy, with a slow pace
straight to me they pass and run motionlessly
they look at me with a red bark
they take my breath sounding like a deep cry
and they moan and get startled that they hide
from the birds, what? So the birds won't see what? Truth.
People in their silence call out their horrible fate
and take hold of the wind's hand.
We're all a blow of the wind, in the tempest.
What do you want to do before is too late? When and where?
Fate always comes first and always, anywhere,
does things on time.
And the words scatter and tumble, piece by piece,
your years which I loved so much, your flesh
teared to pieces by the gods
the years when I loved you so much.
Before you were born, when you were reborn, when
you unfolded me like an enigma and wore me
you, victor of the city, you my king.
Words of guilt like a sword which I strike
and it pierces me deep.
Nothing, nothing, nothing.
What I know I have forgotten, what I saw sleep
turned into an endless nightmare
small black dots that near me and always become larger
the faces, as thick as ever that come closer and closer
footsteps that pass by and run motionlessly
winds with their wings outstretched thorns
a knot in the throat, a blind command.
I was always your curse and your reward, Oedipus.
You were made of ether — yes, you — of earth and of the thick darkness
of love
born not to anyone but to the sky that lights its many eyes during the
night
and the endless city isn't enough, one life isn't enough
to contain a little of truth — silent

like the eye sockets of the dead, vacant, the little salt
left by the storm. Three days, at the three way path, three thieves.
No, don't be concerned, don't look back anymore, don't hang
onto the minute nor the thin rope of a word
that one may leave, no one is capable though one walks only
straight ahead to the widely spread net into which he'll sleep.
Unbroken elongated arms, red rags of eyes, cloths, births
mouths, rags, kisses, you, you.
To complete it on time. What? When and where? Fate is always first,
Fate everywhere
Fate brings everything on time!

MANOLIS ALIGIZAKIS

Manolis (Emmanuel Aligizakis) is a Greek-Canadian poet and author. He's the most prolific writer-poet of the Greek diaspora. At the age of eleven he transcribed the nearly 500 year old romantic poem *Erotokritos*, now released in a limited edition of 100 numbered copies and made available for collectors of such rare books at 5,000 dollars Canadian: the most expensive book of its kind to this day. He was recently appointed an honorary instructor and fellow of the International Arts Academy, and awarded a Master's for the Arts in Literature. He is recognized for his ability to convey images and thoughts in a rich and evocative way that tugs at something deep within the reader. Born in the village of Kolibari on the island of Crete in 1947, he moved with his family at a young age to Thessaloniki and then to Athens, where he received his Bachelor of Arts in Political Sciences from the Panteion University of Athens.

His articles, poems and short stories in both Greek and English have appeared in various magazines and newspapers in Canada, United States, Hungary, Slovakia, Romania, Australia, Jordan, Serbia and Greece. His poetry has been translated in Romanian, Swedish, German, Hungarian, French, Portuguese, Arabic, Turkish, Serbian, Russian languages and has been published in book form or in magazines in various countries.

His translation *George Seferis: Collected Poems* was shortlisted for the Greek National Literary Awards the highest literary recognition of Greece.

In September 2017 he was awarded the First Poetry Prize at the Mihai Eminescu International Poetry Festival, in Craiova, Romania.

OLD COUPLE

Long and narrow rusted table
hardly stands motionless
bleached out tablecloth as though
thrown in debts of river for a long time
cloth faded like her eyes gazing the sea's
agony that reaches the foreign land
where her son has vanished

shade of grapevine thick like a sin
and harsh like a thought pounding
her memory that light may be reborn

and he brings two plates
trembling hands pour wine in two glasses
small plate with olives, piece of feta

and the sigh expertly camouflaged by a smile
the lone cicada that insists to disturb
monologue of their loneliness

finally he sits next to her when
above them the grapevine laughs
as his calloused fingers touch
her wrinkled hand and the sun
somewhere higher than everybody
roars with laughter when the old man says
to her…you forgot to make the salad

In memory of my parents
in their late years of life in the village

BURDEN

He put his bag on the floor,
laid next to me
he raised one leg and
leaned it against the wall
as if to leave on it
a fleshy mark
a faint human trace
the other leg was resting
on the cool cement

suddenly as though he remembered
something very important

he got up
walked to the table
leaned down and smelt
the last bloomed rose
then he let a sigh float
in the darkened room
as if to release
burden of his last breath
and without any word
on the cool cement he collapsed

TENDERNESS

Your fingers
tenderly entangled
with mine

melodious harmony
of ten stars
whispering

I love you

DELPHI

Even this solemn remnant
of the ancient temple standing
like an anchorite in meditation
by the slope of the tired hill
even this they shall defile

remember it — I said

half-breed men with wide shoulder-blades
and hierodules with exquisite cheekbones
swaying their provocative buttocks
for the amusement of the winds
and for the sea's virgin salinity
even this they shall defile

remember it — I said

aimlessly before the innocent statues
they shall desecrate and life the whore
they shall call and with stamina
and unyielding persistence they shall
bury the primeval beauty and after
they exhume the ancestral hatred
and guilt, the pneuma they shall imprison
to be guarded by Herculean arms
and theirs the wealth
of the valley and my kin's reward
bloodshed in streets and neighborhoods
where you and I once roamed and played
making plans for exploits and deeds

and you said —

it would have been better if we stayed
obedient to the holy and venerable
half-truths brought to our lands by easterners
at least they promised a gleaming Paradise

FIRES

Ancient fires still burning
inside the temples

outside the porticos
center of the agora

where an eloquent poet once
orated verses before

the paranoid oligarchy
expelled him from the city

images that come to us
and nothing has really

changed over the eons
except the invention

of bullets to speed
the process of apathy

IMAGE

Like an ancient
repeatedly hymned sin
your body that I crave
to re-explore
gleams in my mind

like that first time
under the shade of the olive tree
whispering softly

yes, yes

TORCH

Scent of your vulva
sublime astringent
next to the oleanders
at high-noon
waist of July
a bright day
the sun erected
avidity

and I said —

my primal concern
deep inside it
to anchor
like a fiery torch

SCANDALOUS

He stops shaving razor floating in air
hand absentmindedly creates a circle in mid-void
like a bird stilled by camera lens

her scandalous vulva visits his mind
from days of that August
on the scorched island
in low tone siesta
in muffled moaning
lest the mirror would crack from tension
in the cool soothing room

before his eyes
finger in circular motion of agony
swirling eroticism
higher and higher
near a shuddering apex
wind pandemonium
lust and a red colored
Lucifer laughs sardonically
as the razor touches his flesh
opening it
like hers
color reddish

WHAT IF

If you didn't get to the train station

at that exact time you wouldn't

have met him you wouldn't have

started dating you wouldn't have

married you wouldn't have

the twins graduating this year and

where would you be now

had you taken the next train?

AXIUM

The point
isn't in the answer
but in the evolution
of the question

and the two of us,
my beloved answer,
erected cypresses
opposite
the blushing of the sun

GOLDEN KISS

He threw his hat on the chair
took off his shirt to reveal
his tan breast where a cross shone
reflecting brightness of the sun

and his heart pulsed in a different mode
when she walked to him and
placing her finger over the venerable spot
kissed his lips saying: I miss you

LOSS

The years I risked
under the spell of the moon
for that lone kiss

March daffodils
autumn chrysanthemums
why have you bloomed?

Now at the edge of
the train station platform
a step forward would mean
an opportunity left behind

and I try to grasp the purpose
of my life based on the speed
of passing time as I stand
opposite the melancholy of
the eternal understanding

no more train whistles
just dust and that
lost kiss

DATE

A blind date
is set for you by fate
to meet your Death
this morning
for this you smile
and tighten your lips
in agony

Bon voyage!

INHERITANCE

He knew I devoted all my
earthly love to him
I pronounced him heir
of the world which I had
concealed from the traitors

for this he dug
his grave deep
he threw in it
the inheritance
soon after he stood
somber on top of the slab and
from the depth
of his lungs
he wailed

in this shadow for eons
we've dwelled
you and I
the two disinherited
you and I
the two exaggerations

LIMPING MAN

Breeze laughed amid
his limping footsteps
nature's unforgiving mistake
struggled out of the sea

eyes full of kindness
irises of a saint
a brave man's graceful stature
in his unbalanced steps
the balance of the Universe
searched for justice
pain of the unlike
in vain danced
in the expression of the man
who limped out of the light waves

in his glance the meaning of disproportional
victorious triumph
against the unjust chaos
his unequal side an unsung song
not rhyming poem
deficient erotic verse
a mortal's hearth full of pain
that begged for analogy
in the syllable of his smile
in the word of his uplifting courage

the limping man unwritten poem
ready to spring out of my mind
to complete the day's
incompleteness

Good Lord, were you drunk
when you fathered him?

Good Lord, have mercy on us,
don't drink again!

CONFESSION

My confession was simple:
father, I said, I'm a sinner
the guilt of the universe sits
heavy on my chest
forgive me that I passionately loved
the bloomed hyacinth and
the flight swings of swallows

and my two greatest sins
my unmeasured love
for the laughter of the child
and the beggars who stood
with their extended hands
filled with good wishes

my confession was simple

straight to the Purgatory
the priest delivered his opinion

AUTUMN

In tree branches
rustle of leaves
definition of fall
soft landing
under my soles
secretly played game
grayish, foggy
October morning
prompts smile
anticipation
of fiery April
resurrection

philosophy of leaves
exegesis
harmony
purpose

POEM

Write a poem for me

you said —

to talk of love

it'll describe your lips

I said —

their smile it will capture

their color it will accentuate
and I bowed in awe

as if before the statue
of naked Eros

JUSTIFICATION

I strode over
fallen branches
victims of last night's
merciless wind
listened to music in tune
with endless perfection
then the chirp of the bird
raised my head
saw it, a chickadee
on the tree limb

justification
this day
alive that I was

FINCH'S SONG

If it wasn't for
the finch's song
he wouldn't know
spring had arrived.

With blurry eyes
he looked through
the open window deep
into the irises of March
and confirmed it;

and in the air ethereal
the scent of a woman's wet mound.

AMORPHOUS

Before I entered the uterus
I was there
smoke of a fire slowly extinguishing
wind hitting your blue window
crack of your being, a tight grip

song of the funeral procession
before I took the shape of life
before I choose my name

I was there
scent of a red rose
the bird's first flutter
before I entered the trap of flesh
the softest wave of the sea I was

lone eagle on rocky promontory
from high up watching over you
before I was born I was
the shapeless freedom
companion of the infinite
a simple sigh destined
to scar your lips

there I was
the joyous chime of a bell
there I was
the indeterminable

BIBLIOGRAPHY

Dionisios Solomos, *Collected Poems*, Philologiki Editions, Salonica, Greece, 1962

Aristotelis Valaoritis, Poems, *users.uoa.gr/~nektar/arts/poetry/aristotelhs_balawriths_poems.htm*

Andreas Kalvos, Poems, *users.uoa.gr/~nektar/arts/poetry/andreas_kalbos_wdai.htm*

Kostis Palamas, Poems, *users.uoa.gr/~nektar/arts/tributes/kwsths_palamas/index.htm*

Constantine Cavafy, Poems, translated by Manolis, Libros Libertad, Surrey, BC, 2008

Yannis Ritsos, *Selected Books*, translated by Manolis Aligizakis, Libros Libertad, Surrey, BC, 2011

George Seferis, *Collected Poems*, translated by Manolis Aligizakis, Libros Libertad, Surrey, BC, 2012

Odysseus Elytis, *Collected Poems*, Ikaros, Athens, Greece, 2005

Tasos Livaditis, *Selected Poems*, translated by Manolis Aligizakis, Libros Libertad, Surrey, BC, 2012

Cloe and Alexandra, Poems, translated by Manolis Aligizakis, Libros libertad, Surrey, BC, 2013

Dimitris Linantinis, *Hours of the Stars*, translated by Manolis Aligizakis, Libros Libertad, Surrey, BC, 2015

Karyotakis-Polydouri, *A Tragic Love Story*, poetry translated by Manolis Aligizakis, Libros Libertad, Surrey, BC, 2016

Manolis Anagnostakis, Poems, http://users.uoa.gr/~nektar/arts/poetry/manolhs_anagnwstakhs_poems.htm

Nikiforos Vrettakos, Poems, *users.uoa.gr/~nektar/arts/poetry/nikhforos_brettakos_poems.htm*

Kiki Dimoula, *Poems*, Ikaros, Athens, Greece, 2009

Miltos Sachtouris, Poems, users.uoa.gr/~nektar/arts/poetry/miltos_saxtoyrhs_poems.htμ

Katerina Anghelaki, *Rook-Poems*, Kastaniotis Editions, Athens, Greece, 2014

Nanos Valaoritis, Poems,

Katerina Gogou, Kastaniotis Editions, Athens, Greece, 2013

George Douatzis, *The Red Scarf*, Mandragoras Editions, Athens Greece, 2016

Haris Vlavianos, *Self-Portrait of the White*, Patakis Editions, Athens, 2018

Phaidon Theofilou, *The Cycle of my Close Cousin*, Athens, Greece, 2017

Dina Georgantopoulos, *Caressing Myths*, translated by Manolis Aligizakis, Libros Libertad, Surrey, BC, 2015

Tolis Nikiforou, *Sunlit Windows*, Mandragoras Editions, Athens, Greece, 2014

Tzoutzi Mantzourani, *Coffee and Cigarettes*, Fildisi Editions, Athens, Greece, 2013

Agathi Georgiadou, *Poetic Adventure*, Metechmio, Athens, Greece, 2006

TRANSLATOR MANOLIS ALIGIZAKIS

Emmanuel Aligizakis, (Manolis) is a Cretan-Canadian poet and author. He's the most prolific writer-poet of the Greek diaspora. At the age of eleven he transcribed the nearly 500 year old romantic poem Erotokritos, now released in a limited edition of 100 numbered copies and made available for collectors of such rare books at 5,000 dollars Canadian: the most expensive book of its kind to this day.

He was recently appointed an honorary instructor and fellow of the International Arts Academy, and awarded a Master's for the Arts in Literature. He is recognized for his ability to convey images and thoughts in a rich and evocative way that tugs at something deep within the reader. Born in the village of Kolibari on the island of Crete in 1947, he moved with his family at a young age to Thessaloniki and then to Athens, where he received his Bachelor of Arts in Political Sciences from the Panteion University of Athens.

After graduation, he served in the armed forces for two years and emigrated to Vancouver in 1973, where he worked as an iron worker, train labourer, taxi driver, and stock broker, and studied English Literature at Simon Fraser University. He has written three novels and numerous collections of poetry, which are steadily being released as published works.

His articles, poems and short stories in both Greek and English have appeared in various magazines and newspapers in Canada, United States, Hungary, Slovakia, Romania, Australia, Jordan, Serbia and Greece. His poetry has been translated in Romanian, Swedish, German, Hungarian, Ukrainian, French, Portuguese, Arabic, Turkish, Serbian, Russian, Italian, Chinese, Japanese, languages and has been published in book form or in magazines in various countries.

He now lives in White Rock, where he spends his time writing, gardening, traveling, and heading Libros Libertad, an unorthodox and independent publishing company which he founded in 2006 with the mission of publishing literary books.

His translation *George Seferis: Collected Poems* was shortlisted for the Greek National Literary Awards the highest literary recognition of Greece. In September 2017 he was awarded the First Poetry Prize of the Mihai Eminescu International Poetry Festival, in Craiova, Romania.

AWARDS

~1st Poetry Prize, Academy of Mihai Eminescu, Craiova, Romania, 2017

~Distinguished Poet and Writer Award, City of Richmond, BC, 2014

~1st Poetry Prize, International Arts Academy for this translation of "Yannis Ritsos- Selected Poems", 2014

~Winner of the Dr. Asha Bhargava Memorial Award, Writers International Network Canada, 2014

~"George Seferis-Collected Poems" translated by Manolis, shortlisted for the Greek National Literary Awards, translation category.

~1st Poetry Prize, International Arts Academy, for his translation of "George Seferis-Collected Poems", 2013

~Master of the Arts in Literature, International Arts Academy, 2013

~1st Prize for poetry, 7th Volos poetry Competition, 2012

~Honorary instructor and fellow, International Arts Academy, 2012

~2nd Prize for short story, Interartia festival, 2012

~2nd Prize for Poetry, Interartia Festival, 2012

~2nd Prize for poetry, Interartia Festival, 2011

~3rd Prize for short stories, Interartia Festival, 2011

BOOKS by MANOLIS

QUEST, a novel, Ekstasis Editions, spring 2018
THE MEDUSA GLANCE, poetry, Ekstasis Editions, spring 2017
THE SECOND ADVENT OF ZEUS, poetry, Ekstasis Editions, spring 2016
CHTHONIAN BODIES, paintings by Ken Kirkby and poems by Manolis Aligizakis, Libros Libertad, 2015
IMAGES OF ABSENCE, poetry, Ekstasis Editions, 2015
AUTUMN LEAVES, poetry, Ekstasis Editions, 2014
ÜBERMENSCH/ΥΠΕΡΑΝΘΡΩΠΟΣ, poetry, Ekstasis Editions, 2013
MYTHOGRAPHY, paintings and poems, Libros Libertad, 2012
NOSTOS AND ALGOS, poetry, Ekstasis Editions, 2012
VORTEX, poetry, Libros Libertad, 2011
THE CIRCLE, novel, Libros Libertad, 2011
VERNAL EQUINOX, poetry, Ekstasis Editions, 2011
OPERA BUFA, poetry, Libros Libertad, 2010
VESPERS, paintings and poems, Libros Libertad, 2010
TRIPTYCH, poetry, Ekstasis Editions, 2010
NUANCES, poetry, Ekstasis Editions, 2009
RENDITION, poetry, Libros Libertad, 2009
IMPULSES, poetry, Libros Libertad, 2009
TROGLODYTES, poetry, Libros Libertad, 2008
PETROS SPATHIS, novel, Libros Libertad, 2008
EL GRECO, poetry, Libros Libertad, 2007
PATH OF THORNS, poetry, Libros Libertad, 2006
FOOTPRINTS IN SANDSTONE, poetry, Authorhouse, Bloomington, Indiana, 2006
THE ORPHANS, poetry, Authorhouse, Bloomington, Indiana, 2005

TRANSLATIONS FROM GREEK TO ENGLISH

KARYOTAKIS—POLYDOURI, The Tragic Love Story, poetry translated by Manolis Aligizakis, Libros Libertad, 2016
HOURS OF THE STARS, poetry by Dimitris Liantinis, translated by Manolis Aligizakis, Libros Libertad, 2015
HEAR ME OUT, short stories, by Tzoutzi Mantzourani, translated by Manolis Aligizakis, Libros Libertad, 2015
CARESSING MYTHS, poetry by Dina Georgantopoulos, translated by Manolis Aligizakis, Libros libertad, 2015
IDOLATERS, a novel by Joanna Frangia, translated by Manolis Aligizakis, Libros Libertad, 2014
TASOS LIVADITIS-SELECTED POEMS, translated by Manolis Aligizakis, Libros Libertad, 2014
YANNIS RITSOS-SELECTED POEMS, translated by Manolis Aligizakis, Ekstasis Editions, 2013
CLOE AND ALEXANDRA-SELECTED POEMS, translated by Manolis Aligizakis, Libros Libertad, 2013
GEORGE SEFERIS-COLLECTED POEMS, translated by Manolis Aligizakis, Libros Libertad, 2012
YANNIS RITSOS-POEMS, translated by Manolis Aligizakis, Libros Libertad, 2010
CONSTANTINE P CAVAFY-POEMS, translated by Manolis Aligizakis, Libros Libertad, 2008
CAVAFY-SELECTED POEMS, translated by Manolis Aligizakis, Ekstasis Editions, 2011

TRANSLATIONS FROM ENGLISH TO GREEK

THE GOLDEN KISS, poetry by Carolyn Mary Cleefeld, translated to Greek by Manolis Aligizakis, Libros Libertad, CCC Communications, 2018
LIGHT IN THE PINENEEDLES, poetry by Karoly Fellinger, translated from English to Greek by Manolis Aligizakis, OSTRIA Publications, Athens, Greece, 2017

BOOKS in OTHER LANGUAGES

ODE TO APHRODITE (Arabian), poetry by Manolis Aligizakis, translated in Arabic by Fethis Sassi, Borsa Publishing, Cairo, Egypt, 2018

THORNS OF THE ROSE, (Romanian), poetry by Manolis Aligizakis, translated in Romanian by Tatjana Betoska, Editura Europa, Craiova, Romania, 2017.

FOGOLY, (Hungarian) novel by Manolis, translated in Hungarian by Karoly Csiby, Parnassus Publications, Bratislava, Hungary, 2017

FUILLES D'AUTOMNE, poetry by Manolis Aligizakis, translated into French by Karoly Sandor Pallai, Editions Du Cygne, Paris, 2017

NABORI SEĆANJA, (Serbian) poetry by Manolis Aligizakis, translated into Serbian by Jolanka Kovacs, Zrenjanin, Serbia, 2016

FRUNZE DE TOAMNA, Poetry by Manolis, translated by Lucia Gorea, AB-ART, Romania, 2016

OSZI FALEVELEK, (Hungarian), poetry by Manolis Aligizakis, translated into Hungarian by Karoly Csiby, Gyp, Hungary, 2015

SVEST, (Serbian), poetry by Manolis Aligizakis, translated into Serbian by Jolanka Kovacs, Serbia, 2015

ESZMELET, (Hungarian), poetry by Manolis Aligizakis, translated into Hungarian by Karoly Csiby, AB-ART, Bratislava, Slovakia, 2014

ÜBERMENSCH (German), poetry by Manolis Aligizakis, translated into German by Eniko Thiele Csekei, WINDROSE, Austria, 2014

NOSTOS SI ALGOS, (Romanian) poetry by Manolis Aligizakis, translated into Romanian by Lucia Gorea, DELLART, Cluj-Napoca, Romania, 2013

BOOKS IN GREEK

THE CIRCLE, a novel, Korotzis Editions, Athens, Greece, 2018

NOTES OF A WET AUGUST, poetry, Koronzis Editions, Athens, Greece, 2018

THE PRISONER, (Greek, PETROS SPATHIS in English) novel, OSTRIA Publications, Athens, Greece, 2017

BLUE IN THE WINDOW (Greek), poetry, OSTRIA Publications, Athens, Greece, 2017

SECOND ADVENT OF ZEUS, Greek, ENEKEN Publications, Thessaloniki, Greece, spring 2017

ATHIVOLES, (Greek), poetry, Fildisi Editions, Athens, Greece, 2016

SONGS OF THE ABSURD, (Greek), poetry, ENEKEN, Salonika, Greece, 2015

IMAGES OF ABSENCE, (Greek) poetry, Sexpirikon, Salonika, Greece, 2015

HIERODULES, (Greek), poetry, Sexpirikon, Salonika, Greece, 2014

YPERANTHROPOS, (Greek), poetry, ENEKEN, Salonika, Greece, 2014

TOLMIRES ANATASEIS, (Greek) poetry, GAVRIILIDIS EDITIONS, Athens, Greece, 2013

FYLLOROES, (Greek) poetry, ENEKEN PUBLICATIONS, Salonika, Greece, 2013

EARINI ISIMERIA, (Greek) poetry, ENEKEN PUBLICATIONS, Salonika, Greece, 2011

STRATIS ROUKOUNAS, (Greek) novel, MAVRIDIS EDITIONS, Athens, Greece, 1981

LONGHAND BOOKS

EROTOKRITOS, by Vitsentzos Kornaros, (rare book-collectible), transcribed by Manolis Aligizakis, Libros Libertad, 2015

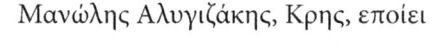

Μανώλης Αλυγιζάκης, Κρης, εποίει